THE SAVAGE SKY

Other titles in the Stackpole Military History Series

THE AMERICAN CIVIL WAR

Cavalry Raids of the Civil War
Pickett's Charge
Witness to Gettysburg

WORLD WAR II

Armor Battles of the Waffen-SS, 1943–45
Australian Commandos
The B-24 in China
Backwater War
Beyond the Beachhead
The Brandenburger Commandos
Bringing the Thunder
Coast Watching in World War II
Colossal Cracks
D-Day to Berlin
Exit Rommel
Flying American Combat Aircraft of World War II
Fist from the Sky
Forging the Thunderbolt
The German Defeat in the East, 1944–45
Germany's Panzer Arm in World War II
Grenadiers
Infantry Aces
Iron Arm
Luftwaffe Aces
Messerschmitts over Sicily
Michael Wittmann, Volume One
Michael Wittmann, Volume Two
The Nazi Rocketeers
On the Canal
Packs On!
Panzer Aces
Panzer Aces II
The Panzer Legions
Retreat to the Reich
A Soldier in the Cockpit
Surviving Bataan and Beyond
The 12th SS, Volume One
The 12th SS, Volume Two
Tigers in the Mud

THE COLD WAR / VIETNAM

Flying American Combat Aircraft: The Cold War
Land with No Sun
Street without Joy

WARS OF THE MIDDLE EAST

Never-Ending Conflict

OTHER

Desert Battles

THE SAVAGE SKY

Life and Death on a Bomber over Germany in 1944

George Webster

STACKPOLE
BOOKS

Published by
STACKPOLE BOOKS
5067 Ritter Road
Mechanicsburg, PA 17055
www.stackpolebooks.com

Cover design by Tracy Patterson

Printed in the United States of America

10 9 8 7 6 5 4 3 2 1

FIRST EDITION

Library of Congress Cataloging-in-Publication Data

Webster, George, 1924–
    The savage sky : life and death on a bomber over Germany in 1944 / George Webster.—1st ed.
        p. cm.—(Stackpole military history series)
    ISBN-13: 978-0-8117-3388-5
    ISBN-10: 0-8117-3388-2
1. Webster, George, 1924– 2. United States. Army Air Forces. Bombardment Group, 92nd. 3. World War, 1939–1945—Aerial operations, American.
4. World War, 1939–1945—Campaigns—Europe, Western. 5. World War, 1939–1945—Personal narratives, American. 6. Flight radio operators—United States—Biography. I. Title.

D790.25392nd .W43 2007
940.54'4973092—dc22
[B]
                                                            2006101097

Table of Contents

Preface

Imagine being blasted by a 170-mile-per-hour gale at 53 degrees below zero. You are 30,000 feet above the earth—higher than Mount Everest—in an open airplane. An electrically heated suit and an oxygen mask keep you alive, but the ice formed by your breath clogs your oxygen mask and makes you gasp for air. Exposed skin freezes instantly. Altitude sickness threatens to suffocate you. Exertion at this altitude doubles you over with agonizing cramps. And someone is trying to kill you.

These were perils faced by crews on B-17F bombers flying over Germany in World War II. The B-17F had open ports in its fuselage that allowed a below-zero gale to howl through much of the plane. Crew members froze to death or lost fingers, toes, feet, and hands to freezing. Others died from lack of oxygen or from altitude sickness. Still others went insane from fear and the knowledge that they had little chance of survival. All of this occurred before hordes of German fighter planes and barrages of antiaircraft shells killed or mutilated bomber crews by the hundreds.

The following pages take you with me on flights over Germany in the winter and spring of 1944, a period of bitter aerial combat in which the Allies destroyed much of the German Air Force prior to the Allied landings in France. We begin with a fearsome December crossing of the North Atlantic, in which our four-engine B-17, out of fuel, lost in a violent storm, and without radio contact, barely reaches the Irish coast. We continue with four months of combat during which five members of my bomber's crew are killed and two are wounded. We end, after twenty-five missions, east of Berlin in a B-17 that is smashed and on fire from German fighter attacks. It has lost so much fuel that it has no chance of returning to England.

Instead, it makes a tense flight northward across eastern Germany to crash-land in Sweden.

If flying over Germany was that bad, why did we do it? Some volunteered for the glamour of flying—and the fact that girls got all giddy over a man wearing wings. For some, it was a feeling that nothing bad could happen (young men's immortality complex). The rest did it because they had no choice. Many gunners on bombers, including four on my B-17, were draftees.

I had no interest in flying. Full of patriotism, I volunteered for Air Force Officer Candidate School in the hope that my scientific training would help my country. But clerical error and high losses of bomber crews diverted me to become a replacement for a dead flyer. I loved my country, but I didn't volunteer to die for it. General George Patton, whom I regard as the greatest American general of the twentieth century, put it well when he told his men, "It's not your job to be the poor son of a bitch who dies for his country. Your job is to make the other poor son of a bitch die for his country."

In addition to giving you an account of a brief period in history that was both thrilling and terrifying, I have another reason for writing. World War II was the supreme event of the twentieth century. It was the greatest war in history, killing millions and causing unimaginable suffering. Now most of those who fought in it are gone, and its brutality fades behind us down the corridor of time. But we must never forget the horror of war, whether on land, on the sea, or in the air. National leaders must be extremely careful about decisions that send young men and women to their deaths. War is not cool. It is fire and blood and death and terror and hopeless despair. General Sherman is reported to have said, "War is hell." He was right. War is worse than your worst nightmare.

Now let's look into the evil face of war. Return with me to the 1940s—to chocolate shakes and cherry Cokes at the corner drug store, Bob Hope's jokes and Glenn Miller's music on the radio, movies at the theater, and an awesome war thundering on the other side of both oceans. Events and conversations are as accurate as I can reconstruct them from official records and memory, but even inaccuracy can't hide the terror that was war in the frigid air above Germany.

CHAPTER 1

Lost above the North Atlantic

It is two hours before dawn on December 5, 1943. We are somewhere past mid-ocean on a flight from Labrador, Canada, to Scotland. Our Boeing B-17G four-engine bomber is in thick cloud 8,000 feet above the icy water of the North Atlantic. The shuddering plane rocks and bounces in a violent storm.

We are also in serious trouble.

"We're lost?" the pilot asks over the intercom.

"Virtually," the navigator says. "I haven't had a star sighting for hours, and we can't get a radio fix. In a storm this bad, I can only guess where we are."

The intercom is deathly silent. To be lost over the North Atlantic in December sends a chill down your spine.

"I'd say we're more than three-fourths of the way across," the navigator says, "but in this weather, we could be a long way from where I estimate we are."

"We damn well better be more than three-fourths of the way across," the pilot says. "There's less than two hours of fuel left. If we don't find land in the next 120 minutes, we go into the water."

"You know how cold the water is down there?" the navigator says. "We better be able to get into those life rafts. Otherwise, we'll only last a few minutes."

"I know," the pilot says, "but when the gas is gone, we go down."

I sit alone in the bomber's radio room, with only a tiny light above my desk. I'm trembling. In my nineteen years of life, I have never faced anything like this. I know that our flight from Labrador to Scotland is at the limit of a B-17's range. Planes usually fly from Newfoundland to Iceland to refuel, and then fly on to Scotland. But tonight, Iceland is closed in with clouds and fog, and the Eighth Air Force in England needs us so urgently that it orders us to fly nonstop across the Atlantic. It is possible to make the nonstop flight, as long as we don't have headwinds, so I assumed that we would fly across the ocean with no problem.

We left Goose Bay, Labrador, on a clear, cold night, but while the bomber droned eastward, a storm front raged south faster than predicted. It hit us hard, wrapping us in thick cloud, buffeting the aircraft with strong winds, and preventing our navigator from seeing the stars to plot our course across the ocean. The pilot used up precious fuel in a futile attempt to climb above the storm to give the navigator star sightings.

To aid navigators in this situation, I usually use the radio to get our position from a direction-finding station in Great Britain. Sounds good, right? But on this stormy night, my radio receiver emits a steady howl that sounds like "wow, wow, wow." It blots out all other sounds. I carefully tune the big radio transmitter at the rear of my cabin and broadcast query after query to the British for our position, but all I hear is, "wow, wow, wow." In the background are whispers of dots and dashes, but they are too weak to decipher. As we continue to fly eastward, the interference grows stronger. I heard that the Germans and Allies jam each other's radios, but I didn't know that the Germans could reach out into the Atlantic to try to kill us. I'm a real innocent.

We're blind, alone, and lost, without communication with the outside world. If we can't find land before we run out of fuel, no one will know where we went down.

While I listen to "wow, wow, wow" on the radio, I gaze around my compartment. It is shaped like a big aluminum can lying on its side. Aluminum girders, the skeleton of the airplane, form a network inside unpainted aluminum walls. The cabin is about seven feet in diameter and has a wooden floor. It smells of oil and metal. On the left side of the cabin, my desk is bolted to the front bulkhead. A powerful radio receiver faces me from the rear of the desk. It is black, and its lighted dials gleam at me. Behind me stands a big, black transmitter, its red lights glowing in the gloom. To my right, a door leads forward into the bomb bay and beyond it into the pilots' cabin. To the right of the door is an aluminum rack of small radios for navigation and talk to nearby planes. Attached to the far wall is a first-aid kit. A medic taught me how to use its contents, including syringes of morphine for wounded crewmembers.

On the rear wall of the radio room, a door leads back into the waist compartment that extends from radio room almost to the tail. It has big windows for machine guns on each side. It also has the entrance to the "ball turret," a globe-like structure that hangs beneath the plane. The ball turret is a claustrophobic nightmare, but a cramped gunner can fire its twin machine guns at planes attacking from below. Beyond the waist, at the rear of the plane, is a tiny compartment where the tail gunner kneels uncomfortably to fire two machine guns.

In this new B-17G, the roof of my compartment is transparent Plexiglas. It is one of the first B-17Gs to head for England, but we will fly bombing missions in a B-17F, which has an open roof that allows a 170-mile-per-hour gale as cold as 50 degrees below zero to sweep through the radio room and the rear of the plane.

Each wall of my compartment has a window. Beneath the window on my left is a hose that I can connect to an oxygen mask when we fly above 10,000 feet. There are cables to connect earphones, microphone, and an electrically-heated suit. The ten crewmembers communicate by means of an intercom system.

Hours earlier, we passed near the spot where the *Titanic* sank into the same freezing water that waits for us if we run out of gas. When I was a child, my grandmother told how *Titanic* passengers went from the comfort of warm cabins to freezing death in icy water. When our plane roared into the night sky from the Royal Canadian Air Force Base at snow-packed Goose Bay, Labrador, we knew that coming down into the North Atlantic in winter would bring us the same fate as the *Titanic* passengers. Even if the plane doesn't smash apart on impact with the ocean's huge swells, it will sink like a stone as water pours in through openings in the bomber. If we survive impact with the ocean, our only hope is to launch two inflatable life rafts that the plane carries.

The red handles that release the life rafts are near the ceiling at the front of the radio room. During training, no one mentioned these controls, but as I stare at them with growing fear, I realize that I don't know how they operate. Do I pull on them? Do I turn them?

Do I push them? One thing is clear. I won't have time to experiment. When the plane hits the ocean and sinks like a rock, I must reach those controls before an avalanche of bone-chilling water sweeps me away. There will be only seconds to find out how to operate them. If I fail, we will freeze to death in less than thirty minutes while we float in our life jackets in frigid water. Even if I succeed, we must fight through rushing water to escape from the plane in the minutes before it sinks. In total darkness, tossed by massive waves of freezing water, we must inflate our life jackets and find the rafts before they float away. If we can climb into the rafts, I hope that one of the gunners held onto the hand-cranked, emergency radio to send a mayday (SOS) call for help. Frigid water will wash over us while the rafts toss like corks on the Atlantic's immense swells, but there is slim chance of rescue. Still, it depends on getting a radio signal to a station in Great Britain and telling the British exactly where we are.

"We're down to ninety minutes of fuel," the pilot calls to the navigator. "Got any good news for me?"

"I wish I did."

Since the navigator can't use star sightings or directions from the radio, he must navigate by "dead reckoning," in which he estimates where we are from our speed and other factors. But it is only an educated guess. On a long flight, headwinds, crosswinds, and a dozen other things can make our actual position far different from the position he plots by dead reckoning.

As I send another query, the jamming stops! A message blazes in with our position. As I acknowledge it, I hear another message for us, but the jamming returns. I'm not certain that I got the second position correctly, but the two messages report different positions for our plane. Puzzled, I read each to the navigator and pilot.

"Both of those operators had fast hands," the pilot says, and I remember that he had been in the Army Signal Corps before he became a pilot, so he was listening to the Morse code as I received it. "I got the first position the same as you got it, but I'm not sure about the second."

"Neither am I," I say. "The jamming came back and made it hard to read."

"The first position puts us far north of where I estimate us to be," the navigator says. "It says that we'll run out of fuel in the ocean northwest of Scotland."

"So we'll have to make a major change in course to the southeast," the pilot says.

"But the second position," the navigator says, "if you guys got it accurately, puts us just about on the latitude that I estimate, but the longitude is farther west. Headwinds could cause that."

"So the second message has us heading toward Scotland," the pilot says, "but we aren't as close as you estimate we should be."

"That's right."

There is silence on the intercom.

"What do you think?" the pilot asks.

"I can't figure out how we can be so far from my estimated position," the navigator says.

"How about you, radio?" the pilot says to me.

"Direction-finding stations are supposed to be pretty accurate. If they're that good, how can the two positions be so different? Both messages were addressed to us."

"You think there's something rotten here?"

"It's strange that the jamming let up just as that message came through so clearly. Jamming was steady before that and has been since. That has been the only break in the interference."

"It's suspicious," the navigator says. "Maybe the Germans lowered their jamming long enough to get the first message out to lure us toward them. If we get close to the French coast, they could shoot us down easily enough."

"Do you recommend that we stay on your course or that we head southeast?" the pilot asks. The way he says it makes my mouth go dry. Our lives depend on this.

"I don't trust the clear message," the navigator says. "I recommend that we stay on our present course. I don't see how I can be so far off."

"That's right," the copilot says. "I think the Germans are trying to fake us into heading toward them."

"I agree," I say. "There's something strange about the first message. It's too good. I trust our navigator."

"Thanks for the vote of confidence," the navigator says. "I hope I deserve it."

"We'll stick with your position," the pilot says, "but it's a crap shoot. If we're wrong, we'll sure as hell go down in the ocean. No matter where we are, we only have about sixty minutes of gas left."

I am frightened. It's a terrible feeling to know that the only thing keeping you from the freezing water below is a dwindling supply of gasoline in the plane's almost-empty tanks. It never occurred to me that I might die in the war. In the movies, brave airmen come through "on a wing and a prayer" to the sound of triumphant music at the film's happy ending. Now it seems likely that we will crash into the ocean, and I face the cold reality of dying.

I can imagine the flight engineer hovering behind the pilot and copilot while he makes certain that the bomber isn't wasting an ounce of fuel. Below the flight deck, the navigator and bombardier huddle in the nose compartment.

We drone on in silence

Finally, the pilot calls me.

"We have about twenty minutes of gas. Try your best to get a mayday call out that somebody can hear."

I'm so terrified that my hand shakes when I send the message.

"I'll keep sending maydays," I say. "Maybe one will get through."

"When we run out of gas and head for the ocean," the pilot says, "screw the key down to send a constant signal that somebody may be able to get a fix on. I'll tell you when we're going down. Are the other guys asleep?"

"They're back in the waist compartment, sleeping on our luggage. I looked in on them about an hour ago, and all four were sound asleep."

"OK, don't tell them about this until we're close to the time we go down. I want the intercom clear for my orders. Make sure that two of the guys have the survival kit and the portable radio."

"Are you ready to launch the rafts if we need them?" the navigator asks.

"I hope so. Nobody ever told me how to do it. I hope it's straightforward."

"Before we hit, I'll come back and help you," the flight engineer says.

"I'm letting down slowly," the pilot says. "It gives us a little more range, and we're closer to the water when we run out of gas."

The door from the waist compartment behind me opens, and a sleepy Greg Araujo, our ball-turret gunner, comes in pointing to his watch.

"What's going on?" he says. "We should be in Prestwick, Scotland, by now."

"We've had bad headwinds. I guess we're still over the ocean. The pilot's trying to get us to land, but there's only fifteen minutes of gas left."

"Jesus!" His face turns pale. "Can I do anything to help?"

"Yes. When we hit, hang onto that yellow bag of survival stuff. If I can get the rafts launched, we'll sure need it."

He grabs the bag and heads back into the waist compartment.

As I desperately try to break through the jamming, the pilot calls.

"Our fuel gauges say that our tanks are empty. At best, we have ten minutes of gas. Have you been able to get a message through?"

"No."

"I was afraid of that." There is a note of hopelessness in his voice. "We're down to 500 feet, and we've dropped under the clouds. Look outside. You can see the ocean. At least it's a little lighter."

I look out the window. Heavy, dark clouds hover just above us, like the low ceiling of a cave. Surprisingly close beneath us are huge, angry waves of a turbulent ocean. We can't survive a landing in those massive swells. It will be like hitting a mountain. The plane will smash into pieces, and we will die. I've never been so terrified in my life. My heart races and I shake as I peer ahead.

"Any sign of land?" My voice is almost a plea.

"No," the copilot says.

"I've never flown when the gas supply was this low," the pilot says. "Look at those gauges! The engines should cut off any minute."

I work desperately to get a message through the howling on the radio. Trying to hold down panic, I remember the lead weight attached to several hundred feet of antenna wire trailing behind the bomber. The plane's regular antenna extends from the wings to the top of the tall rudder. It's adequate for most uses, but the trailing antenna allows me to send a much more powerful signal. Still, I have little hope that my calls are getting through the jamming.

Panic surges through me. To fight it, I concentrate on the things that I must do quickly if we survive our crash into those mountainous waves.

"What's that?" I hear the navigator say over the intercom.

"Look's like something in the water," the copilot says.

I press my face against the window and peer ahead, but I can't see a thing. Wait! There it is! A black object is in the ocean. It appears and disappears as huge swells wash over it. Is it a boat? Is it flotsam from a torpedoed ship? Is it a raft loaded with flyers hoping for rescue, as we soon may be? While the bomber races toward it, the object grows, but I still can't figure out what it is.

"It's a rock!" the pilot says.

We roar over it, and through a swirl of mist, I see a shiny, black rock washed by huge waves. It appears to be ten or twenty feet across its top.

"Look! Here come more rocks. Hey, one's pretty big," the navigator says with excitement in his voice. "There should be land ahead."

"I don't see any land," the pilot says. "Shit, we don't have any fuel left."

"Coastline!" the navigator roars.

I gaze ahead. A long coast emerges from the haze far ahead. I beg the plane to keep going. Time stands still. We'll never reach that coast, and we'll smash into those waves so perilously close beneath us. The coast creeps toward us. Finally, I hear a cheer as we sweep over cliffs and sail just above rolling hills of the greenest countryside that I have ever seen. With a start, I remember the lead weight and long antenna trailing below the plane and quickly press a switch for an electric motor to reel it in. Letting that weight smash through someone's home is not a good way to introduce us to the people in this lovely, green country. I gape at roads and winding lanes and forests and meadows and what looks like a gray castle far off in the misty distance.

"There's an airfield," the navigator yells.

"These engines will stop any second," the pilot says. "Fire red flares. I'm going straight in, no matter what they say."

I hear the bang of the flare gun as the flight engineer fires a flare. Immediately, a green light blinks from atop a squat, gray building on the edge of the airfield. A brown runway stretches out before us. The engines throttle back to a quiet whir, and the pilot eases the plane down for a wonderfully soft landing.

"Jesus, that was close," he gasps.

A yellow truck waits at the end of the runway as we roll to a stop. On its rear is a sign, "Follow Me." It leads our bomber to a parking spot near another squat building. Several Royal Air Force officers in blue uniforms wait there. As the pilot parks the plane in a designated spot, the engines cough and stop.

In the silence, I sigh. I don't think that my heart will ever slow down. When I climb stiffly from the bomber after a nerve-racking twelve hours and fifteen minutes in the air, I hear an officer tell Rex Townsend, our pilot, that we are at the RAF Coastal Command base at Enniskillen, Northern Ireland. He says that its aircrews fly anti-submarine patrols. I see twin-engine bombers dispersed around the airfield. They are sky blue on the underside and gray above, with the British roundel on wings and fuselage. The strong headwinds stopped our flight far short of its destination at Prestwick, Scotland. We barely made it to the Irish coast.

An RAF officer approaches me and introduces himself as a communications officer.

"I hear you had a bloody bad time with Jerry's jamming," he says.

"It was so strong that I couldn't hear anything," I say. "I don't see how planes get across in bad weather when they have that much interference."

"Usually, there is little jamming here, but I believe Jerry may have tried out a powerful directional beam last night, and you were in it."

"That's just our luck."

"I beg your pardon? Oh, yes, bloody bad luck. Of course, it is also possible that an atmospheric fluke caused it, but we must be alert to everything Jerry does. He is always trying something new. As soon as we get you settled, let's pop by my office and do a report on it. Excuse me for a moment. I must speak with that intelligence chap."

He hurries off to speak with another RAF officer who has been talking with Rex Townsend. As I stand beside the big bomber in a misty rain, I stare at the emerald hills beyond the airbase and utter another sigh of relief, but I can't stop trembling. It was a close call.

CHAPTER 2

Irish Interlude

Still shaken by our close call with the cold Atlantic, I climb into a gray Royal Air Force truck that carries us to comfortable quarters, where we have a breakfast of porridge (oatmeal), toast, orange marmalade, and tea. It tastes wonderful, although my hand shakes badly when I lift my mug of hot tea.

After breakfast, the gunners wander off, but pilot, copilot, and navigator stumble away to bed. I know how they feel. I've been awake for twenty-five exhausing hours. I crawl under gray, fuzzy blankets and am asleep in seconds.

When I wake up in the evening, I step outside into a blackout that hides the field. Dinner is boiled mutton (not lamb), boiled brussels sprouts, and bread. I am starved, but my stomach rebels violently, and I quickly achieve a lifelong dislike of mutton and brussels sprouts. The bread, however, is edible. Still tired, I return to bed to nurse my unhappy stomach.

The next morning, I wake to sunshine. The emerald countryside glistens. When I go to breakfast, I find no crewmembers. There's nothing to see on the airbase (if you've seen one airbase, you've seen them all), but outside the fence, Northern Ireland beckons.

Trying to be suave, I saunter up to the gate. Two blue-uniformed RAF guards in white belts and white gloves regard me with a mixture of curiosity and amusement. Dropping all pretense of being casual, I point outside the gate with a questioning look. A guard waves me through and goes back to his conversation. Just like that, I'm outside.

I wander down the road, gazing at a landscape of brilliant green. Grass, shrubs, trees, fields, and hills are so green that they take my breath away. The vegetation is not plain green. It's a riot of emerald and jade and olive and lime and pea green and sea green.

No wonder people call Ireland the Emerald Isle. Drops of water on leaves and blades of grass sparkle like diamonds in the sunshine.

A man driving a truck stops and offers me a ride. Riding on the left side of the road is unnerving, but it takes me into Enniskillen. People fill the streets. I'm soon the center of a cluster of jovial Irishmen who can't resist teasing a Yank who has nothing better to do than gape at their town. But to me, Enniskillen is a picture postcard. Ancient stone buildings with bric-a-brac trim line cobblestone streets. Parks are as green as the hills in the distance.

A half dozen Irishmen offer to show me the town. The obvious leader is Michael, a short, round man with a fringe of black hair around his bald head, a cherubic face, and a booming voice. He wears a white shirt, gray vest, and black pants that have seen better days. We visit Enniskillen Castle, a stone edifice with twin towers that rise high above the ground. It is the first genuine castle that I've ever seen. The castle's keep, which Michael tells me is its stronghold, dates to the 1400s. This awes me, because Columbus didn't discover America until 1492. I gape like Mark Twain's Innocent Abroad.

After the castle, I stroll with the Irishmen along Darling Street and Henry Street. They say that it was formerly called Beggar Street. We gaze at shops, and I return cheerful smiles from townspeople. My friends tell me that the lower end of High Street was once called Margaret's Gutter, after a woman who sold produce there. They show me the Town Hall, Saint Macartin's Church of Ireland Cathedral, Saint Michael's Catholic Church, the Butter Market (a sort of farmers' market), and the Diamond, a place for fairs and public gatherings. Michael tells me that John Wesley preached there to a "riotous crowd of sinners" in 1773.

With the onset of evening, my friends steer me into a pub. It's something out of the movies, with dark wood, aromas of malt beverages, and eruptions of laughter from a mixture of townspeople and RAF uniforms at tables and the bar. On one side of the room, several men entertain a noisy group of onlookers while they throw darts at a dartboard.

I want to show my appreciation to the men, so I offer to buy drinks. They accept and call for Guinness. I have no idea what Guinness is, but I guess that it is beer or ale. Michael suggests that it would be "enormously kind" of me to buy drinks for everyone. I gulp and nod, wondering whether I have enough money to pay for it. Michael rises.

"This fine Yank is buying for the house."

A cheer shakes the walls. My friends ask if I am hungry. Soon, meat-filled pastries appear, wrapped in newspaper. Everyone has another round of Guinness, and I find that drinks are inexpensive by American standards. I buy round after round. We toast Northern Ireland, Great Britain, the United States, King George, President Roosevelt, the RAF, and the U.S. Air Force. By now, things have become hazy, and I am having trouble saying the things that I want to say. Two RAF pilots guide me to the door while I wave goodbye to the cheering Irish. I try to help the RAF gentlemen stay on their feet while we engage a taxi, because I believe that they are quite drunk. I have difficulty finding the taxi's door, but what can you expect in a blackout with two drunken pilots?

As the taxi purrs down a dark road, we approach a broad meadow. Bathed in bright moonlight, eerie fingers of fog rise from it like a scene from a Dracula movie. The driver turns from the road leading across the meadow and enters a gloomy lane that circles it.

"Can't you take the direct route?" one of the RAF officers asks with a frown.

"Oh, sir, it's late," the driver says. "I'd be daft to cross that meadow now. The little people, you know."

I can't tell whether he's serious, or whether this is a clever way to get a bigger fare, but the meadow did look spooky with those skinny fingers of rising fog.

We leave the taxi at the airbase gate. I want to lie down and take a nap, but the RAF officers hold me up until they get me to my quarters.

"It might be wise to have some of your chaps with you if you plan to be in Enniskillen at night," one says.

"Why?" I say, trying to get his face in focus.

"The IRA, the Irish Republican Army, is active just over the border," one says. "They want to kidnap a Yank for some deviltry, so you must be alert. There jolly well could have been IRA in the pub tonight."

I try to digest what he said, but the effort is too much, so I thank the RAF officers and stumble inside. Why won't the undulating floor hold still until I can get into bed?

The next day, I return to Enniskillen. Michael promised more sightseeing. As I stroll on High Street, a young woman with tight, brown curls and blue eyes confronts me.

"Are you the Yank that Michael took to see the lot of our sights yesterday?"

I nod.

"Well, my name is Helen [she pronounces it "Hilin"], and Michael asked me to take you to visit Windmill Hill, if you've a mind for more sightseeing."

She leads me out of the city. After the RAF officers' warning, I worry. Could Helen be leading me into an IRA trap? But no one is there when we reach the breezy top of Windmill Hill, crowned by The Redoubt, the ruins of a fort built in the 1600s. It has a grand view of Enniskillen and the River Erne. Green hills and valleys stretch away forever. We sit, and Helen tells me the fort's history and peppers me with questions about America. Her goal is to migrate there as soon as the war ends.

Enniskillen is on an island between two big lakes, Upper Lough Erne and Lower Lough Erne. The lakes and city form a breathtaking vista. Helen turns to me.

"I like to sit and enjoy the scenery. If you've a mind to, we can sit for a time."

We fall silent. Helen probably dreams of America, while I ponder the bewildering path that led from my university to the top of a hill in Northern Ireland.

It began in November of 1942. I was a university student, working toward a career in biochemistry. But Selective Service was drafting millions of men into the army, and I heard that the draft board in my home town planned to draft me. Most draftees went to the infantry, but I knew that I would be a terrible infantryman. Still, I was patriotic and wanted to help my country if it needed me. Could my scientific training be useful? It was something that few people had.

The opportunity came in late November. Two U.S. Army Air Force lieutenants spoke to a campus audience about openings in the air force in administration, intelligence, and technical areas after you completed officer candidate school. After an aptitude test, a lieutenant took me aside and grinned.

"Congratulations," he said. "Your high score makes you eligible for direct entry into officer candidate school, provided you pass the physical."

A sergeant typed my enlistment forms, and the lieutenants and I signed them.

"Take these to a recruiting station," he said, "and you'll go in as a volunteer officer candidate. Ninety days in Miami Beach, and you'll be a second lieutenant."

South Haven, Michigan, my home town, was too small to have a recruiting station, so I went to the recruiting station in Kalamazoo, forty miles away. There, I got a hostile reception.

"Too good for us enlisted men, huh?" the sergeant said, nose to nose, while he spewed alcoholic breath over me. "You want to be a goddamn officer. You ain't old enough to command shit."

He typed forms, attached the lieutenant's papers to the back of his forms, shoved them into a brown envelope, and told me to take them to the National Guard Armory.

I entered the armory in Kalamazoo at 8 A.M. on December 2, 1942. An army corporal took my papers and had me join a line of pale men moving along a hallway. They were draftees and were unhappy with being forced to leave their families to enter the army. The man ahead of me told of leaving his wife and two children an hour ago.

"It was awful," he said. "We all cried. I don't know how we can do it."

The man behind me was single, but he worked a farm for his elderly parents, and he didn't know how they would manage without him. Other men in line had equally-sad stories. I began to see a dark side of war that had not been in the newspapers.

First stop was a medical laboratory. Two men with dead-white faces lay on cots at the rear.

"I bet they passed out," a man behind me said. "Don't look, or you will too."

While I wondered why the sight of a man on a cot would make me faint, a medic took my blood. Thud! The man behind me fainted. The medics immunized me for typhoid, tetanus, and small-pox, examined me, and pronounced me fit for military service.

Busses took several hundred of us to Fort Custer, an army base near Battle Creek. Starting my military career at a post named for General Custer didn't seem to bode well for the future. Fort Custer looked like a Siberian prison camp, as wind whirled snow around hundreds of grim, white, two-story barracks. The future looked even worse when sergeants made several hundred of us stand shivering for an hour in snow and freezing wind, while they went inside an office to sort our papers. Later, we put on wrinkled uniforms reek-ing of mothballs, filled bags with uniforms and equipment, com-pleted forms, and took tests. We were a sorry-looking bunch.

But something was wrong. I met six volunteer officer candidates that were leaving within the hour for Miami Beach. They wore VOC tags and had special treatment as budding officers. I asked the ser-geant in charge of my barracks to let me go to the personnel office to straighten out my records so I could go with them.

"You ain't goin' nowhere, shithead," the sergeant, thoroughly drunk, said.

The next day, I hauled my bags through deep snow, as hundreds of recruits trudged to a railroad siding. We looked like Napoleon's retreat from Moscow. We boarded old coaches with hard, straight-back seats. For three days, the train crept through Illinois, Kentucky, Tennessee, and Alabama. The only food for breakfast, lunch, and dinner was canned sauerkraut. We ate it from the can, or we starved. That much sauerkraut gave everyone severe diarrhea. Day and night, a line of men waited in agony to get into the tiny bathroom at the end of the car. I developed a lifetime dislike of sauerkraut.

The train took us to Keesler Army Air Field on the Gulf of Mex-ico near Biloxi, Mississippi. Doctors treated diarrhea and gave us a searching medical exam. Sergeants got our uniforms cleaned, pressed, and decorated with Air Force insignia. A personnel ser-geant frowned at my file and took it to a lieutenant.

"Some dumbass stapled your OCS forms to the back of your file," the lieutenant said. "Normally, we would ship you to Miami

Beach, but you're one of the few recruits physically qualified for combat flight. You're also the only one with aptitude for Morse code. Most men can't learn it. The air force's top priority is flight crews, so training you to be a radio operator on a bomber takes precedence over training you to be an officer."

My world crashed, thanks to a drunken recruiting sergeant.

I was supposed to have six weeks of basic training at Keesler Field, but being slated for a bomber crew put me on a fast track. I only had time to learn how to salute before I boarded a train three days later to ride in first-class luxury, without sauerkraut, on a train to Chicago. At the Air Force Chicago Technical School, I lived in a handsome room with marble bath in a high-rise hotel (later the Conrad Hilton) on Michigan Boulevard in downtown Chicago. It overlooked Grant Park and Lake Michigan. The air force had commandeered it for a technical school. I dined in the gold-trimmed grand ballroom on cuisine prepared by hotel chefs and lived a life of relative luxury.

Morse code was easy. The first day, three of us memorized thirty-six combinations of "dah" and "dit" that stood for letters of the alphabet and numerals zero through nine. We got ever faster at sending and receiving Morse code while teachers aided the many students who had trouble. Maybe it's genetic. Off duty, I explored Chicago's art museum, natural history museum, aquarium, planetarium, and museum of science and industry. Dottie Dickerson, a pretty girl who graduated from high school with me, worked in Chicago, and we sampled Chicago's nightlife. I tried to get back on track to Miami Beach. A sympathetic lieutenant prepared a transfer order, but school ended with a diploma that said I was a qualified air force radio operator.

On a bomber, the navigator, bombardier, flight engineer, radio operator, and gunners had to learn to fire a machine gun, so I went west for an appointment with a machine gun. A Santa Fe train gave me a first-class ride. Santa Fe trains did not carry dining cars, so it stopped at Kansas City, Dodge City, and other towns. At each, the passengers went into the station for excellent meals served by the famous Harvey girls. The train finally left me, at 3 A.M., on a road near Kingman, Arizona. A truck was supposed to be waiting to take me to the airbase. No truck, so I walked along the dark road until the truck appeared. The driver said that the road crawled with rattlesnakes at night.

Kingman Army Air Field baked in the sun in the Hualapai valley in northwest Arizona, between the Hualapai Mountains and the Cerbat Range. The mountains and desert were awesome, and there were unending numbers of bugs, lizards, and snakes for me to watch for entertainment. Days were blistering hot. Dozens fainted during afternoon calisthenics.

The main event was to fire a big, black .50-caliber machine gun, with a belt of six-inch shells. The target was a bed sheet mounted on a car that ran round and round on a track a hundred yards away. The car rounded the curve toward me. I grabbed the handles on the gun and pulled the trigger. The gun spat fire and kicked upward toward the sky, taking me off my feet. Each time I fired, it did the same.

"I don't think I hit the target at all," I said to the instructor.

"It don't matter," he said. "In a B-24, you radio guys sit behind the pilot and don't have a gun. On a B-17, you got a piss-ant gun in the roof of the radio room that couldn't hit shit, so you're best off to just leave it alone."

I fired for day after day, but my shots went skyward. Some are probably still in orbit around the moon. After two weeks of it, I moved to Yucca Army Air Base, a tiny, remote field so overrun by rattlesnakes that the base doctor had an amazing collection. I put on flying coveralls, helmet, goggles, and parachute. Feeling like an actor in a Hollywood movie, I strode out onto the flight line to face a long row of North American AT-6 single-engine trainers. The rear cockpit of each had a machine gun. My pilot was a big, jovial lieutenant. A mechanic strapped me in, the pilot waved, the engine snarled, and away we went. I was flying! In the air, I gaped at a panorama of mountains, mesas, valleys, and desert. A rare road crossed the empty landscape, and the double-track Santa Fe Railroad drew a bold, black line from east to west. I was an airborne tourist and drank in the beauty of Arizona until the pilot called that it was my turn to fire the machine gun. Below, a plane pulled a bed sheet on a long cable. We dove. I fired. We did it for a week, but I didn't hit the target.

"I don't think I ever hit the target," I told the pilot. Maybe they would send me back to officer candidate school.

"You did OK," he said. "You didn't throw up, and you didn't wet your pants."

No one told me that I had to wet my pants. If I had, would I be on my way to officer candidate school? Too late.

Despite the fact that I never hit a target, the air force gave me silver wings, wristwatch, sexy leather jacket, sexier sunglasses, and flight clothing. It promoted me to sergeant (three stripes) on flight status, which added 50 percent to my higher pay.

Another train ride on the Union Pacific Railroad through the dusty, little town of Las Vegas, Nevada, and the beautiful metropolis of Salt Lake City took me to Ephrata Army Air Field in central Washington. There, the air force assembled my flight crew.

Rex Townsend, the pilot, was a handsome Californian from Sacramento. Soft-spoken and amiable, he wanted to fly fighters, but the air force assigned him to a B-17.

Gunnar Swanson, the copilot, was a lanky, genial Scandinavian from Manhasset, New York. His calm manner and good advice became a big help to me.

Ken Kinsella, the navigator, was a big, jovial sophisticate from Washington, DC. He had a booming voice, a never-ending smile, and a stock of funny songs.

Ralph Ballmer, the bombardier, was a short, cherubic comedian from Toledo, Ohio. He kept me laughing from the moment I met him.

Lloyd Lyons, the flight engineer, was a drawling Virginian from Blacksburg. He quickly showed that he knew the workings of a B-17 bomber.

Greg Araujo, the ball-turret gunner, was a husky, cheerful Hispanic from Kansas City. I admired his courage for volunteering to fly in the cramped ball-turret beneath the plane.

Ed Norton, a slim Pennsylvanian, was a waist gunner. He was older than the rest of us, and his black hair had silver threads, but he was a source of good advice for nineteen-year-old me.

Ken Tasker, the other waist gunner, was a Kansas farmer. He got airsick but hid it because he wanted to fly so badly. I couldn't understand wanting to fly, but I admired his grit.

John Kindred, the tail gunner, was a quiet fellow from Saint Louis. The best way to describe him was thoughtful.

From the moment that we met, we were together. We ate together, relaxed together, went to orientation classes together, and talked endlessly. The air force felt that bomber crews would perform their jobs better if we bonded and trusted each other. Our first job was to become familiar with every inch of a B-17 bomber.

The B-17 bristled with eleven fifty-caliber machine guns. The press named it a Flying Fortress and said it could fight its way through swarms of fighters to put tons of explosives on a target with pickle-barrel accuracy. We actually believed this. Its top speed was 300 miles per hour, but it cruised at 170. Its range was nearly 2,000 miles.

On Friday, the thirteenth of August 1943 (another bad omen), we donned our sexy leather jackets and sexier sunglasses to climb into a B-17E for our first flight. Up we climbed into the blue and went sightseeing in the Cascades past Mount Rainier to Seattle. The city was tucked neatly between Puget Sound on the west and Lake Washington on the east. We circled Seattle many times at 3,000 feet while I did my tourist thing of gazing raptly, admiring everything that I could see in the city.

After a month of flying to Seattle, we moved to Kearney Army Air Field in central Nebraska. There, we again flew around leisurely. I assumed it was how we trained. The countryside was amazingly flat, with the Platte River snaking below us. Only in western Nebraska did the ground become rough, and Rex showed us Chimney Rock's skinny finger pointed skyward and spectacular Scott's Bluff that rose above the Platte River.

Rex liked to fly about twenty feet off the ground and scare the pants off of everyone we met. The high point came when he flew down the main street of an Iowa city and turned left at the town square. Since the base never sent me a practice message, I spent my flying time sightseeing, while the gunners slept in the rear of the plane. The media made us into glamour boys and the B-17 Flying

Fortress into an invincible, glamourous plane. Amazingly, we believed this, too.

Toward the end of training, we had to fly at 20,000 feet. A 170-mile-per-hour blast of below-zero air came in through the open roof of the radio room. I froze. I had never been so cold. I also had to breathe oxygen through a mask. It was difficult and surprising: the heroic flyers in movies didn't wear oxygen masks.

With that, training ended. We would fly a new B-17G to Syracuse, New York; Presque Isle, Maine; Goose Bay, Labrador; and across the Atlantic to Prestwick, Scotland, to join the Eighth Air Force. A nonstop flight was dangerous, because it was at the limit of a B-17's range, but storms ruled out a landing in Iceland, and the Eighth Air Force badly needed us and our new B-17G.

This puzzled me. If bombing missions were so easy, why did they need us so desperately?

CHAPTER 3

A Death Sentence

E nniskillen, Northern Ireland. The day after I reminisce on Windmill Hill, we climb into the B-17G and take off into low clouds and rain for a brief flight across Northern Ireland's hills to Langford Lodge, a U.S. Air Force base outside of Belfast. Air force mechanics take away our new B-17G to modify it for combat. After an all-day wait, a truck carries us through the bustling city of Belfast to a busy dock. Loaded with baggage, we stagger up a gangplank onto a ferryboat crowded with civilians and British soldiers. Benches fill the ship's cavernous interior, and we find seats among the people that pack the benches. As night descends upon Belfast, the steamship slips from the harbor and sails into the blackness of the Irish Sea. The water is rough, and the ferry pitches and rolls so much that you must either sit on a bench, or hold the railing on the wet deck in darkness. Many people get seasick and run outside. The ferry shows no lights because of the threat of German submarines, and I shudder at the thought of how a single torpedo could blow the little ship sky high.

When we land in England late at night, I see that the ferry terminal adjoins a busy railroad station. It has no waiting room. Instead, multiple tracks under a shed adjoin a brick building that has a window where you buy tickets and a window where you buy hot tea. It is cold in the train shed, so hot tea (served British style in mugs with milk and sugar) is welcome. Amid clouds of steam, the quaint (to my eyes) engines and cars in the train shed are right out of a Hitchcock movie. Passengers hurrying on the platforms look like characters surrounding Richard Hannay in *The Thirty-Nine Steps*.

An American transportation officer gets us two first-class compartments on an overnight, southbound express. It introduces me to British trains and their three classes of passenger cars. First class has elegant, roomy compartments with comfortable seats. First-class passenger cars are comparable with the best in the United States. Second-class compartments are plain, and third class is a cattle car, with wooden benches in open cars for passengers. Our compartments have doors on the outside walls that allow us to step from the station platform into the compartment. The far side of the compartment has glass windows and a sliding door that opens onto a corridor running along the side of the car. The compartment has two plush sofas that face each other. Each holds four persons. Again, I feel like I'm in a Hitchcock movie.

Rex Townsend says that we are on our way to the U.S. Air Force Reception Center at Stone, England. A railroad worker slams our outside door. A uniformed man on the platform blows a whistle and waves a baton at the engineer. The engine whistle whoops and away we go. I try to sleep, but can't. Too much has happened too quickly. I sit with eyes closed and listen to the soft conversation of my fellow crew members.

In early morning, we step off the train, and a truck takes us to the reception center. Air force men that have just arrived, mostly by ship, fill the place. We stay in a former girls' school, and the rooms are bright and clean. Food is poor, and I meet Spam, the canned meat that I will face so often that I still smile when I pass it at the market. As canned meat goes, Spam is edible, but the problem comes when you face it day after day. Still, it gives the air force a way to feed us meat without danger of spoilage. I meet desert butter, a waxy butter substitute that cannot be melted or spread and tastes like house paint. There also are foul-tasting powdered milk and powdered eggs.

The first disturbing event occurs when I meet a radio operator who is passing through the center on his way home. He tells me happily that he finished his twenty-five missions.

"I feel like the luckiest son of a bitch in the world," he says. "I didn't think there was a chance in hell that I would finish."

"Why not?" I ask.

He looks at me, and I see something in his eyes. Is it pity? Is it sadness?

"Two other crews came in with us as replacements," he says, "and three more came in the next week. Our crew is the only one of the six that got through twenty-five missions."

"What happened to the other five?"

He stares at me, and a look of pity is definitely there.

"Blew up, burned up, how the hell should I know? They didn't make it."

"How can it be that bad?" I say. "I'd have heard about it."

"Wait and see," the veteran says. "They didn't want you to know, or you'd all go AWOL in the states. When I get off the boat in New York, I'm gonna kiss the ground. I'm that lucky."

He turns to leave.

"I hope you make it," he says, with pity in his eyes again.

A cold feeling creeps through me. Is this why the air force rushed me through training so fast? Am I slated to replace a dead radio operator? Back in the United States, is someone rushing through training to replace me? Is it that bad? Suddenly, I'm scared.

After three days at Stone, a train carries us south to the U.S. Eighth Air Force base at Bovingdon, a village near London. The daytime ride is my first chance for a good look at the English countryside. Spellbound, I watch passing fields, forests, and villages. I see cottages with thatched roofs that look like those I saw as a child in books of nursery rhymes. I smile at little automobiles and boxy trucks driving on the left side of the road, police officers in tall hats, red telephone booths, red, double-deck buses, and lots of people on bicycles. I see signs advertising Bovril and others saying, "My Goodness, My Guinness!" The landscape is wonderfully neat and attractive, and the villages look like movie sets. With a thrill, I reflect that I'm in England—land of Shakespeare, King Arthur, and my ancestors.

Bovingdon Air Base is the Eighth Air Force's Combat Crew Replacement Center. It is a set of runways, a group of battered B-17 bombers, a collection of drab buildings, and a cluster of tents. A captain gives a welcoming lecture and tells us that they will train us for combat, teach us British procedures, and assign us to a Heavy Bombardment Group (termed a Bomb Group). Bovingdon is grim, muddy, and cold in December of 1943. Its low, gray buildings are ugly, but they are palaces compared with the tents in which we live. They must be left over from World War I, because the canvas is rotten and pierced with rips and holes. A cold rain falls, and water pours in through the openings. The tents have no floors, only sticky mud that clings to everything. I can't keep things dry, including the cot on which I try to sleep under cold, rain-soaked blankets. I wake up the first night with a puddle of chilly water between my feet at the foot of my bed.

Although the radio operator at the Stone Replacement Center stunned me with the news that his crew was the only one of six that completed twenty-five missions, I am not prepared for the instructor's words when a class of radio operators begins training for combat flight.

"For all practical purposes, you got no training in the U.S.," the instructor says. "You'll need a load of training before you have any hope of getting through a combat mission. Even with training, about half of new crews don't survive the first six missions."

A cold fist grabs me. I thought that we would sail over Germany, brushing aside fighters and dropping our bombs. I'm a real innocent, but it's the impression that I got from movies, radio, newspapers, and even from air force instructors in the United States.

"I was told that a B-17's guns can take care of fighters," a radio operator says.

"That's horseshit." the instructor says. "Until you have plenty of fighter escort, the Krauts will shoot you down. They shoot down our guys on almost every mission."

He looks around at the now-silent class of radio operators.

"They didn't tell you, but the average life of a B-17 over Germany is eleven missions. You have to finish twenty-five, so your odds of getting through are damn poor."

As he talks, my mind races. If we are worse than average, we won't even finish eleven missions. Even if we are better than average, we could go down on our fifteenth or twentieth mission. Only if we are incredibly lucky can we have a chance of finishing twenty-five missions. Little wonder that the radio operator at Stone gazed at me with pity in his eyes. My chance of finishing is almost zero. Coming here is a death sentence!

"The Eighth Air Force began bombing operations over Europe on August 17, 1942," the instructor says, "but no crew completed twenty-five missions until the *Memphis Belle* did it in May of 1943. During eight months, every other crew was lost before reaching twenty-five missions."

"If it's this bad, how do I quit?" someone says. "I was drafted into this, and I got a wife and three little girls at home. I don't intend to get myself killed."

"You can't quit," the instructor says. "They'll arrest you for desertion in the face of the enemy. Maximum penalty is death by firing squad. If you're lucky, the court martial might take pity on you and give you twenty years in prison."

We are in a trap. How did it happen? I never heard of these losses in the United States. It looks to me that the Pentagon kept the rate of loss quiet to get fellows to join the air force. Only a fool would volunteer to fly twenty-five missions if there was almost no chance of surviving them. The instructor's words give me a sleepless night under water-soaked blankets.

Bovingdon's proximity to London allows us to see air raids. I stand outside my tent in the blackout and gaze south at London's many searchlights probing the sky among bright flashes of hundreds of antiaircraft shells. Big flares of light on the horizon tell of bombs dropped, and the southern sky turns orange from fires.

On Christmas Eve of 1943, I sit in cold, wet darkness in my tent and dream of past Christmases, with a tree and lights and decorations and carols and presents and Christmas dinner. Tonight, there is blackness, cold, and rain.

Next day, Bovingdon's mess hall amazes me with turkey, dressing, mashed potatoes, and cranberry sauce, but it still doesn't seem like Christmas. The day after Christmas, our stay ends just as we begin training. The bomber groups need replacements so badly that they must train us as best they can. It's a bad feeling to know that we will replace men that were just killed.

Bombers in the Eighth Air Force are assigned to one of three air divisions. The 1st and 3rd Divisions fly B-17s. The 2nd flies B-24s. The B-24 can fly faster than a B-17 and carry more bombs, but it can't take as much punishment. Each air division is composed of several combat wings. Each combat wing has three bomb groups, and each bomb group has four bomb squadrons.

We join the 1st Air Division's 40th Combat Wing, and it assigns us to the 92nd Bomb Group. The 92nd is the oldest heavy bomber group in England, and its ground personnel are veterans, many of whom arrived in July of 1942. At the same time, three other flight crews are assigned to the 92nd Bomb Group. Their pilots are Robert Lehner, Charles Nashold, and William Parramore. Remember those names and the fact that the average life of a B-17 over Germany is only eleven missions.

CHAPTER 4

Blimey! Home, Sweet Home

The 92nd Bomb Group occupies a former RAF airfield outside the village of Podington in Bedfordshire, about fifty miles north of London. The forty men of the four crews assigned to the 92nd Bomb Group get acquainted while we ride a London, Midland, and Scotland train to Wellingboro, the railroad station closest to Podington. We look like we were assembled by Hollywood casting. We are tall and short, slim and husky, baby-faced and graying, talkative and silent, New Yorkers and country boys. Some joke or talk of sports, but there is an undercurrent of concern. How can anyone ignore the news that the average life of a bomber over Germany is eleven missions, but we must complete twenty-five? Unless we are very lucky, the chances are that most of us won't make it through twenty-five missions. Who, among the fellows sitting in the compartment with me, will die? Which ones have only a few weeks of life remaining? It's an awful feeling.

For most of the trip, I talk with Herb Moomaw, radio operator for Robert Lehner's crew. Herb is a big, smiling, intelligent fellow with a calm voice and positive outlook. Talking with him makes me feel better.

"The missions may be rough, but I bet we come through all right," Herb says. "It'll give us something to tell our grandchildren."

"Hell, I don't even have kids yet," chuckles a gunner sitting across from us, "but if any of these English women need help, I'm available."

This chatter continues while the train rushes through an ever-changing panorama of fields, forests, villages, and towns. It stops at St. Albans, Luton, and Bedford. At each station, British men in fine suits and derby hats mix with men in tweeds and gray caps and women wearing everything from furs to cloth coats. Groups of

British soldiers, probably on leave, carry packs and rifles. I see no American uniforms on the platforms.

The train pulls into Wellingboro, which appears to be a medium-size town of brick and stone buildings. Army trucks wait to carry us to our new home. The air base is more attractive than I expected, on land bordered by trees and farmers' fields. The Orlebar family owned the western portion of the airfield. We pass its dignified, Queen Anne–style mansion, Hinwick House, just before we reach the airbase gate. I learn later that it was built for Richard Orlebar around 1700. Lord Luke owned the land which is now the eastern part of the airfield.

The airbase has a bright look, far more attractive than Bovingdon, with trees, grass, walkways, and paved roads. Offices, shops, and living quarters are in one-story British buildings or Quonset huts, which are structures of ribbed metal that look like huge pipes half buried in the ground. Some buildings are gray, but many are a pea green that blends with the countryside.

After military police pass us through the gate, I see the 92nd Group's headquarters on my left. To the right is a side road lined with living quarters for flight crews and base personnel. If you continue on the main road, you pass buildings that house support units until you reach a hangar, a two-story control tower, and the flying field. The field has three runways circled by a taxiway. Branching off the taxiway are about thirty tracks dispersed around the field. They lead to concrete pads on which B-17s park. The layout reminds me that bombers scatter around the field to minimize loss from German air raids.

The 92nd Bomb Group consists of the 325th, 326th, 327th, and 407th Bomb Squadrons, plus military police, fire, medical, and other units. I am tense about what lies ahead when the base commander assigns us to the 327th Bomb Squadron. With Araujo, Kindred, Lyons, Norton, and Tasker, I settle into a pea-green building next to 327th Squadron headquarters. Townsend, Swanson, Kinsella, and Ballmer are in a pea-green building across the street. Shower and bathroom facilities are in a nearby structure. Except for the hotel in Chicago, the living quarters are superior to any military housing I occupied in the United States. The place is clean, bright, and roomy. It houses a mix of flight crews and clerks. The clerks are a cheerful lot and give us a warm welcome.

One of the residents is John Sloan, the group historian. To my young eyes, he appears to be a million years old, and I wonder why he is even in the air force, especially overseas. To my question, he directs me to ask the Cuyahoga County, Ohio, draft board. John is an erudite writer, and I quickly find that I like nothing better than to talk with him. We spend evenings discussing history, literature, and the arts. (His book, *The Route as Briefed,* is a record of the 92nd Group's missions, triumphs, and tragedies.) Dick Shaw is another gem. From Newtown, Ohio, just outside Cincinnati, he is a clerk at group headquarters and a cheery gold mine of information. Al Coppage, a short, stubby gunner, provides entertainment with non-stop chatter, most of it funny. His foil is Earl Varner, a North Carolina gunner who loudly drawls strong opinions on everything from powdered milk to British royalty.

Living is surprisingly comfortable. Combat crews have a separate mess that serves better food than that served to the base personnel. The combat mess is a bright cafeteria, with white walls decorated by colorful squadron insignia. A cafeteria line runs along one side of the room, and tables fill the rest. Instead of eating from the military's metal trays with depressions, combat flyers have white, ceramic plates, cups, and bowls. Spam is here, but a chef does remarkable things with it. There is desert butter and powdered milk, but he makes chocolate ice cream from powdered milk, which kills the milk's repulsive flavor, and his cooks make sensational pudding cakes.

We have a Red Cross Club for relaxation, with coffee, sandwiches, cakes, music, library, pool tables, ping pong, and a quiet place to write letters. Two attractive Red Cross women operate the club. A tan dog helps them. He begs for food and gives you a slobbery kiss if you give him some.

A movie theater has a screen, a noisy projector at the rear, and rows of wooden benches for a roomful of film critics. Movies are welcome, except war movies with Hollywood heroes, who draw boos and obscene epithets. A rumor is that the government requires Hollywood to make these films for propaganda at home. On the other

hand, whenever a romantic film has a panting love scene, the pro-
jectionist stops the movie and runs the scene over and over, while
the audience hoots, hollers, squirms, and moans, "Oh, baby!"

In addition to movies, USO shows arrive periodically and bring
terrific entertainers from Hollywood and Broadway. They put up
with a lot of hardship to play for us, and everyone loves them.
Cheers are deafening.

A loudspeaker in my building provides popular music by the
Armed Forces Network, news from the BBC, and music with propaganda from Axis Sally, a German who often ends her program by
playing "Lili Marlene," a sad song popular with the German Army.

The base personnel are superior to those in the United States.
They all seem eager to do a good job and give us the best chance
possible to fly our missions successfully. Thus, good people and
good facilities make life on the airbase better than at airbases in the
United States. It would all be ideal if it wasn't for the fact that we
have to go out and be killed. Veteran crewmembers assure us that
our chance of surviving twenty-five missions is not good, but since
we can't do anything about it, the best thing to do is to not think
about it.

Herb Moomaw and I spend hours talking of home and the war
and what the twenty-five missions ahead of us may be like. Others
talk of these things, but many talk nonstop about women and sex.
Some have had amazing sexual experiences, and they say that London is a vast sexual playground. Although I dated several girls in my
hometown, I had no experience with sex, so I listen with interest.

The group is lenient about us leaving the base. The village of
Podington is tiny, and I wonder how the villagers cope with all the
Americans. Several miles north is the small town of Rushden.
Northwest is the bigger town of Wellingboro, but it is off limits to
us. It contains a U.S. Army supply unit staffed by black soldiers. The
enterprising fellows tell local girls that they are American Indians in
order to get dates. I admire their style, but when our boys from the
South heard of them dating white girls, they grabbed their pistols to
go into Wellingboro and kill blacks. Headquarters quickly placed
Wellingboro off limits to airmen from our base, except for trips to
and from the railroad station. Instead, the 92nd Group busses us to

the large city of Northampton. Veterans say that it is good because there is far more to do in Northampton, with theaters, restaurants, pubs, stores, and lots of girls.

The 92nd Group must need us badly. As soon as we get unpacked and settled in our quarters, training for combat begins. Although the group needs us now, it must get us ready to fly a mission with a chance of returning. Our squadron commander says that our gunners have not had a fraction of the gunnery training that they need, so Greg Araujo, Lloyd Lyons, Ken Tasker, Ed Norton, and John Kindred go to a gunnery range at The Wash, on the east coast of England, for intensive training. Rex Townsend and Gunnar Swanson practice formation flying. Ken Kinsella studies British navigation systems, and Ralph Ballmer views photos of German targets and simulates bombing.

Major Capdeveille, the group communications officer, sends me to a building near the flight line. I quickly learn the radio procedures during a mission and find that the main change in the radio room of a combat-ready B-17 is the addition of a shelf above my desk. It holds a secret British IFF (identification friend or foe) transmitter. This black box identifies us as an Allied plane to avoid us being shot down by British fighters if we are ever alone when we approach England. Inside the IFF is enough dynamite to destroy it. If it might fall into enemy hands, I push two red buttons on it, and—*BOOM*—it's wrecked. I hope it's all that is wrecked: I'm not keen on setting off dynamite inside an airplane.

We use secret codes that change daily. Messages are in five-letter groups. The daily decoding key is on a thin square of rice paper inside a clear, plastic holder. If I think that it will fall into German hands, I must chew up and swallow the rice paper—just like Hollywood, except the rice paper tastes terrible.

To my surprise, I find that operating the radio is only a tiny part of my job. First, I must keep a detailed log. I knew that I would have to record radio messages, but I also must record everything that I see, especially things on the ground. This includes boat, rail, and road traffic, fires, and anything unusual. Apparently, many radio operators don't take time to observe and log what they see, so I am urged to watch and record everything that I see while we are over enemy territory. I am going to be a big snoop.

Next, I learn to operate a large camera installed in the floor of the radio room. At least one camera-carrying plane goes on each mission. It takes a series of pictures during bombing to show where the bombs hit. I also learn to use a hand-held camera to photograph anything interesting. Whatever I record seems to be interesting to the people in our group intelligence office.

Finally, I must distribute "chaff" when we approach a target. Chaff, called "window" by the British, is a mass of thousands of aluminum foil strips that remind me of the icicles you put on a Christmas tree. The Germans use electronic means to aim the antiaircraft guns that blast our bombers from the sky. A cloud of chaff throws off their aim by causing a false reflection for their electronic locators. Chaff comes in paper cylinders, with hundreds of foil strips in each. As we approach a target, I rip open one cylinder of chaff after another and feed it out through a chute in the side of my compartment.

I go to the medical section to learn how to survive below-zero temperatures in the 170-mile-per-hour wind that roars in through the open roof of the radio room and out through the waist gunners' open windows. Even the heaviest sheepskin won't keep me warm, so I get an electrically heated suit of fuzzy, blue material. It reminds me of a toddler's cold weather pajamas. Heating wires run through it as in an electric blanket. An electric cord plugs into an outlet next to my seat in the radio room. Electric boots and gloves plug into sockets at the ankles and wrists of the electric suit. Freezing is a deadly problem in a B-17F. Even the new model of oxygen mask that I brought from the United States accumulates ice so fast in the intense cold that it clogs up your oxygen supply. A gunner in the 91st Group just died when he didn't notice that ice had blocked his mask. Captain Furniss, our flight surgeon, modifies my mask but warns that I must check it regularly to clear out ice while flying at high altitude.

Even if the oxygen mask works, low atmospheric pressure at high altitude causes "altitude sickness," producing headache, nausea, and poor coordination. I will fly at altitudes equal to standing on top of Mount Everest. In severe cases, the low pressure could cause fluid to leak from my bloodstream into my lungs and brain, killing me. Exertion at high altitude will amplify altitude sickness and double me over with cramps.

Captain Moneymaker, the escape officer, has me don a white shirt, tweed jacket, and blue tie. An assistant rearranges my hair to look European and takes my picture. I get four passport photos of my European self to be used for false identity papers in case our bomber is shot down. They sew a tiny compass into the collar of my flight suit. I will carry a larger compass in my pocket, along with lots of French and German money, maps printed on silk, and a big chocolate bar. If I am shot down over Germany, I must slip through the countryside until I find a railroad and can sneak aboard a boxcar labeled as headed for France. The French Resistance should then get me to Spain.

At squadron operations, I learn that each squadron sends out a formation of six or seven B-17s. Three squadrons fly together as the 92nd Bomb Group of eighteen to twenty-one bombers. The fourth squadron gets to rest or flies with the odd squadrons of two other groups to form a composite group. Three groups fly together to form a combat wing of fifty-four to sixty-three planes.

I learn that the Germans have hundreds of antiaircraft guns around cities. The gunners can aim at us or fire straight up to form a barrage through which we must fly. The Germans have 2,000 fighter planes in France, Belgium, Holland, and northern Germany. They are the FW-190, ME-109, and ME-110 aircraft, armed with cannons and machine guns.

To counter them, we have some 600 machine guns in a combat wing, and we have the P-47, P-38, and P-51 fighters to protect us. The P-47 can only escort us a little past the German border, but the P-38 can go farther, and the P-51 can escort us anywhere. We have an adequate number of P-47s, fewer P-38s, and only a small number of P-51s.

That finishes training. With the rest of my crew scattered, Major Kalhorn, the squadron executive officer, grins and suggests that I visit London for two days. I gasp. Me, on my own in London? It has huge numbers of people, royalty, famous buildings, shows, restaurants, and stores. I also heard that it has great numbers of girls. Maybe I can find a nice girl who would like to go to places with me. It's worth a thought. Excitement grips me. I'm going to London!

CHAPTER 5

London

Imust carry a gas mask with me to London. It is in a little canvas bag that slings over my shoulder like a lady's purse. There is fear that Hitler will unleash nerve gas or mustard gas on London. The chemical warfare officer says that even a tiny drop of nerve gas would kill me. Likewise, when he places a microscopic drop of mustard gas on my arm, it raises a half inch blister. I'm convinced. This is serious stuff.

The base has frequent transportation to the railroad station at Wellingboro. Trains of the London, Midland, and Scotland Railway run often, so I buy a first-class ticket just before a train rolls to a stop at the station. I step into a handsome compartment containing several English gentlemen in well-tailored charcoal suits, white shirts, and black derby hats. Each reads a newspaper and ignores me, which is fine because I want to gaze at the countryside.

The train leaves Wellingboro and speeds down the track, blasting past stations and stopping only at Bedford, Luton, and St. Albans. Between stations, I watch the changing panorama of meadows, forests, rolling hills, and villages. It's like a big movie set that shows the British countryside. Even in January, it is pretty.

As the train enters London, I gasp when it slows and passes block after block of wrecked homes, stores, factories, and churches—all destroyed by German bombs. I gape at blackened skeletons of buildings, with twisted frameworks and bare girders that look like bony fingers pointing toward the sky. Some blocks are massive piles of rubble. Some have a single building destroyed, as though a plane dropped one bomb. Great piles of debris close many streets. In other places, the rubble has been removed, leaving vast, empty spaces. Many buildings are only blackened frameworks. Some blocks are totally destroyed, and next to them are blocks of untouched buildings. The desolation is awful.

A striking thing about the wrecked areas is the absence of people. But in one block, firemen's hoses pour water on sporadic flames of smoldering ruins that send up clouds of black smoke. It must be from a raid last night. Here, I see a crowd of onlookers. Some watch the firemen. Many cry while consoled by others. Children cling to mothers. Some women hunt through the rubble of buildings. Others stand gazing at the ruins or shuffle down the debris-strewn street. I assume that the buildings held apartments that were their homes. As the train continues into the city, it is heartbreaking to see massive gaps that bombs have blown out of block after block of London.

The train pulls into St. Pancras station with a screech of metal wheels on metal rails. The gentlemen in my compartment open the door, and I follow them out onto a grimy platform of the busy station. At two dozen other platforms, trains have either just arrived or prepare to leave. Beyond the hot, hissing, steam engine at the head of my train is a red-brick facade. Then, I am outside, facing a line of shiny, black taxis. The street is jammed with a madhouse of trucks, taxis, cars, and red, double-deck busses, fed by crowds of travelers pouring from trains. Fascinated, I watch how they all drive on the left. I had heard officers at the base say that the Park Lane is an excellent hotel, if you can get a room there, so I climb into a taxi.

"Where to, captain?" the driver shouts.

"The Park Lane, please."

He slaps down the lever on the meter and roars off down Euston Road. We careen onto Tottenham Court Road and turn onto busy Oxford Street while I gape at buildings, elegant shops, signs, traffic, and sidewalks crowded with people, including flocks of pretty girls. This is exciting! My heart beats fast because it is also scary for a small-town boy alone in London. A turn onto Park Lane and another onto Piccadilly bring us to the white pillars at the entrance to the Park Lane, across from Green Park. With a thrill, I see Buckingham Palace just beyond the park.

As I leave the taxi, I see a finely dressed gentleman talking with the uniformed doorman. He watches while the doorman looks at me as he would an insect.

"Are you seeking accommodations at the Park Lane?" the gentleman says.

"Yes, sir."

"I regret that all of our rooms are taken," the doorman says.

"Oh," I say, disappointed to be turned away from such a handsome hotel. I didn't even get inside the door. "Could you possibly suggest another hotel? This is my first time in London. My bomb group gave me two days here before I begin bombing missions."

"You seem frightfully young," the gentleman says. "Might I ask your age?"

"Nineteen."

He shakes his head and turns to the doorman.

"I believe there may be a room available, don't you?"

"Yes, sir." The doorman grabs my bag. "If you will follow me, sir," he says as he heads for the door.

"Thank you," I say to the gentleman.

"Good luck, lad."

The lobby is handsome and filled with well-dressed British men and women, and with officers in the uniforms of a dozen nations. The room price makes me gulp, but the pleasant room helps calm my anxiety about how few men complete twenty-five missions before they die.

The first order of business is sightseeing. I leave the hotel and stand on the wide sidewalk to absorb the sights and sounds of London. Piccadilly is a broad boulevard filled with cars and busses. People are well-dressed, and the neighborhood seems upscale. It reminds me of photos I have seen of boulevards in Washington, DC. The only things that spoil the picture are numbers of silver barrage balloons floating high overhead to prevent low-level German bombing. Signs everywhere point to the nearest air raid shelter.

Since it is just beyond Green Park, I walk over to Buckingham Palace, a huge, impressive structure of gray stone with a paved courtyard in front. A tall, iron fence, trimmed in gold, surrounds the palace and courtyard. A guard in a British Army uniform stands beside an ornate, black and gold gate in the fence. Next to him is a tall, narrow guard box, which I assume he enters when it rains.

"I thought the guards here wore red coats and tall hats," I say to a pipe-smoking gentleman in tweeds beside me.

"They do in peacetime, lad, but they won't wear them again until the bloody war is over."

Inside the courtyard, near the palace's entrance, is another guard and guard box. The guard near me stands like a statue. Several giggling, teenage girls try to make him smile, but two police officers, also guarding the gate, shoo them away. While I continue to admire the soldier's ability to stand so still, he stomps his heavy boot three times, shoulders his rifle, and marches back and forth before he stops and again becomes a statue. A throng of civilians and military along the fence peers in at the palace. I am about to turn away when people press in behind me with excited talk of the king. I gaze toward the palace and see a black limousine pull away from an entrance. The limousine heads for the gate where I stand, gaping as usual. The crowd now presses so close that I couldn't leave if I wanted to go. Guards swing open the gates. Where did so many police officers come from so quickly? The limousine rolls through the gate, and King George VI, in naval uniform with much gold braid, gazes through the limousine's window at me. I give my best salute. The king smiles and returns the salute while the crowd cheers and women wave white handkerchiefs. A rotund gentleman in gray tweed beams and claps me on the back.

"His Majesty was pleased to have a Yank salute him," he booms. "Good show!"

Completely unglued by exchanging salutes with King George, I stroll down Birdcage Walk (the English certainly have interesting names for streets) to Westminster Abbey, a massive edifice with two soaring towers. Multiple statues are set into its outer walls. I studied about Westminster Abbey during a course in world history, and now I get goose bumps when I walk into the real thing. The cathedral's immense, echoing interior seems to soar to the heavens. It is ornately decorated with statues, plaques, pennants, oak pews, and enormous, stained-glass windows in its thick walls. I remember that it dates from the eleventh century. It was the coronation site for

William the Conqueror in 1066 and for most English kings and queens since then. It is the burial place for British monarchs and a whole catalog of legendary persons. Their grave markers fill the walls and floor of the Abbey. I can't walk without stepping on a marker for some great person. The Poets' Corner contains the remains of giants of English literature. Awed, I search the area and find markers for writers and composers that I have admired all my life. In addition to its grandeur, Westminster Abbey is peaceful, and I spend hours wandering through it.

Across from Westminster Abbey are the Houses of Parliament, with Big Ben soaring into the air. Because of the war, Parliament is closed to visitors, but it is a handsome structure resting on the Embankment along the Thames. The river hums with boats and barges of all sorts, and silver barrage balloons fill the sky along its course, since the London docks downstream are frequent targets of German bombers.

A taxi driver calls to me and offers a tour of London. The price sounds good, so I hop into his cab. First stop is the Tower of London, dating from the eleventh century. The grim structure is awesome, and my driver delights in grisly descriptions of famous executions within its ancient walls. Next, we visit St. Paul's Cathedral, a massive structure with an enormous dome. The driver tells me that Sir Christopher Wren spent thirty-five years supervising its construction. Now, damage from German bombs mars its beauty, but it still stands solidly. We halt briefly at St. Clement Danes Church on The Strand, while the driver cheerfully recites the nursery rhyme, "Oranges and lemons, the bells of Saint Clemens." We visit The Old Curiosity Shop on Portsmouth Street. Above the door is a sign that says, "Immortalized by Charles Dickens." A thrill runs through me at seeing it. Down an alley off Fleet Street, Samuel Johnson's house is a narrow, four-story brick with white-trimmed windows. I'm becoming overloaded with history, so the taxi deposits me back at the Embankment.

In late afternoon, I wander up Whitehall past the Horse Guards to reach busy Trafalgar Square. In the center of the square is the towering monument to Lord Nelson's naval victory over Napoleon's fleet off Spain's Cape Trafalgar. After admiring it, I continue on to the circular roadway at Piccadilly Circus and west on Piccadilly to the Park Lane. I return to my room as a contented tourist.

Dinner that evening is at the Café Royal, a highly recommended restaurant just off Piccadilly Circus. The décor is elegant, and the tables are filled with British men in tuxedos and women in lovely gowns, as well as with high-ranking British and American officers. How did I get in here? But the fact that I'm not a general doesn't seem to bother my elderly waiter, who suggests items from the menu and brings me a glass of dry sherry. The prices make me choke, but the excellent food and relaxation are worth it. After dinner, I hurry to the theater district around Leicester Square and find a thoroughly enjoyable musical production.

Later, I just get into a luxurious bed when the mournful sounds of air raid sirens echo over the moonlit roofs of London. Should I go to an air raid shelter or stay in bed? I hear the sound of distant guns firing, and I think that I hear the far-off drone of airplanes. But the wonderfully comfortable bed wins out. I won't trade it for a cold, drafty air raid shelter, so I snuggle down under the covers.

After a fine breakfast the next morning, I take a taxi north to Madame Tussaud's famous wax museum on Marylebone Road. Inside are incredibly lifelike figures in wax. I gape, as usual. There are movie stars, musicians, famous people of all sorts, statesmen, military men, American presidents, and the Royal Family. The figures are so realistic that a woman walks up and asks a guard a question, only to realize that it is a wax figure. I peer into the face of the still form of a nearby guard that I assume is also wax, only to have him suddenly grin impishly at me. Down in the cellar is a dark Chamber of Horrors inhabited by figures of infamous murderers. I read the story of Jack the Ripper and look at a chilling letter that he supposedly wrote to the London police. Upstairs, a hallway containing previous British monarchs impresses me. As it goes back in time, the light becomes dimmer until you reach the earliest kings in semi-darkness.

I have a lunch of fish and chips, with lots of malt vinegar, at a little shop on Baker Street. A search for 221B Baker Street, the fictional home of Sherlock Holmes, is fruitless. This sends me by taxi to the British Museum on Great Russell Street, where I go up the

steps and past impressive columns to an awesome place where I
spend the remainder of the afternoon happily wandering through a
few of its chambers. I only see a fraction of the museum, but I
promise myself that I will return.

I spent so much money on a luxury hotel and expensive dinner
the previous day that I decide to see if I can find something lower-
priced for dinner. After a sumptuous, hot bath in a huge tub at the
Park Lane (a far cry from the cold, communal showers at the airbase), I get into a clean uniform and step outside into the darkness
of a London blackout. The sidewalk teems with shadowy figures. I
see soldiers and sailors from a dozen nations. There are teenage
girls who giggle and flirt with men in uniform. Despite heavy make
up, some of the girls appear to be no more than twelve or thirteen.

As I continue along Piccadilly toward the traffic circle at Piccadilly Circus, the sidewalk becomes jammed. For the first time in
my life, I see prostitutes. Hundreds of women and girls stand close
to the buildings, trying to catch the eye of a passing soldier or sailor.
They wear eye-popping, short skirts in the dank, chilly weather, and
they lead eager soldiers and sailors away in droves. I had heard that
sex and liquor are major items wanted by men in uniform. The
number of drunks in uniform is impressive.

Veteran flyers at the base told me that Soho is the Bohemian
district of London, and you can get almost anything there. It's a
blacked-out warren of narrow streets and alleys near Piccadilly Circus. Soho has restaurants, stores, pubs, cafes, and hundreds of
upstairs houses of prostitution. Prostitutes fill its streets. But there
are also tantalizing aromas coming into the darkness from little
restaurants of all sorts—French, Italian, Spanish, Hungarian,
Indian, even Chinese. The smell of spicy tomato sauce stops me outside a place that shows only a dim light from a crack in tightly
closed drapes covering the windows. Inside is a tiny Italian restaurant with ten tables. There is no printed menu. The waitress is an
attractive woman, probably in her forties, with curly, black hair and
a nice face. She describes a pasta dish. Her speech has a heavy
French accent. The dish sounds better than air force food, but she
glances at the other diners and leans down to whisper to me.

"The owner has prepared veal that is delicious. It is expensive, but you Americans are wealthy."

From what I have been told, the veal must be black market. I nod. I also gape. When she leans down to whisper, the wide neck of her uniform drops down, and I stare at two big breasts. There is no bra, just bare breasts. Hypnotized, I continue to stare. She sees me staring, and I turn red with embarrassment, but she straightens up with a smile.

"I think you will enjoy everything that I give you."

The veal dish and a glass of wine are wonderful. The waitress stops several times to see if all is well.

"You are obviously French," I say during one stop, "but you are working in an Italian restaurant."

"One does what one must. I left France when the Germans over-ran our country. My husband was killed fighting for France. I am alone, so I must work. The owner has been kind to me." She glances toward the door. "This is better than the work those women do in the street."

"But do they make more money than you?"

"Do you think they keep the money that men pay for their services? The pigs that own them take the money. The women are slaves. They cannot escape. I receive my meals and gratuities."

As the restaurant gradually clears out, we spend more time talking.

"You are alone, yes?" she says.

I nod. "I want to enjoy myself as much as possible before I begin to fly bombing missions against Germany. I didn't realize it will be so rough. From what I hear, most of us won't survive them."

She stares at me silently. Then she cocks her head to one side and smiles.

"I enjoy our conversation. Would you like to continue it? If you get a bottle of wine, we can go to my room. My name is Yvette."

I grin and nod. Conversation would be nice.

Soon, the restaurant closes, and Yvette quickly cleans it. My bill, including a bottle of wine and a generous tip for Yvette, takes most of the cash that I brought with me to London. As we walk through the blackout, the streets have cleared out, but many prostitutes still work. We pass several doorways in which a prostitute and a soldier are having sex.

"Those women do not even have a place to take a man," Yvette says. "They live on the street."

Yvette has a one-room, third-floor flat. There is a sofa, table with two chairs, bed, tiny stove, and heater. The toilet is down the hall, and I go there to use it. When I return, Yvette has changed into a flowery, silk wrapper that leaves no doubt that she is nude under it. I gulp. I don't think she's interested in conversation. Wine is already in two glasses. After we drink some, she takes my face in her hands and kisses me. No woman ever came at me like this before. I've never done it. I hope I don't make a fool of myself.

"You are so young," she says, "but I will give you a night of happiness before you go to fight the Germans."

The next morning, Yvette is pleased that she seduced a nineteen-year-old virgin. As for me, exhausted but happy, I decide that sex is better than I ever imagined. Yvette wore me out with her need for more and still more.

I sleepily take the train back to Wellingboro and catch a ride to the airfield. Our gunners have finished training at The Wash and are in London on leave. When they return, the crew is complete again.

"I don't know what the missions are going to be like," Ralph Ballmer says to me, "but once I get back home, I'm going to stay there."

On January 9 and 10, we fly training missions at 20,000 feet over England. I don't think that I will ever be accustomed to the intense cold and that awful 170-mile-per-hour gale roaring in through the open roof of my compartment. With the wind chill, instant freezing of accidentally exposed skin worries me constantly.

Herb Moomaw and I talk at dinner many nights. He teases me about Pearleen, my friend from high school, and my claim that we are only friends. He thinks there is more to it than we are willing to admit. I stoutly maintain that I care deeply for her, but we are just friends. He says that the world doesn't work that way.

On January 11, Rex Townsend flies as copilot with a veteran pilot on a bombing mission to Oschersleben, Germany. When he returns, his face is pale, and he tells us that it was very bad. Four hundred German fighters rose to attack the bombers. The 92nd Group was under constant assault and lost two B-17s.

After hearing reports from veteran crewmembers about how bad it was, I am frightened. The other members of my crew wear serious faces. We know that we're close to the time when we will face the Germans. During the brief time that we have been in the 92nd Bomb Group, it has flown eight missions and lost seven B-17s with their crews. That's seventy men. It is a scary prelude to combat.

The next morning brings somber news that a member of our squadron committed suicide by shooting himself during the night.

"I'm surprised that there aren't more suicides," a veteran gunner says. "If you fly, you get to the point where you get tired of waiting for the Germans to kill you, and if you don't fly, you get mighty low from seeing your friends go out and not come back."

"Suicide seems awfully drastic," I say.

"Yeah, more often the guy goes nuts, and they take him to the booby hatch. Doc says they don't know if those guys will ever recover. They just sit and stare at a wall."

On January 20, 1944, after dinner, the crew strolls back to our squadron area in winter's twilight. We must check the bulletin board in squadron headquarters each evening to see if we are scheduled for a mission the following morning. For the past week, we have not been on the schedule. But tonight, when we troop into squadron headquarters and gaze at the bulletin board, a chill grips me. I see our names—Townsend, Swanson, Kinsella, Ballmer, Lyons, Webster, Araujo, Norton, Tasker, and Kindred—posted on the bulletin board. We are scheduled to fly a combat mission tomorrow morning. My mouth is suddenly dry.

As they say in the movies, "This is it."

CHAPTER 6

This Is It

January 21, 1944. I toy with a breakfast of two fried eggs, fried Spam, toast, orange marmalade, and coffee. It's a good breakfast, but I'm going on a bombing mission for the first time, and I'm nervous. No, I'm not just nervous, I'm scared stiff. Butterflies in my stomach threaten breakfast. I try to hide my trembling hands when I'm not eating.

"First mission, huh?" a veteran flight engineer across the table says, eyeing my pale face. "I kid you not. It ain't no fun. If you don't remember nothing else, remember this. If your plane catches fire, get the hell out. You got between thirty seconds and a minute before the fire gets you or she blows up."

He isn't making me feel any better. He grins.

"The good news today is that take-off ain't until noon. That means we ain't going far. We don't dare come back after sunset, or the Germans will follow us back and shoot us down when we put on our lights to land in the dark."

"A short mission is good?"

"It's the goddamn best you'll get."

"But won't there still be German fighters and antiaircraft?"

"They'll always be waiting for us, but if we don't go too far, our fighters can cover us pretty well. Generally, flak ain't as bad near the coast as it is above the big cities in Germany, so be thankful for a short mission. You won't get many."

Still, the jitters won't go away. My watch shows almost 10 A.M. when everyone trudges to a nearby building. Military police guard the door. After they check my identity, I join a crowd in the briefing room, a large chamber filled with rows of benches. Flyers occupy every seat. A black curtain covers a map at the front of the room. My mouth is dry and my heart is thumping while I wonder what is behind it. The room buzzes with talk as combat crews speculate on where we are going. It's just like a movie.

Conversations die when several captains and lieutenants walk to the front of the room and face us. An intelligence captain pulls back the curtain. The red line on the map that marks the route we will follow runs south only as far as the Pas de Calais on the French coast. We won't go to Germany today. Smiles and sighs of relief fill the room. The flight engineer at breakfast turns around, grins, and gives me a thumbs-up.

"Your targets are two of the secret Operation Crossbow sites at Le Plouy Ferme and Bellevue," the intelligence officer says, pointing to a spot on the map.

Did he say secret? He has my full attention. My first mission and we are already dealing with something secret. This really is like the movies.

"Today, the Eighth Air Force will hit thirty-six of the ski sites that the Germans are constructing for their new secret weapons," the intelligence captain says. "Your job is to destroy them. Anything you observe about the site will be useful, so keep your eyes open. It will be a difficult target to see. The Germans are masters at camouflage. Here is a drawing of the target."

He projects a sketch on the screen of a thin track, resembling a railroad track that is several hundred yards long. It looks like a ski resting on its side, with the curved part of the ski at the south end and the rear end of the ski pointing north toward England. It looks like some kind of launching guide, but what do they intend to launch? Are we talking about something that could wipe us out?

"You will assemble in the usual fashion," he continues, "and the bomber train will proceed to the south coast, passing over Hastings on the way out."

Hastings: That's where William the Conqueror landed in 1066. My nervousness fades in the excitement of being able to see Hastings. I'm an airborne tourist at heart. The thought is interrupted as the officer continues.

"From Hastings, you will cross the Channel to your IP here." He points to a spot on the map that is the IP (initial point) where the bomber formation turns toward the target for its bombing run.

"From the IP, you will approach the target and bomb. Your with-drawal route will bring you back near Hastings and from there to our base."

The flak officer describes antiaircraft batteries that defend the target. Since I have no experience with antiaircraft fire, I'm not sure what to expect.

With a bad feeling, I hear him say that several hundred German fighters can rise to attack us. To counter it, our escort will consist of 500 short-range P-47s, 50 medium-range P-38s, and 50 new long-range P-51s. Of course, they will be spread for 200 miles along the French coast while they try to guard almost 700 bombers divided among thirty-six targets. Also, fuel consumption will cause only part of the fighter force to be with us at any time. Ten squadrons of British Spitfire fighters will cover our return across the English Channel.

After a stop for my last chance at a bathroom for hours, I go to the equipment room near the airfield to get dressed for the mission. It has a counter in front of rows of shelves of equipment, and it smells of leather and canvas. A supply clerk runs to bring me an armload of my flying gear.

Over flying coveralls, I pull on a blue, wooly suit with electric heating wires to keep me from freezing in the intense cold that I will soon face. I remove my shoes and pull on dainty, wool slippers, also containing heating wires, and plug the boot wires into recepta-cles on the ankles of my electric suit. Over these, I pull on leather, sheepskin-lined pants, jacket and boots. I look like an Arctic explorer.

I strap on a yellow life jacket in case we go down in the water. If we do, I must pull two cords on the life jacket, and two cartridges will fill it with carbon dioxide gas to make it float. Over the life jacket, I buckle on my parachute harness, making certain that the straps are tight. If they are not tight, the straps can hurt me badly when my parachute opens. The parachute is in a separate, canvas pack. It is a chest chute, rather than a parachute that attaches to my back. In an emergency, I must snap the parachute pack onto clasps on my harness. Before I jump, I must remember to do it. I heard of flyers so panic-stricken when fire engulfed their bombers that they jumped without a parachute. That scares me.

I grab a canvas bag containing a sheepskin-lined helmet with goggles, earphones, and oxygen mask, a throat microphone, silk gloves, and leather gloves that plug into the wrists of the electric suit. I also check my escape kit, containing silk maps, compass, German and French money, a chocolate bar, and passport photos of me as a European civilian. The kit fits into a pocket in my flying coveralls.

In a guarded room nearby, I get a bag containing the day's secret codes written on rice paper and encased in transparent, plastic holders. In case of trouble, I must remember to eat the rice paper. I put my shoes in the equipment bag. If I have to parachute into Europe, my flying boots are a dead giveaway, so I will carry shoes down with me. After I check everything, I waddle out to a waiting truck, carrying bags and parachute.

By now, it's a chilly 11:15 A.M., and pale sunshine of a January morning bathes the airfield. The scent of farmland around us permeates the air, but as I near the truck, I smell canvas and oil. As soon as our crewmembers are aboard, the truck grinds its gears and rumbles along narrow roads until it rounds a curve, and the airfield opens before us. I gaze at runways surrounded by the circular, perimeter track. Off the perimeter, B-17 bombers park among trees for concealment. To our left is a black hangar, and nearby is the gray, two-story control tower with a wind sock. The truck roars around the perimeter, turns sharply, and squeals to a halt with the nose of a battered B-17F towering above it. We jump out and gaze up at the plane that will take us to France.

Painted dark brown, our B-17F squats on a concrete pad like a giant, winged lizard. It smells of oil, gasoline, hydraulic fluid, and metal. A gas-driven generator, called a putt-putt, runs noisily beneath the big bomber, its cable plugged into the underside of the plane's nose to provide power until the engines start. I get a shock when I see patches all over the plane that cover a chilling number of places damaged by enemy gunfire. This is the real thing.

A half dozen mechanics in greasy coveralls greet us, and the crew chief assures Rex Townsend that the ship is in good shape. Townsend, Swanson, and Lyons examine the maintenance record and begin a careful inspection of the aircraft. One by one, my fellow crewmembers climb into the plane through a door near the tail. Ed Norton is twenty yards away, having a last cigarette. I stand in the morning light and admire the country beyond the fence. Even in winter, the fields and trees are pretty.

I climb into the B-17 and walk forward through the waist to the radio room. A radio mechanic and a photo technician are there. The mechanic has finished his check and says that the radios are in good shape. Corporal Muddy Waters, the photo technician, wishes me luck and hands me a big, hand-held camera before they both leave. I place the secret codes on the desk next to a blank mission log on my clipboard and put my chest chute on the floor next to a heavy vest of armor.

I pull on a leather helmet with goggles and gray, rubber oxygen mask. The mask hangs from one strap of the helmet until I need to snap it onto the other side of my helmet to cover my nose and mouth. Making certain that the plastic earphones in the helmet are comfortable on my ears, I snap on the helmet's chin strap and fasten a throat microphone around my neck. Its elastic strap has two, tiny microphones that fit against both sides of my throat. It's uncomfortable to wear, but it keeps my hands free while I talk.

I look through the forward door of my compartment into the bomb bay. A dozen 500-pound bombs hang from racks there. This is the first time that we have carried bombs, and it is the nearest that I have been to one. They are big, ugly, dark-brown things, armed and ready to explode. We carry more than two tons of explosive. Our bomber alone can destroy a city block or a factory. Think of the destructive power of the sixty bombers in our combat wing. No wonder the Germans are desperate to stop us.

Through the door on the far side of the bomb bay, I peer into the flight deck in time to see Rex Townsend climb into the pilot's seat. Gunnar Swanson follows and waves to me before he turns and slides into the copilot's seat. Electric motors begin to whine. The plane's doors slam. No turning back now. My mouth is dry. I'm trembling.

I plug cables from earphones, throat microphone, and electric suit into receptacles on the plane's wall. An inch-thick hose from my oxygen mask snaps into a long hose connected to a meter on the wall beside my desk. The meter has a red ball in a vertical tube. When I snap on my oxygen mask, the ball will rise and fall with my breathing. This is called a demand system, since it supplies oxygen as I breathe in, but next to the ball is a valve that I can turn to increase the flow of oxygen if I need it. There is a yellow tank of portable oxygen lying on the floor behind my seat. I can plug my oxygen mask into it and carry it with me in case I have to go to another compartment of the bomber while we fly above 10,000 feet. That altitude is the cut off. Below it, I can breathe normally. Above it, I must wear an oxygen mask. The higher we climb, the more difficult it is to breathe, even with an oxygen mask. Oxygen is critical. If I don't get enough, I will develop anoxia, which leads quickly to unconsciousness and death.

As I check to see that I haven't forgotten anything, I hear a B-17 engine start up across the field, then another, and still another. Outside, mechanics finish the strenuous job of turning the propellers on our plane. The smell of gasoline is strong.

Rex opens his window and calls, "Clear!"

"Clear!" the crew chief says, as a mechanic stands ready with a fire extinguisher.

One engine whines and coughs into a roar. The second follows, then the third and fourth. The plane vibrates from the power of the spinning propellers. Rex runs each engine up to roar at maximum power while he, Gunnar, and Lloyd watch the instruments. The engines slow for a minute, then Rex guns them, and we begin to move. The mechanics wave as the big plane ponderously leaves the parking pad and crawls to the perimeter track. With squealing brakes, Rex turns the B-17 onto the perimeter track and joins a procession of bombers lumbering along like a column of elephants. We brake to a stop, and the line of bombers sits with spinning propellers while waiting for a signal.

There it is! The first B-17 thunders down the runway. As it picks up speed, the second and then the third begin their runs. They seem to take off almost nose to tail. Brakes squeal as the column of bombers moves forward, each turning onto the runway and roaring away. The plane ahead of us turns and rumbles off. Rex steers us onto the runway. The engines thunder. With a jolt, we move forward and roll along the runway faster and faster, but the plane is sluggish with tons of bombs and hundreds of gallons of fuel. Trees at the end of the runway race toward us. I have a moment of panic before the wheels lift off, the ground falls away, and the B-17 passes over the tree line. We are off the ground at a few minutes past noon.

Our plane climbs steadily. Ahead and above, B-17s that took off before us move in a wide circle to allow each bomber to catch up. As it does, it fits into a V formation with two other planes. Rex slides our plane into place, and the 327th Squadron's six-plane formation, with one V following the other, is complete. Another squadron's six-plane formation is a mile away. It circles to let our formation fit in with it. We all circle as we climb, and a third squadron's six-plane formation fits in with us to make the 92nd Group's eighteen-plane "combat box" with a shape that lets all guns bear on attacking fighters.

In the distance, the 305th Bomb Group's eighteen-plane formation makes a wide circle. As I watch, our group joins it, followed by an eighteen-plane array from the 306th Bomb Group. This makes the 40th Combat Wing's huge, fifty-four-plane combat box that spreads across the sky. Now, the bombers' guns cover each other, and 594 machine guns protect the fifty-four bombers in the formation.

"We're at 10,000 feet, gentlemen," Ken Kinsella says from his navigator's desk. "It's time to go on oxygen."

I hook the gray, rubber mask over my face. The odor of rubber is unpleasant, and the ice-cold oxygen in my lungs makes me shiver. The red ball in the oxygen regulator jerks up and down with each breath that I take, showing my nervousness. As we continue to climb, the air blasting past me from the open roof becomes frigid. I have never been so cold. Ken Tasker and Ed Norton in the waist compartment stand beside big openings for their machine guns. They look frozen in the hurricane of icy wind. The gale batters me with a subzero fist. What is the wind chill of a 170-mile-per-hour wind at twenty degrees below zero? Awful, I bet.

Frost forms on the compartment walls, and breathing the frigid oxygen is like a January night in Minnesota. If it were not for the electric suit, I would freeze to death. I never imagined how scary it is to have my life depend on an electric cord and an oxygen hose. If either fails when we are over Europe, the pilot will have to let me die, because our bomber cannot leave the relative safety of the formation. It's a frightening thought, but German fighters watch for a lone bomber and will shoot it down, killing everyone.

A haze covers London in the distance to our left, but Big Ben is visible. I think of people going about their business in London, and flyers sightseeing, as I did recently, unaware of the armada passing to the west of them. Peering ahead, I watch our fifty-four planes slide in behind another fifty-four-plane formation. A fifty-four-bomber array pulls into position a mile away on our right, followed by a fourth, to form a mass of combat boxes. Others join until the sky fills with hundreds of bombers. I have never seen so many planes! All these planes, with their guns and bombs, look so incredibly powerful that it seems as though nothing can stop them.

We continue to climb, and it gets even colder, while the massive fleet wings south. Below, scattered clouds dot the English countryside, but the bombers bask in cold sunshine, their spinning propellers making glistening whirls. The clouds below us are white and puffy. The sky above is brilliant blue.

Our giant procession crosses the south coast of England. I gaze down eagerly at a pattern of neat, green fields, roads, railroad tracks, towns, rivers, and a surprising number of lakes. Somewhere within my view is the place where the famous Battle of Hastings was fought in 1066. I can't take my eyes off the landscape until the gray water of the English Channel is below, and we thunder on toward France.

The French coast appears ahead and draws closer by the minute. It gives me a strange feeling to know that there are German soldiers along that coast gazing up at our approach and ready to shoot us if they have the chance. Greg climbs down into his cramped, gun turret below the ship. John Kindred crawls back into the tail. Ken and Ed grab their machine guns on either side of the waist compartment. Sharp bursts of gunfire echo through the formation as gunners test their guns. Our gunners cut loose with a terrific racket. I don't bother. I'm not interested in being swept off my feet when the gun in my compartment's roof whips upward to the sky. Now all the gunners watch for German fighter planes.

As we roar on south, the leading formation crosses the French coast. Dozens of orange flashes burst around it, leaving ugly, black puffs of smoke. Those are big explosions! This is for real! One of those bursts could blow our plane apart. The multiple flashes of antiaircraft shells send me into a frenzy of buckling on my body armor. The armor's canvas jacket encloses overlapping strips of thick steel and is heavy on top of my other clothing. It is difficult to move. I gasp from the effort and remember that exertions at high altitude can double me over with cramps.

"Opening bomb bay doors," Ralph Ballmer calls on the intercom.

That's my signal to open the door from my compartment to the bomb bay and crouch in the doorway. The effort makes me gasp for oxygen.

"Bomb bay doors are open," I call as I gaze 15,000 feet straight down through the open doors of the bomb bay. This is no place to be if you are afraid of heights. Ragged openings in clouds show the French countryside. It is a pretty picture of meadows and forests and roads and rivers and cottages and even a village.

Antiaircraft shells explode around us, startling me. A wave of fear surges through my body. Orange flashes seem to be right next to us, and the plane rocks, but we pass through the bursts. Clouds hide much of this portion of French landscape while we wheel around, searching for the target. From glimpses that I get through breaks in the clouds, the area appears to be peaceful. Camera poised, I search the ground below and take pictures for intelligence, but I see nothing that looks like a ski or a straight track. The Germans hid the target well.

While our formation wheels around again for a second try to find the target, I see groups of four-engine B-24 bombers in the distance. As I watch, single-engine planes fly around and through the B-24s like angry hornets. They are German fighters. Bombers and fighters are firing at each other. From this far, the streaks of firing look like sparks from a Fourth of July sparkler. Fighters and bombers fire furiously. My heart races with fright. Someone is going to get hurt over there. Two fighters bore in toward a B-24, and sparks from their wings hammer the bomber. I gasp as the B-24 catches fire and shudders before it turns over and spirals down crazily. Another, and still another, of the big planes trail flames before falling from the sky. Each time the German fighters sweep through a B-24 formation, a bomber blazes with orange fire and tumbles downward. Where are the parachutes? Just as the flight engineer told me at breakfast, the fire spreads so fast that the crew doesn't have time to get out. A chill grips me as I watch the bombers die, like lumbering cattle attacked by packs of wolves. I think of the agony of the crew members as each burns to death. Fear clutches me at the thought that the same thing will happen when the Germans attack us.

Our group moves over the target area again, and I scrutinize the ground without success. Nothing down there looks like a ski. Our bombers complete their second wheel over the target area and Ralph Ballmer closes the bomb bay doors. We head north over the Channel, still carrying our bombs.

"They can't see our target, so we're going home," Townsend says.

I shed my heavy armor after we leave the French coast behind. Above us, British Spitfire fighters sweep through the sky to cover our withdrawal. While we cross the Channel, we descend below 10,000 feet. Off comes my oxygen mask. What a good feeling! Ice had formed in its bottom, partly blocking the openings that bring oxygen into the mask. I must remember to check it regularly. How can I remember all the things that are essential to keep from dying? The masks leave deep grooves in everyone's face.

I grin when we cross cliffs along the English coast and fly low above pretty fields, forests, hills, towns, and villages. We came through our first mission safely. It was the best kind of training mission that we could have. We went through all the actions of a mission with minimal danger. The group soon thunders over our airbase. One by one, the bombers peel off and land. When our turn comes, Rex Townsend sets the plane down as light as a feather and taxis around the perimeter track to our parking pad. To my surprise, Podington feels like home. We crawl from the plane to welcoming grins of the ground crew, and I give my camera to a photo technician. Rex Townsend walks over and slaps me on the back.

"Well, that was your first one," he says with a satisfied smile. "Let's hope a lot more are like that."

"Let's hope they're all like that," Ballmer says, with a wide grin on his cherubic face. "Let's hope they're even easier!"

That gets a snort and a grin from Townsend, who walks away, shaking his head while Ballmer beams.

A truck speeds us to a noisy building filled with tables where intelligence officers question us about the things we saw. No one saw German fighters near us, and the antiaircraft fire startled the heck out of me, but it was what veteran crews expected.

What did we accomplish today? The 92nd Bomb Group achieved nothing, since it could not find the camouflaged target and had to bring bombs back. Our crew achieved a lot, since we experienced a real mission without facing German fighters. I heard that many crews go down on their first mission from mistakes of inexperience. We were spared that. I learned the routine of a real mission, not a practice one. I found out how cold it is in the frigid gale that blasts through my compartment and how even a few hours at high altitude take a lot out of you. I'm exhausted. What will a long mission do to me?

At dinner, I try to relax while I listen to conversation, but the sight of B-24 bombers going down unnerves me. I can't erase the picture of them twisting like mortally wounded animals before falling in flames. The Eighth Air Force lost five B-24s and one B-17 today, and veterans say that this mission was as easy as they get. I have to survive twenty-four more. How long before we meet those deadly German fighters?

The idea of secret German sites fascinates me, and it doesn't take long to wheedle information from a new friend in group intelligence. The sites are for something the Germans call "V-weapons." The rails are to launch unmanned, flying vehicles, called V-1, which carry a huge amount of explosive and dive into a target. The goal is to launch hundreds, even thousands, of these against us. But the shocker is that there are other areas—such as one at St. Omer near the French coast—that are huge construction sites for some big weapon. No one can tell me what it is, but it is called V-2. There is a rumor that it is a kind of Buck Rogers rocket that will be unstoppable and destroy us, but that sounds crazy. Rockets are in the future—maybe by 1980, not 1944. Whatever the weapon is, Operation Crossbow's objective is to destroy the V-1 and V-2 weapons before they get into action. If today is any indication, it won't be easy.

My mind keeps coming back to how cold and exhausting it was up there. If it gets any worse, I don't know what I'll do.

CHAPTER 7

Lynch Mobs in Germany

January 29, 1944. A flashlight in my eyes jars me awake. A voice comes from blackness behind the light.

"Breakfast at four and briefing at five. You awake?"

"Yes, thanks. I'll get right up."

Since our first mission on January 21, we have trained hard, and I'm exhausted from yesterday's five-hour practice flight in a sub-zero gale 20,000 feet above England. If I don't get up now, I'll go back to sleep, so I leave my warm nest under blankets for the room's chill. As I shiver, I know that I'll soon be a lot colder. I have never felt such cold as that caused by the subzero wind that pummels me from the open roof of the radio room. I don't want to face it again, but there is no choice.

In faint moonlight from the window, I nervously pull on flying coveralls, heavy socks, shoes, and sheepskin-lined jacket. I try to be quiet so I don't disturb men asleep in my building, but I hear the disembodied voice going from place to place, waking flyers. They cough, curse, groan, and mutter. Zippo lighters click for cigarettes that betray the smokers' tension. I'm just as tense, but I tremble instead of smoking. I can't forget that the 92nd Bomb Group has lost seven bombers in the short time that I have been here. We have about 250 flyers, and during that time we lost 70. That's almost a third of us.

I gaze at photos of my mother, my little brother, and my friend Pearleen. I hope that I return to see them tonight. The thought of never seeing them again puts an ache in my throat, but what can I do?

I step outside into the frosty air of English winter. It is 3:40 A.M., and U.S. Eighth Air Force Station 109 is silent under a clear sky and pale moon. The hum of a far-off plane, probably an RAF night-fighter on patrol, fades in the distance, leaving only the sound of a truck that idles nearby, waiting for us. I smell fields and haystacks beyond the nearby fence. A distant cottage is dark, the farmer and his family asleep. Black trees huddle over the cottage like witches around a cauldron.

I run twenty yards to the chilly, communal bathroom, and then clamber into the back of the truck. As minutes pass, the other crewmembers climb aboard, one by one. They grunt or nod sleepily.

"Let's go," Lloyd yells to the driver when the last man, Ed Norton, finishes his cigarette and climbs in.

Gears grind, and the truck pulls away to bounce through darkness along narrow roads, past sleeping barracks and dark buildings tucked in amid English farms. Across a broad pasture, I catch a glimpse of B-17 bombers, dispersed like sleeping dinosaurs among clumps of trees.

Lloyd turns to me.

"You got the pills, in case anybody needs them?"

I nod. The medics issued a supply of DL-amphetamine (Benzedrine) capsules to us. If we're too sleepy, the amphetamine will wake us. I heard that many, veteran flyers take sleeping pills at night and amphetamine in the morning. Will I become like them and have the "shakes" and nightmares so badly that I will have the same cycle of sleeping pills and amphetamine? I hope not.

The truck stops next to a squat building. I jump out with the rest of the crew and pass through black curtains into the glare of light in the combat mess. I blink at the noisy cafeteria, with colorful insignia on white walls. On one side, behind a long, cafeteria counter, white-clad workers serve a line of flyers. Two servers fry eggs, while the rest place food on white plates held by flyers. Tables of flyers fill the room. Aromas of coffee, toast, fried eggs, and fried Spam wash over me. Fresh eggs are in short supply in England, so they only go to combat crews before a mission. Otherwise, it's those awful, powdered eggs.

Before I can have food, Captain Furniss, our flight surgeon, waits with a wicked grin and a paper cup filled with bitter paregoric. When I question him about paregoric, he tells me that it's an alcoholic solution of opium and camphor that dates back to eighteenth-century medicine. Opium causes constipation. There are no bathrooms on a B-17, so the paregoric will bind me up for hours until we return. Then, Captain Furniss will be waiting with a cup of castor oil to send me to the bathroom faster than a cat chased by dogs. I swallow the paregoric and grimace.

"Yuck, that's terrible stuff," I say.

"Go get breakfast," he says with a benign smile, "and don't forget to pee before you get on the plane. If you have to do it at 25,000 feet, you may freeze something you don't want to lose."

I give him a worried look and head for the serving line to get my breakfast and carry it to a table.

"They bind us up with paregoric and clean us out with castor oil," a veteran gunner at the table complains. "They knock us out with sleeping pills and wake us up with pep pills. By the time I finish my missions, my insides won't be worth shit."

"That's better than the alternative—not finishing your missions," a gunner says.

"The generals don't care," someone says. "All they want is for us to carry that load of bombs and drop it on the target. They don't give a shit if we're screwed up for the rest of our lives. We're expendable."

With that pleasant thought, I continue to eat two fried eggs, three slices of fried Spam, three slices of toast with orange marmalade, and coffee. After the cup of paregoric, breakfast tastes fantastic. I must eat it all because I won't get anything more until we return in late afternoon.

While I eat, I talk with Herb Moomaw. He and his crew are going today. Since our crews traveled together from Bovingdon to the 92nd Group in late December, Herb and I have talked a lot. I've made a lot of friends, but Herb and I tend to pal together. We talk of things we hear from home, and how great it will be to get back there. Herb's talk of home reminds me that, for each fellow facing a bombing mission, there are moms, dads, wives, children, brothers, sisters, and sweethearts, all worrying that their loved one will survive each day. I have to get away from that thought quickly.

One thing that I notice is an absence of smiles and laughter. Many flyers eat silently. Some pick at their food. Each man likely wonders whether he will get back. Chaplains circulate, talking to the men. The flight surgeon treats stuffy noses, clogged ears, and upset stomachs, all of which can be big trouble at high altitude.

I am tense when we trudge into the briefing room past military police. I don't know what to expect, and the unknown is always scary. This time, when the intelligence captain pulls back the curtain covering the map of Europe, everyone groans. The red line on the map goes southeast in Germany to Frankfurt. Eight hundred bombers, including those of the 92nd Group, will bomb factories turning out war materials. Frankfurt is a big city and important industrial center. If we destroy its factories, it will help cripple German industry and end the war so we can go home.

Because Frankfurt is important, we will face a heavy barrage of antiaircraft fire and 600 German fighters. Eighth Air Force bombers will have an escort of 90 P-38s, 500 P-47s, and 40 P-51s, but the 500 P-47s can't fly as far as Frankfurt. It sounds like we're in for a big fight.

"One final thing," the intelligence officer says, "and it's important. German civilians have begun to kill our unarmed flyers when they parachute into Germany after their plane is shot down. The Germans have hung our guys from the nearest tree and beaten them to death with shovels and clubs. According to the Geneva Convention, you should be taken prisoner and treated humanely. Our information is that the German Army is doing that, but the trouble is coming from German civilians. Beginning with this mission, you will carry your Colt .45 caliber pistol with three clips of ammunition. If you parachute into Germany, try to escape. If you can't, try to surrender to the German Army. If civilians corner you, defend yourself."

The room is deathly quiet. We already face hazards from cold, high-altitude, lack of oxygen, German fighters, and antiaircraft. Now, we must add lynch mobs waiting on the ground, if we can get out of a burning plane before it blows up.

"I repeat that you should try your best to escape if you are shot down. Don't kill civilians unless your life depends on it. If you kill a civilian, it means execution if the German Army later captures you, so you're between the proverbial rock and hard place."

When we reach our B-17, we all stop and gaze at the battered wreck that we will fly today. It is so patched that it has patches over patches. If it was a used car, you would junk it, but the 92nd Group was ordered to get every bomber into the air today. We are a new crew, so we get the junk. Lloyd scowls while he examines the B-17F's maintenance record and questions the crew chief. Rex and Gunnar look unhappy. The crew chief says that he has done the best that he can. He thinks that they have the plane in flying condition. Lloyd looks doubtful and says that he doesn't think the bomber can fly a mission, but a lieutenant colonel comes by in a jeep and stops to talk with them. He says that engineering officers have judged the plane fit to fly. Lloyd still looks doubtful.

After a 7:15 A.M. take off and more than an hour spent climbing and assembling the massive bomber formation over England, I gaze down from 24,500 feet at the patchwork landscape of Belgium. Broken clouds prevent me from seeing anything noteworthy on the ground. Just ahead is the German border. The radio room is colder than I could imagine. An icy gale that blasts me and takes my breath away is colder than the first mission. My frosty oxygen mask digs into my face. The frigid oxygen feels like needles in my lungs and makes me shiver all the more. Today, instead of bombs that other planes carry, our bomb bay holds thousands of propaganda leaflets. I scan one, using my rudimentary German. It tells the Germans that they will suffer worse bombing until they overthrow Hitler and his Nazis.

Encased in electric suit, sheepskin clothing, life jacket, parachute harness, and heavy armored jacket, I can hardly move. Dozens of cylinders of chaff sit beside me, ready to try to confuse German radar at Frankfurt. Despite heavy gloves, I hope that I can open the packages of chaff quickly and fill the sky when we near the target.

High overhead, our escort of P-47 fighter planes reaches the limit of its range. The fighters leave white trails in the blue sky as they turn back toward England. Now, we have 90 P-38s and 40 P-51s to protect 800 bombers spread over miles of sky. We are on our own for the rest of the way to Frankfurt and back.

Look out! I see a swarm of planes coming toward us from high in the southwest. They must be German fighters. But, before I can call out, the intercom crackles with tense talk between pilot and copilot.

"It's no good," Rex Townsend says, "and it's getting worse. We're going to have to abort and try to make it back."

Further conversation tells me that something serious has gone wrong with the bomber's engines. It sounds like we've lost the superchargers that make it possible for our engines to operate in the thin atmosphere of high altitude. It may be that the engines are failing. We're already lagging below and behind the 92nd Group. Enemy fighters destroy stragglers, so it will be suicide to go on. But can we make it back?

The big B-17 banks sharply and turns until the nose points north. I watch the armada of bombers go in the opposite direction and become smaller behind us as they head south toward Frankfurt. We are alone. If German fighters see us, they will blast us into a fiery torch spinning down, like the B-24s that I saw on our first mission. With a dry mouth, I scan the sky behind us for German fighters. There they are! They make a wide circle as they dive on the bomber train that we just left. If they look our way, we will be a tempting target. They disappear from my view, and I hold my breath, waiting for John in the tail to yell that they are coming at us.

We fly in bright sunshine while I continue to hear worried conversation between pilot and copilot. They are having no end of trouble. Even unflappable Gunnar Swanson sounds tense. The crew is quiet. Our B-17 continues to lose altitude. If the engines quit, we will parachute into Germany and its lynch mobs. If we can reach Belgium, we may make contact with the underground and evade capture. My mouth is as dry as dust as I glance at my parachute lying on the floor and feel the pistol strapped to me. I gaze down at the hostile land below. It looks cold and snowy, so I mentally urge the bomber to stay in the air.

We reach Belgium. No time to be an airborne tourist while I spend an eternity watching the Belgian coast creep toward us. How could we be moving so slowly? Finally, the coastline passes beneath us, and we are over the North Sea. My heart slows to a mere gallop. I snap on the IFF transmitter to tell British fighters that this lone plane is friendly, and I encode a mayday message to transmit if the engines fail and we go down in the cold water of the North Sea. The English coast comes into view. We move toward it until our low-flying plane limps over land. We made it!

Despite the bomber's trouble, Rex Townsend sets it down gently on the runway of the quiet airbase. Rex, Gunnar Swanson, and Lloyd Lyons confer immediately with engineering officers. The engineers are not happy that Rex had to bring the plane back. Ignoring them, a grinning Ken Kinsella strides over and slaps me on the back.

"Rex got us back OK, and we were over enemy territory, so we get credit for another mission," his voice booms.

"Two down, and twenty-three to go," I say.

We have lunch in the mostly deserted combat mess, and I try to relax. The crew members are strangely quiet, but we finally unwind and Lloyd tells a joke. We don't mention the flight.

After the 92nd Group returns in the afternoon, I hear that it faced vicious attacks by German fighters. The Eighth Air Force lost twenty-nine bombers and fifteen fighters on the mission to Frank-furt. One of the B-17s was from our group. Crews from other planes in the 92nd Group don't think anyone on the lost bomber survived. Its pilot was James Holdren of the 407th Squadron. The news makes me numb. I saw the crew at breakfast this morning and talked with one of them. Now they are gone.

What did the 92nd Group accomplish? Along with other groups, it dumped tons of bombs through clouds on Frankfurt. It wasn't precision bombing, but it destroyed a lot of factories and buildings and homes in the city and made life more difficult. It likely killed women and children, but I try not to think about that.

On my way back from dinner, I stop at squadron headquarters and look at the bulletin board. There's an alert posted for a mission tomorrow, and it lists my crew to fly.

CHAPTER 8

Terror

January 30, 1944. It seems as though I just went to sleep when the voice wakes me in darkness. At breakfast, I scan my fellow diners' faces and wonder who will die today. Despite the cheerful combat mess and fried eggs, fried Spam, and toast for breakfast, everyone looks glum. Most of the fellows flew yesterday, and hours at high altitude are exhausting.

As we enter the guarded briefing room, my mouth is dry while I wonder what lies ahead. The curtain pulls back. The red line runs east across Germany to the city of Brunswick where we will drop our bombs on an aircraft plant. If we smash it, we will reduce production of the fighter planes that kill us. I guess that is an incentive.

We take off at 8:30 A.M. on a cold morning, and spend an hour getting the sixty-three planes of the 40th Combat Wing into formation. Our combat wing then joins an armada of bombers thundering eastward over the North Sea while we climb above 10,000 feet. I buckle on my oxygen mask while my cabin gets steadily more frigid, and I lean against the sub-zero gale roaring through my cabin. It is like a hurricane at the North Pole, and it extracts every bit of heat from my body.

Soon, our bomber is 23,000 feet above the German countryside, heading toward Brunswick in north central Germany. I cannot see where we are, because solid cloud blankets the earth below. More cloud forms a ceiling just above us, so we are like the meat in a sandwich. Actually, it is like being in a dark, miles-long cavern, with the ceiling just above your head. The bombers' engines leave long trails of thick, white vapor, called contrails (condensation trails). They are impressive but are a headache for gunners, because German fighters can hide in the trails and sneak in close to fire at our B-17 from behind. We know they are lurking close by to kill us.

They can pop out any moment, like the murderer in a horror movie. Our gunners speak to each other tensely while they gaze in all directions. As usual, I can hardly move in my heavy clothing and armored jacket. It's freezing—colder than last time—and I shiver from cold and fear.

But as we fly on, I begin to feel warm and comfortable. Maybe I'm getting accustomed to the cold. It's not so bad after all. I'm getting sleepy, and everything is fine. Flying this mission is easy. It feels so good to put my head down on my desk. I'll just close my eyes for a few minutes. No! Something is wrong! I sit up, and my befuddled brain recalls the warning from Captain Furniss, so I unhook my oxygen mask and peer inside. Ice has closed the oxygen inlets. I have only seconds to remove the ice before I pass out from lack of oxygen. I squeeze the mask and dig desperately with my gloved fingers. Everything is getting dark, and I don't feel cold at all. I feel so pleasant, and I just want to close my eyes and sleep. The ice plops from my mask onto the deck. I jam the mask over my face and turn the valve to pour oxygen into the mask while I breathe deeply until I am awake again. I shiver. Ice in your oxygen mask is big trouble.

"Look out!" Lloyd yells.

Explosions surround us. Machine guns hammer. Orange streams of gunfire flash above my head, followed by silver fighters slamming past so close that I'm terrified that one will collide with us. About forty fighters dive through our combat wing's bombers. Rex has our plane pitching and weaving to try to spoil the fighters' aim, while our gunners fire red strings of bullets. Even through my oxygen mask, I smell smoke from the guns. Fighters' wing guns shoot orange streaks of fire around us. Gunfire is everywhere. Terror grips me as gunfire smashes into a nearby B-17, and it bursts into flames. Silver fighters flash past. Their fire hits another B-17, and it explodes in a boiling, orange fireball. Two German fighters race by. I see black crosses on their wings, swastikas on their rudders, and pilots huddled in cockpits. Farther away, four fighters dive toward a B-17, and batter it with so much gunfire that pieces fly from it like a minor explosion. Fire erupts from its wings. In an instant, it blazes from wings to tail. I see a flash and look to my left to see a B-17 engulfed by fire. Inside, men in agony are burning to death. The plane flops onto its back like an animal in torment and explodes in a huge fireball. The guns of B-17s converge on a fighter off to our right. Its cockpit shatters, and fire spouts from its engine as it flutters down like a wounded hawk.

"Watch out!" Lloyd shouts.

Our B-17F lurches and twists crazily as Rex takes violent evasive action. Lloyd fires sharp bursts from the twin machine guns in his top turret. Ballmer and Kinsella fire the nose guns. German fighters streak past while machine guns hammer all around us. It seems like the fighters will destroy us all, but the firing dies out.

"All clear ahead," Lloyd says.

I can hear relief in his voice. My breathing is becoming difficult. I remove my oxygen mask and dig globs of ice from it. How can you fight under these conditions?

"The enemy fighters peeled off and headed down into the clouds," Greg calls from the ball turret on the underside of the bomber. "OK, they're gone."

"Watch that they don't come back," Townsend warns.

"We're coming up on the IP," Ken Kinsella says.

Within minutes, the huge formation makes a majestic turn and begins to fly straight and level on its bomb run. My watch shows that it's almost noon. Directly ahead of us is a wall of black smoke that blossoms with orange flashes from hundreds of bursts of antiaircraft shells. The Germans are throwing up a big barrage of antiaircraft fire. We fly into the black cloud amid a storm of explosions that violently pummel our B-17. This sends me into frantic activity. Bomb bay doors opening. Start camera. Spread chaff.

"Bomb bay doors open," I yell and dive for the chaff.

I hear loud bangs and snaps as shells explode close by and send shrapnel ripping through our plane. Terrified, I tear open tubes of chaff and stuff them into the chute that carries them outside. Faster and faster I work, and I see a twinkling cloud of silver expanding behind us like a Christmas snowstorm. My gloved hands fly. The last of the chaff goes out. Antiaircraft shells don't seem to be coming quite as close. Maybe the chaff is effective.

"Bombs away!" Ballmer shouts, as the plane jumps upward, relieved of its heavy load.

"All bombs away," I confirm as I look down through the bomb bay at the solid layer of cloud below us. Our bombs disappear into the clouds.

"Bomb bay doors closing."

"Doors closed," I report and shut my door to the bomb bay.

That's the trouble with winter weather. We had to dump the bombs into the clouds. I hope they hit the aircraft plant, but we may have scattered them all over Brunswick. Each of those 500-pound bombs makes a heck of a blast. Our combat wing dropped more than 600 of them. They probably messed up Brunswick pretty badly. How many homes and schools and hospitals are those bombs hitting right now? It gives me a bad feeling. General Sherman was right. War is hell. I shut off the camera and shiver.

We turn away from Brunswick and head for England, three and a half hours away.

A few minutes later, I peer at the clouds overhead and wonder whether enemy fighters will dive at us from them.

A nearby B-17 in the 92nd Group has dropped below the bombers in its squadron. As the plane tries to regain its position, it climbs up beneath another B-17. I watch in horror as it rises toward the belly of the other B-17.

"Watch out!" I yell.

But the pilot must not see the B-17 above him. While I stare aghast at a tragedy that I can't prevent, the B-17 smashes upward into the other plane. There is a flash and one plane disappears in a fireball. The other B-17 spins down like a wounded bird into the clouds below. I don't see anyone get out. Twenty of our fellows died before my eyes.

The rest of the return trip is tense. Our gunners scan the sky for fighters, but none appear. After Rex Townsend makes another soft landing at our base, everyone's face is pale and smudged. We were at high altitude in bitter cold for seven hours. I'm almost too exhausted to walk. John Kindred's face is white, and his hands tremble as much as mine.

"Are you guys OK?" a pale Gunnar Swanson says, looking closely at each of us.

"That was a lot tougher than the first two," Townsend says, "but we'll be OK."

Later, I learn that the Eighth Air Force lost twenty bombers and five fighters. Despite bad weather, German fighters were able to get up and attack us. They did lots of damage to the bombers of the 40th Combat Wing, but that's not the only way you get killed, because two of the bombers lost were the colliding planes from the 92nd Group. I saw the crewmembers of those bombers at breakfast this morning. Two were in line just ahead of me getting fried eggs. We talked about how bad the paregoric tastes and how cold it is on the missions. One gunner said that he didn't think that he would ever warm up again. Now they are dead.

This is awful, and I suspect that it is going to get worse.

CHAPTER 9

Cold

As a cold, dark February of 1944 begins, I have survived three bombing missions, and they have taught me lessons. First, a below-zero gale at 170 miles per hour is almost unbearable. Second, hours at high altitude are more exhausting than I could imagine. Third, there are too many ways to die: freezing, lack of oxygen, altitude sickness, mechanical failure, lynch mobs, gunfire, burning, explosion, and shrapnel from antiaircraft shells. Worst of all, watching acquaintances die almost daily are reminders of how poor my chances are of completing twenty-five missions before something kills me. The savagery of the missions has been a shock. It is difficult to keep an optimistic outlook, even though I have flown only three missions. Veterans in my building say that I haven't seen anything yet.

It looks like every mission will be different. I didn't expect that. I thought they would be the same routine of flying to a target, dropping bombs, and coming home. Instead, each has its own character and dose of terror.

After talks with John Sloan and intelligence personnel, I now see how we fit into the grand scheme of things. During World War I, bomber aircraft supported troops on the ground—something like airborne artillery. But between the wars, our air force generals developed the idea of strategic bombing, where we help defeat a nation by bombing and destroying its essential industries. They further developed the idea of precision bombing to minimize civilian casualties and not waste bombs by scattering them away from the targets. This requires daylight bombing, so the United States built four-engine, long-range bombers that were armed with many machine guns. The theory was that these bombers can defend themselves while they fly to a target, but the Eighth Air Force has found that they cannot do so without suffering big losses. They need fighter escort, so fighter planes are being brought to England as soon as they and their pilots are ready. Right now, there are not enough fighters, but strategic bombing must proceed, so we suffer big losses. Despite that, we are attacking the German aircraft and oil industries to cut production of fighters.

Rain, mud, and cold fill the days. In this English winter, there is no snow, but weather is miserable. I lean into chilly wind while I trudge along wet, mud-streaked roads for meals and errands. A truck roars past, splattering dirty water and forcing me off the concrete into sticky mud that coats my shoes. Cleaning gummy mud from shoes has become normal activity several times each day. Eighth Air Force alerts us for missions and cancels them because of foul weather.

Letters from home are bright islands in the gloom. My mother writes of how much she and my little brother miss me. She says that my cat, Ginny, misses me badly. He sits patiently, staring at the front door, waiting for me to return. I love Ginny. Despite his name, Ginny is a big tomcat, and heaven for him is to lie on my lap and purr. I miss the three of them so much that I ache inside. I suspect that every fellow in my building has the same feelings.

From his home in Indiana, my father sends advice, based on his time in the trenches in France in World War I. "Keep your head down" is his warning. I don't know how to do it in an airplane, but he means well. He says that they ate beans and hardtack in the trenches. I don't know what hardtack is, but I suspect that Spam is a big improvement over it.

Pearleen writes cheery letters about life in nursing school at the University of Michigan and urges me to be careful. Her letters radiate sunshine. I doubt that she knows how much they help to make dark days brighter. We dated during high school. We never considered ourselves girlfriend and boyfriend, but we are good friends, and Pearleen means a lot to me.

Friends from high school and university write newsy letters about home and classmates who are in the Army, Navy, or Marines all over the world. I read each letter many times and keep it to read more. After I read them, I dream of home.

The other bright spot is a university correspondence course. Darkness, cold, death, and fear fade when I study, but the warm glow from letters and the memory of Ginny curled up purring on my lap vanish when Ed Norton comes in and says that we are scheduled to fly a mission in the morning.

February 3, 1944. My mouth is dry as I enter the briefing room. It is already crowded with flyers. Where will we go today? I sit down as the briefing officers stride to the front of the room. When the intelligence captain sweeps the curtain away, the red line heads east across the North Sea to Germany. We will bomb submarine pens at the German port of Wilhelmshaven. He says that the submarine blockade of Britain is a bad problem, so we will try to destroy submarines.

They will have fighters and a big antiaircraft barrage waiting for us. The briefing officer says that we will bomb from around 30,000 feet to make it more difficult for Wilhelmshaven's scores of antiaircraft guns to hit us. This is higher than we have ever flown, and it brings acute danger of altitude sickness, but it is better than being hit by an antiaircraft shell.

It's cold on the ground when we lift off the runway at 8 A.M., and it becomes steadily colder as we climb high above the clouds into a frigid, blue sky. As our B-17F ascends into its place in the circling array of bombers, breathing becomes more difficult. Finally, all planes are together, and the bomber fleet continues to climb while it thunders out over the North Sea.

Submarine pens are concrete structures, like giant pigeonholes, where submarines park for safety against air attack. The roof above each submarine is sixteen feet thick, so we must score direct hits if we hope to penetrate the roof and destroy submarines.

Despite electric suit and sheepskin-lined clothing, I have never been so cold. I can't stop shivering, and I feel as cold as if I was standing naked outside on a winter night in Minnesota. When we reach 29,500 feet, I'm in agony from the cold, and I shiver so badly that I can't write in my log. The radio room is white with ice. Frost covers walls and radios, even my desk and chair. It coats my log and pen. The 170-mile-per-hour blast freezes me. My oxygen mask can't keep my face from being painfully cold, and I fear that it is freezing.

The mask clogs with ice every few minutes, cutting off oxygen. I gasp for air like a fish out of water, while I tear off the mask in a frenzy and dig out ice. I must get the ice out fast because air pressure at this altitude is so low that I will be unconscious in minutes. I have a panicked feeling that I'm going to die.

Ken Kinsella says that at 29,500 feet, he measures a temperature of 53 degrees below zero. No wonder I'm freezing. I am in a wind chill of more than 130 degrees below zero. I am so cold that it is unbearable. I have to find a way to get away from the cold. My eyes dart around like those of a hunted animal seeking escape, and my panicked brain tells me to get out of the airplane, but we are above the North Sea, and all I would do is freeze to death in the water. There's no escape. I desperately clear ice from my oxygen mask. Each time that I take off my mask, my face burns in the icy blast. I know that it's not burning. It's freezing.

The gray German coast comes into view. It looks forbidding as we approach. I imagine sirens blaring there, people running for shelters, and antiaircraft guns ready. We cross the coast, but clouds partially obscure the ground, so I can't see much that is going on down there.

"Look out!" Lloyd yells.

ME-109 fighters pop from clouds and are on us in seconds. A cold fist grips me. My heart races. The 92nd Group's guns fire sharp staccatos, and our guns fire noisy blasts. Red tracers spurt toward the fighters like multiple Roman candles on the Fourth of July. The fighters' guns spit orange fire through our formation. I duck as strings of fire zip past overhead. Some fighters flip over and dive away, and some race past. I look to see if any of our planes are burning, but everyone seems to have weathered the attack.

"We're at the IP," Kinsella calls at around 11 A.M. "Get ready with the chaff."

A menacing, black cloud from a huge barrage of exploding antiaircraft shells fills the sky ahead. Inside are hundreds of orange flashes of bursting shells. Wilhelmshaven must have a million antiaircraft guns down there. I discharge chaff furiously to produce a sparkling, silver cloud that fills the air behind us.

We plunge into a hell of fire and blasts. They buffet our plane, causing it to pitch and rock. With a bright flash, a shell bursts beside us and sends shrapnel ripping through our B-17. A piece zings past my head and leaves holes on both sides of my compartment. Terrified, I release chaff even faster. Despite heavy gloves, my hands are a blur of action to add to the twinkling cloud of chaff. Explosions batter our bomber like blows from a prizefighter. Loud snaps signal pieces of shrapnel tearing through the plane. One of these shells is going to blow us to pieces!

"Bomb bay doors open," Ballmer calls. His voice is strained.

Gasping for oxygen, I open my door to the bomb bay and kneel in the doorway to gaze almost 30,000 feet straight down at the port of Wilhelmshaven. It clings to the west side of a large bay. Dozens of smoke generators send long fingers of smoke over the city and harbor, but they fail to hide it. Hundreds of tiny lights blink all over the city. These are flashes from antiaircraft guns firing up at us. The bomber rocks and pitches as it is pummeled by explosions. Our load of bombs drops from the bomb bay. The B-17 jumps upward.

"Bombs away!" Ballmer calls.

"All bombs away," I confirm.

Hundreds of bombs from our combat wing explode on Wilhelmshaven's dock area in an inferno of fire and destruction. I hope they destroy submarines. I also hope the Germans down there are in shelters and not caught in that firestorm.

Our armada turns from the target and begins to descend as soon as we are away from the German coast. The North Sea looks gray and rough far below us while the unbearable cold gives way to somewhat bearable cold while we descend. I feel better when we sink below 10,000 feet and my oxygen mask comes off. I feel still better when our bombers thunder low across the English coast. The frost in my cabin melts. I write furiously in my log to record everything that I saw, now that the log is no longer covered by frost. I am still writing when Rex Townsend sets our plane down after seven hours of incredible cold.

"Have you ever been so cold?" Herb asks at interrogation.

"I didn't think I'd survive. I thought I'd either freeze or suffocate."

"I heard that guys got fingers and toes frozen. A doctor said they'll lose them. One guy's electric boot stopped working. His whole foot is frozen. I guess he'll lose it."

"If your electric suit stops working, you're going to freeze, but I figure most of the suits work OK."

"Things like that make a mission tough, but we'll come through. I figure there'll be lots of easy missions."

"That was mission number four. Twenty-one left."

We both laugh.

"Yeah, we're knocking them off, aren't we?"

We head for dinner. I developed a bad headache during the mission, so I get aspirin from Captain Furniss. I would hate to have a headache during a mission.

CHAPTER 10

Goodbye, Herb

I have flown only four missions, but I have learned a lot from talking with veteran crews that have survived twelve or even twenty missions. They say that the air force and news media in the United States misled us. The B-17 Flying Fortress is no fortress. It's a first-rate airplane and can survive much punishment, but German fighters can shoot it down easily, and its eleven machine guns are little protection. The gunners try hard and frequently destroy a fighter, but our pilots take violent, evasive action by throwing the bombers all over the sky to avoid the fighters' gunfire. This spoils the gunners' aim, and their bullets fly in all directions. I guess our commanders, being pilots, don't trust the gunners, so they decree this wild, evasive action. Real protection for us comes from an escort of our fighter planes. When we are beyond the range of our escort, we lose lots of bombers.

Thus, we don't fly unscathed to a target and return in the best Hollywood tradition. We die from freezing, anoxia (lack of oxygen), altitude sickness, gunshots, shrapnel, being trapped in a burning plane, and explosion. I can't get it out of my mind that my chance of surviving twenty-five missions is so small, but if I refuse to fly, I face execution for desertion. What a dilemma to face: death if you do and death if you don't. No wonder fellows go insane. Most of us are depressed. I see it in pale faces and trembling bodies at briefings. I see men praying. A few try to joke, but I note that they are pale and fidget at the same time. As for me, I'm frightened out of my wits. I wish my headache would go away. I've had it for three days, and it's killing me.

Weather is bad over Germany, so our armada of bombers flies over France to Chateaudun, a pretty city on the banks of the Loire, some sixty miles southwest of Paris. Wildly twisting vapor trails in the sky high above us tell of battles between German and American fighter planes up there, but we have no attacks by German fighters. Still, a storm of antiaircraft fire shakes our B-17 while we bomb a German airbase outside the city.

When we return home and I climb down from the bomber, I am exhausted from bitter cold and high altitude. I guess it's the same as being on top of a 16,000-foot mountain.

"I enjoyed seeing Chateaudun," I tell Ralph Ballmer.

"You're not supposed to enjoy it!" the bombardier says, jumping up and down with mock outrage on his pink face. "You're supposed to fight the Hun!"

This makes me laugh, so he stomps away with a satisfied look.

The next day, we bounce and rock through heavy storms to Nancy in eastern France, but bring our bombs back when clouds cover the German airfield there.

"Do you realize that we've completed six missions?" I tell Herb at dinner, trying to raise his spirits. "That's 24 percent of the way toward going home."

"Twenty-four percent sounds better than six missions," he says, with a grin. "That's a quarter of them already. If we can have good weather, we'll be half through in no time."

But the weather becomes so bad that there is no thought of flying. Rain peppers the roof and clatters against windows with each gust of cold wind. I would like to go out and take walks to see Podington and Rushden and other nearby villages, but the weather is too miserable. Herb and I laze around and talk of home.

As we amble back from dinner that evening, we see an alert notice on the squadron bulletin board. A cold fist grips me. It means that the Eighth Air Force has scheduled a mission for tomorrow. Resigned to another day of bitter cold and fright over Europe, I scan the notice. To my surprise, my crew is not flying. I hear an unhappy sigh. Herb's crew is on the schedule.

"Maybe it'll be another one to France," I say. "They may want to go back to the airfield at Nancy and finish the job."

"Could be," Herb said. "Well, I'll get another mission in and be that much closer to going home."

With a wave, Herb heads off to get some sleep before a 3 A.M. awakening. I go to my building and end up discussing English writers with John Sloan. I didn't know bomb groups had historians, but I'm glad that they do because I like to talk with John. He was a professional writer back in the United States, and I am a rapt listener when he discusses the art of writing.

Early the next morning, the thunder of bombers taking off wakes me.

"Good luck, Herb," I whisper as I snuggle under blankets and go back to sleep.

I go to breakfast with Ken and Greg. Ken and I laugh at Greg's jokes while we douse our powdered eggs with enough ketchup to kill their taste, and then enjoy very good toast with orange marmalade. Back at my quarters, I write letters to my mother, to Pearleen, and to several girls that I knew in high school or the university. It seems that every girl that I ever dated has decided to write to cheer me. Bless them. They help make dark days brighter. I relax with study of my university correspondence courses and listen to news on the BBC.

Dick Shaw comes by to invite me to join the 92nd Bomb Group's Quiz Team. Based on the popular "Information Please" radio and motion picture shows back home, the game pits two teams of five persons against each other to answer questions on any subject. The team with the most correct answers wins. There are teams representing each bomb group as well as headquarters of the combat wings and Eighth Bomber Command. It sounds like fun, and I'm happy to join Dick, John Sloan, Abe Judson, and Ken Moxley on the team.

In late afternoon, a sergeant from group operations comes into our building. He is one of the many administrators that live here. A Brooklyn native, he is a great source of information.

"Our guys were supposed to bomb Frankfurt today, but it was a royal screw up," he says. "We lost three planes before the 92nd Group gave up and came back."

He gazes at me seriously.

"I hate to tell you, but your friend Herb's plane is one of the three that went down. Guys on other planes don't think anyone got out."

I sit stunned. Herb was here last night talking with me. Now he is gone. I think of his family, and the pain it will cause. I also realize that it could have been me.

The calamity for the 92nd Group began at take off, when the group leader had engine trouble and couldn't get off the ground. The deputy leader took over, but had trouble and had to turn back after the group crossed the enemy coast. At that time, the group was flying into the sun and became disorganized. By the time the leader of the high squadron took over, the group, minus two planes, was thirty miles from the bomber fleet. A lone group was a tempting target, so thirty German fighters attacked and quickly shot down three bombers, including the new leader and deputy leader. The leader of the low squadron took over and saw that the group, alone and missing five planes, would be raw meat for German fighters, so he turned the remaining planes around and came back. The Eighth Air Force lost thirteen bombers today. Herb's crew, piloted by Robert Lehner, was one of four (including mine) that joined the 92nd Group on December 27, 1943. How long before the next crew of the four is lost?

Bad weather closes in again. Meteorologists predict that it will stay for days. The crew heads to London for forty-eight hours. Ken Tasker and I visit more of London's attractions, go to the motion picture *Yankee Doodle Dandy*, starring James Cagney, about the life of composer George M. Cohan, attend a British musical in the Leicester Square area, shop at the Selfridge department store on Oxford Street, and eat at the Café Royal Grill.

We meet three fellows who trained at the air base at Kearney, Nebraska, at the same time that we did. They have shattering news. Most of the fellows that we knew at Kearney are dead. Some were in B-17s that exploded after being hit by fighters or antiaircraft guns. Some were in bombers that burned so fast that the fellows couldn't get out. Others were in planes that went down, but their fate is unknown.

Fellows I know are dying fast. How much longer do I have?

CHAPTER 11

Jane

After we return to Podington, the weather continues to be bad. Nothing ventured, nothing gained, so I go to 327th Squadron Headquarters and persuade the first sergeant to get me another forty-eight hours in London. I loved London, and I want to see more of the British Museum. Our first sergeant is a first-rate person, but I really don't expect him to do anything but laugh at my request. To my surprise, he agrees to arrange it with our executive officer. An hour later, I have a forty-eight-hour pass to London. Within minutes, I am riding to Wellingboro and the train to London.

This time, I have a card given to me by an impeccably dressed clerk behind the registration desk at the handsome Park Lane, and I have no trouble getting a handsome room. I even get a smile and tip of the hat from the doorman. After cold showers at the airbase, I luxuriate in a long, hot bath before taking a taxi back to the British Museum.

That night, when I have dinner at the Italian restaurant in Soho, the owner shakes his head and says that Yvette no longer works there. In darkness outside, I meet a gunner from the group. He is drunk, and his breath reeks. We chat while we observe a soldier and prostitute having sex in a nearby doorway. As we continue to talk, we discover that three couples are in nearby doorways doing the same thing, despite the passing crowds of people.

"Wow!" I say. As always, I'm the big-eyed innocent.

"Ain't that disgusting?" he says, drenching me in more alcohol breath while he leers at them. "I'd never do that in public. Come on, I got something better. If you don't like it, you can wait for me, and we'll go have a drink."

I have nothing better to do, so I follow him through Soho's dark alleys until he stops and knocks on a door. It opens a crack, and he slips a pound note inside. This is like movies that I've seen of speakeasies during Prohibition in the 1920s. The door opens, and we enter a dim hallway that reeks of perfume. The thin, rat-faced guy that opened the door smirks at us. I didn't know that Englishmen could look so creepy. He looks like he wouldn't hesitate to put a knife in us. What have I got myself into? At the end of the short hall, another door leads into a dimly lit room that is attractively furnished with sofas and tables. Three American officers converse with two women. The women wear short, thin wraps of flowered silk. One wrap is open, exposing a nude body, but the woman pays no attention. With great brilliance, I realize that I'm in a house of prostitution for the first time in my life. I gape, as usual. An unsmiling blond woman hurries up to us.

"You're the bloke who wants Maria," she says to my companion. "She'll be ready for you in a few minutes." She turns to me. "You want the same thing?"

I shake my head. I don't know what she's talking about.

"I'll just wait for him," I say.

"You don't want a woman?" She gives me a knowing look. "You queer? I can get you a nice, young boy."

"No, thank you."

She scowls at me and hurries off.

"This place is damn expensive," my companion says, "but it's worth it. They got beautiful women instead of the pigs that most of these places have."

"The girls over there are quite pretty."

"For a price, you can get almost anything here. I figure I'm not going to make it through these goddamn missions, so before I go, I'm going to do everything I ever wanted to do."

The madam hurries up.

"She's ready."

My friend jumps up, breathing hard. As the madam pulls back a heavy curtain to a hallway, I gape at a naked girl waiting by a door about five feet down the corridor. When I say girl, I mean a young girl. She is no more than eleven or twelve. She has long, black hair, dark eyes, and flat breasts. Before the curtain closes, I see my friend grab the girl hungrily and fasten his mouth to hers.

"Didn't you know that some men like little girls?" a soft voice says in my ear.

I jump a mile and turn to look into brown eyes a few inches from mine in a gorgeous face surrounded by shoulder-length, auburn hair. I always heard that prostitutes are coarse and fairly ugly. This woman is not. She sits close to me. Her perfume envelops me like the coils of a python. Where did she come from? Tongue-tied, all I can do is shake my head. She smiles and draws closer.

"How old are you?" she says, rubbing my upper leg with a mani-cured hand.

"Nineteen."

"I wager this is your first time in this sort of establishment. Madam said you're waiting for your friend to finish."

I nod.

"Well, business is slow tonight, so we can talk if you like. My name is Helena. You blokes always want to know how we got to be whores, so let's dispatch that first. My husband is in the British Army in Burma. I was lonesome and bored, so I had an affair with an American colonel and developed expensive tastes. My husband's pay won't support them, and my lover had to return to America, but he directed me to this place, and I'm happy here. I have a ravenous appetite for sex with men or women, so I make the money I want and have the sex I need to satisfy me."

"Ravenous"? This woman must have had some schooling.

"What about you?" she says, cocking her head. "Are you mar-ried?"

I shake my head.

"I thought not. Do you have a girl back in America?"

"Not a girlfriend. There is a girl, and she's my very good friend. I like her a lot, but she doesn't want to get serious, and neither do I. When I see how many guys don't come back from the bombing mis-sions we fly, I think it's the best way to be. I don't want a girl to be heartbroken if I don't make it."

"Then you should take the opportunity while you are in England to learn as much as you can about women. When you return to America, you can do wonders for her. You may be sur-prised at what she wants." She looks at me archly. "Why don't you pay for a session with me? We can merely talk if you like, and I will teach you many things that you should know about how to please women."

I'm not sure that I want to do this, but she leans over and kisses me. I have never before been kissed like that by a woman so beautiful. While I sit stunned, she places my hand on her breast and kisses me again while the blonde hurries up to relieve me of a large chunk of money. Helena takes my hand and leads me through the curtain and down the hallway to a bedroom. The minute we are inside, she slips out of her wrapper and reclines her nude body on the bed. She is beautiful.

"Get out of that scratchy uniform and lie down beside me," she purrs. "I'll teach you everything you need to know about pleasing a woman."

The next night, after I spend the day in the British Museum, the gunner and I have a good dinner at the Café Royal Grill. It's not as elegant, nor as expensive, as the dining room upstairs, but the food is excellent. His hand quivers as he lifts his glass of wine.

"I got the shakes," he says, "but what can you expect when you know you ain't going to make it?"

"Don't talk like that. Guys get through twenty-five missions. Just before I came overseas, we had a visit from the crew of the *Memphis Belle*. They did twenty-five missions and came home just fine. We'll both finish and go home."

I'm not sure that I believe it, but it helps to say it. He shakes his head and signals for more wine.

"Don't kid a kidder, buddy. The odds are against us. That's why I'm screwing every woman I can. I always wondered what a really young girl would be like. That little bitch last night was hotter than most grown women. It was worth the money. How did you like that whore you had?"

"She was very nice."

"She must have been. When I left, the madam said you were still with her."

"I learned a lot."

I didn't tell him that I had an awful lot to learn.

"Tell you what, old buddy," he says, "let's go to a show. I need to look at some naked women and get charged up. There's a whore with the biggest knockers you can imagine at the place we went last night. Come on with me."

"I think I'll pass tonight."

"Come on, buddy, at least go to the show with me."

I nod reluctantly. What kind of a mess is he going to get me into this time?

He leads me to one of the many theaters in the general area of London's Piccadilly and Leicester Square. London has a curious law. A woman can be completely nude on stage if she stands motionless. She can sing and dance as long as she wears clothing. But for a strip tease, the lights go out. When the lights come back on, the woman stands like a statue with one item less of her costume. This continues until she is nude, but stationary. While we watch a stage full of women alternately sing and lose their clothing this way, my friend pokes me and leers drunkenly.

"These are beautiful women. They're not like you see in a burlesque house back home. Look at that red head there in front. She looks like a goddamn Venus. Man, I'd like to get her in bed."

This guy has a one-track mind. He leans over toward me with a wicked leer, and I get another blast of alcohol breath.

"Old buddy, which one of them women do you like best?"

I gaze at the stage full of nude women and shake my head. I certainly am a long way from South Haven, Michigan.

"I think the one with long, blond hair in the back row is really pretty."

He peers drunkenly at her.

"Yeah, she's a looker all right." He turns to me again with that wicked grin. "I bet you can't meet her."

"I bet I can't either. That woman is downright beautiful. I'm not in her league."

"Buddy, I'll make a bet with you. If you get her to have a drink with you, I'll give you fifty pounds. If you don't, you give me ten pounds."

"You're crazy. You can't be serious."

He scowls, and I see that he is very serious and unpredictable in his drunken state.

"Buddy, I didn't think you were yellow," he says.

How did I get myself into this? He is no longer grinning, and I don't like the look on his face. Maybe it's the wine. I am still not accustomed to drinking, and my head seems to be floating somewhere above my body. I don't want to be called a coward, and I don't want to have trouble with a drunken gunner.

"OK, it's a bet," I say. I'm already prepared to lose ten pounds.

With a sigh, I get up, stagger up the aisle, leave the theater, and stumble in darkness through a dirty alley that smells of urine until I find the stage door. What am I doing? This is crazy, and I don't do crazy things.

But two five-pound notes slipped to a rumpled, gray-haired man guarding the stage door have a surprising effect. They not only get me backstage, but the man also leads me into a big, dressing room reeking of cigarettes and perfume. It swarms with scantily clad women fixing their makeup. They stare at me and laugh when I turn beet red. To my dismay, the doorman takes my arm and leads me to the blonde.

"Jane, this Yank wants to meet you."

"Jane, you have an admirer, but I can't say that he looks like much," a busty brunette shouts, and the women laugh.

Up close, heavy makeup hides the blond woman's looks. I can't tell whether she is young or old. I also can't tell whether she is "really pretty," as I thought, because her face is a painted façade of stage makeup. Now, she wears round, silver-rimmed glasses while she peers intently into a big mirror to apply more makeup. I can't help but stare at her almost nude form. She has firm breasts and a slender body. I notice a faded, exhausted look in her blue eyes when she ignores me and turns to the doorman.

"Making money again, Henry?"

He laughs and walks away. She turns to me and gives me a cold glance.

"If you think I'm going to sleep with you, you wasted your money. I have another show to do, and I have no time for sex-starved Yanks, so please leave."

"That's telling him, dearie," another blonde yells. The women laugh and look at me as though I'm some kind of insect. Thoroughly embarrassed, I feel my face burning as I turn to go. All the alcohol-induced bravado that got me this far is gone. I feel the sting of shame and rejection.

"I didn't want to sleep with you," I mumble.

What am I doing here? This is terrible. How did I get myself into this? I don't dare tell her that it was a bet. I've never done anything like this before in my life. I want to crawl into a hole somewhere. No, I just want to get away.

"I only wanted to meet you," I say. "I think you're very pretty."

This gets a surprising cheer from the other women. A famous author once said that a good deed for a day is to whistle at a plain girl. With all that makeup, I can't tell whether she is plain or beautiful, but I suppose everyone likes to be admired, so I just figuratively whistled at her. My words have an unexpected effect. As I turn away, she puts her hand on my arm to stop me. Her voice is gentle.

"If you only want to meet me—no sex, mind you—I could use a bite to eat after the next show."

I turn back and see a wary look in her eyes. I suspect that this girl has had lots of bad experiences with men who see a nude woman on stage as an easy object for sex.

"I'll be waiting," I say. "You pick the restaurant, and we can talk."

"Good for you, Yank!" a woman yells. "Mind you, show respect for this one. She's a lady, she is."

After I collect my bet and watch the show again, I meet the blonde at the stage door. She wears a worn, gray coat with a kerchief tied over a knot of blond hair. She wears glasses, and I assume that she wears them all the time, except when she is on stage. There's nothing glamorous about her. Strangely, that makes me feel better. For the first time, she smiles a little and takes my arm. The weather is cold and rainy, so we huddle together while she directs me to a tiny café on one of the dark alleys in Soho. Inside, we face each other over a table so small that we are knees to knees. Without makeup, she has a pretty face—not beautiful, but pretty, with nice features and blue eyes. I mentally guess that she is five or six years older than me. The café is Greek, and as we eat, we talk about our lives—mine growing up in Michigan and hers growing up in Here-fordshire. She stands nude on stage because it pays better than clerical and similar jobs, and she doesn't want to be a prostitute, although there is much pressure to recruit her. She does not have the sophisticated boldness of the prostitute, Helena. Instead, there is something wistful and appealing about her. She looks stricken when I tell her of my poor chance of surviving my remaining missions. We talk on and on. I haven't enjoyed myself so much since I entered the military. When the café prepares to close, the girl surprises me.

"Would you like to come along to my flat for a cup of tea?" she says. "We could talk a bit more, if you've a mind to."

"That is really kind of you. I'd love it."

She suggests the Underground, but I hail a taxi to take us to her address in the north part of London. Her place is twice the size of the one that Yvette had and is more attractive. Jane has two rooms—a combined kitchen and living room and a separate bedroom. She tells me that "the loo" is down the hall. Everything is neat and attractive in her living room. Unlike Yvette and Helena, she does not smoke, so the air is fresh, with a touch of perfume.

Over tea, we talk more. We laugh while I tell her how girls back home regarded me as very smart, but not interesting. Talking with her is pure joy. I'm having a wonderful time. But finally, realizing how late it is, I get up to leave.

"Must you?" she says.

"You need to get some sleep, since you have to work again tomorrow."

She gives me a strange, bold look.

"Stay here," she whispers and quickly stands. Her arms encircle me while she kisses me and kisses me and kisses me.

The next morning, I awaken to see blue eyes staring at me from a foot away. Jane's blond hair flows across the pillow. While I gaze at her, I realize that the terrible headache that has tortured me continuously for many days is gone.

"You're staring at me," I say with great brilliance.

What do you say to a pretty woman with whom you have just spent the first really passionate night of your life? With Yvette and

Helena, we were having sex. With Jane, we were making love, and it was tender and wonderful.

"I've been watching you sleep," she says. "You needn't believe it if you don't wish, but I almost never go to bed with men. Last night was special. I will remember it always, but I fear I exhausted you. I simply couldn't get enough of you."

"I thought you were the most wonderful thing that could happen to me, but I'm sure you found that I'm not much of a lover. I'm not at all experienced."

"You were smashing. I loved our night together." Suddenly, her head pops up, and she peers at a clock across the room before she quickly puts on her glasses to peer again. "Do you realize how late it is? Didn't you say you had a train to catch?"

I pick up my watch from the bedside table.

"I have a little over three hours before the train leaves. If you'd like, there's plenty of time for us to go somewhere for breakfast."

Jane catapults from the bed. I couldn't tell when I was in the audience at the theater, and it was dark last night in her bedroom, but now I see that she is a genuine blond.

"You can bathe down the hall, she says. "The water will be frightfully cold, I fear. It always is."

Cold is something that I don't need.

"Do you have a snooty sort of dress? Put it on quick, and we'll go to my hotel, the Park Lane. There's a big tub in my bathroom with plenty of warm water."

"You have a room at the Park Lane? I've never been there, but I know it's appallingly expensive."

"While I'm still alive, I may as well spend the money they pay me on living comfortably."

"Please don't talk that way, but do you know what our comedians say is wrong with you Yanks?" she says with a giggle. "You're overpaid, oversexed, and over here."

Jane dresses quickly. With glasses, a smart dress, and sleek, blond hair in a tight bun on the back of her head, she looks every bit the sophisticated, English lady as we descend from a taxi and sweep through the crowded lobby of the Park Lane. In my room, we are soon in the huge bathtub.

"This is heavenly," Jane says and gives me a look that I can't fathom.

Later, at breakfast, I gaze with distaste at Jane's bronze-colored kipper.

"I couldn't handle smoked herring for breakfast," I say. "It has its head and tail on. I think it's staring at me. Yes, it's definitely staring at me."

"Nonsense!" she giggles. "It's delicious, and much better than the tasteless porridge you are eating."

"I grew up eating it, except we call it oatmeal."

All too soon, time runs out. Jane insists on riding with me in one of London's shiny, black taxis to Saint Pancras railroad station. On the way, she clings to me. I am surprised, but it feels wonderful, and I don't want to leave her.

"Could I see you again when I get my next leave in London?" I ask, prepared for a polite turndown.

"I would like that very, very much," she says, gazing at me intently through her glasses. "Would you like me to write to you?"

"That would be wonderful," I say, and quickly scribble for her my English address at Air Force Station 109.

"I think you could use a bit of cheering up. You have it all calculated with your bloody statistics that you're going to die, but I wager that there are many chaps who finish their twenty-five missions just fine. Remember that when you get into your aircraft, and also remember that I want you back soon, so we can have another night of it. If you wish, we could get to know each other better."

What an invitation!

At St. Pancras station, the taxi driver looks away and waits patiently during our many kisses. Jane's eyes are wet with tears. Does she really like me this much after only one night and morning together? I thought that kind of thing only happens in Hollywood movies.

"Mind yourself and don't get hurt," she says. "I want you back again."

One more kiss and I turn to the driver.

"Take her back to her place," I say, as I give him double fare and double tip.

The last thing that I see is Jane waving from the taxi.

On the train, reality sets in. I'm shy, devoted to science, and from a small town in a part of Michigan so conservative that almost all businesses close on Sunday and many churches ban dancing. I had a strict upbringing and had never done more than kiss a girl until a couple of weeks ago. Now I've slept with a woman who stands nude on stage, and she says she wants to see me again. I don't know much about romance, but I would give anything to see her, although I can't imagine why she even looks at me. She must have dozens of handsome men after her every night and all the dates she wants. Has she already forgotten me? If so, two good things still came from my night with her. She took away my headache, and she made me feel that I might be able to make it through twenty-five missions. She was quite wonderful.

Three days after I return to the base, I am astonished and delighted when a small, pale-blue envelope arrives with a letter from Jane. I answer it immediately, and another letter comes back from her. That sets us on a course of letters about everything, and I find that Jane is intelligent and witty. Her letters are chatty. They are also encouraging—something that I need. She writes four or five times each week, and her letters become brilliant rays of sunshine.

Now, if I can only survive these darn missions . . . but there's a rumor that we are going to set off on a lot of bad ones. The invasion of France is coming in May or June, and the Allies must wipe out the German Air Force if the invasion is to succeed. That means hitting heavily defended targets inside Germany to stop aircraft production and to act as bait so our fighters can shoot down German fighters. I have a cold feeling that grim days lie ahead.

CHAPTER 12

Killer Influenza

The loudspeaker wakes me as it echoes through the building's silent darkness.

"Attention! Attention! Condition yellow."

It is 1:30 A.M. Condition yellow means that German planes are nearby. It changes to red if they are on top of us. We are supposed to run outside and dive into an underground bomb shelter. I checked the shelter once in daylight. It is narrow, black, and cold. An inch of icy water covers its muddy floor. I'll stay where I am and take my chances with bombs, thank you. I didn't go to a shelter in London, and I was all right. It can't be as hazardous as flying on a mission over Germany.

I hear cigarette lighters clicking all over the building. You can tell when smokers are nervous. They reach for a cigarette. How do they survive the tension of a seven or eight hour mission without being able to smoke?

I lie in darkness and listen to the drone of a plane. It is undoubtedly German. At this time of night, things always seem bleak. The war stretches ahead forever. According to tonight's news on the BBC, Allied troops have bogged down in Italy's winter, and Soviet forces are moving at a snail's pace in deep snow. The Allies promise that they will invade France and defeat the Germans, but I see no sign of it. Americans fighting in the Marshall Islands in the South Pacific are more than 1,000 miles from Japan, and the Japanese fight for every inch of any island we try to capture. Despite bombing of German factories and airbases, veteran crews tell me that they don't see any weakening of German opposition, and I keep losing friends that die in burning B-17s.

The German plane is closer, almost overhead. I suspect that everyone in the building is listening to it drone closer and closer.

It's foolish, but you have a helpless feeling that the German bomber is going to drop a bomb exactly on you.

To get my mind off this fear, I ponder a vexing problem. We crewmembers are supposed to bond in an all-for-one and one-for-all unit, and the ten of us have grown close. Townsend, Swanson, Kinsella, Ballmer, Lyons, Araujo, Tasker, Norton, and Kindred are wonderful fellows and seem to be almost like family to me. But I keep secrets from them. During training, I didn't tell anyone but Rex Townsend that I wanted to leave the crew and go to officer candidate school. I also kept from them that I wheedled an extra forty-eight hours in London that they didn't get. They deserved it as much as I, so I worry that some could resent it. When you face death, time to relax is precious. Since I kept the additional time in London a secret, I have to destroy Jane's letters, because my crew would wonder when I had a chance to meet a British woman. This would seem trivial under other conditions, but the pressure we are under causes crewmembers to fly into a rage over small things.

The sound of the aircraft fades. It didn't drop any bombs on us. The loudspeaker announces an "all clear." I turn over, pull the blankets up, and sink into sleep.

While bad weather keeps us from flying, I visit Cambridge University. A supply sergeant must go to an airbase near Cambridge to pick up material. He'll be gone all day. We aren't scheduled for a mission, so it only takes a pack of cigarettes to persuade him to let me ride as far as Cambridge. Next morning, we head out in a truck. He knows the roads and the trick of driving on the left. We tell jokes while I do my usual sightseeing. I get off the truck in Cambridge with a promise that I will be waiting when he comes through the city in late afternoon. In the meantime, I have a day to look at one of the world's great centers of learning. A gray-haired gentleman in scarf and tweed jacket points me in the proper direction, and I spend hours strolling and gazing at university buildings. It is pure heaven to feel the atmosphere of a university again.

I have a lunch of fish and chips that fill a big cone of newspaper and have a liberal sprinkling of malt vinegar. While I eat, I sit on a stone bench and watch university people pass by until several young men note my uniform and gather around to converse. They want to know how people in the United States view the British. We speculate on the postwar world. None of us has a clue, but it is fun. They give me a guided tour of the university, including the library, which grew from a small collection of books in the early 1400s. They tell me that Cambridge University consists of thirty-one colleges.

At St. John's College, we visit the Bridge of Sighs over the River Cam. The students say that it was built in 1831, and its name was inspired by the famous bridge in Venice, where condemned prisoners sighed as they were led across it to be executed. I get a good look at it from St. John's Old Bridge. Like its namesake in Venice, this Bridge of Sighs has barred windows, but they are designed to prevent students from entering at night, rather than to prevent escape.

We visit King's College, an awesome collection of buildings surmounted by the towering chapel. The students tell me that Henry VI laid the first stone of the King's College of Our Lady and St. Nicholas in Cambridge on Passion Sunday in 1441. King's College Chapel is a huge structure. The students say that it was intended by Henry VI to show the power of royal help for a college. The interior is breathtaking. It took over a century to build and was completed in 1547.

We briefly visit Queens' College, founded in 1448 by Margaret of Anjou. If I understand the students correctly, a series of English queens have been patronesses of the college, the latest being Queen Elizabeth. The main college site sits astride the River Cam, the two halves joined across the river by the Mathematical Bridge. When you cross, you get the impression of going from the twentieth century to the fifteenth. The Mathematical Bridge was originally built in 1749 and rebuilt twice. The students say that several old wives' tales have grown about the bridge. One is that it was built by Sir Isaac Newton, even though he died in 1727. Another is that the structure requires no bolts to hold it together, which the students say is nonsense.

There is also time for quick visits to Jesus College, a remarkably peaceful place, which was founded in 1496, and Clare College, founded in 1326. The ages of all of the colleges amaze me. Their beauty impresses me even more.

By the time my friend picks me up, I purr like a happy cat. It was a great day, and I ride back to Podington supremely happy.

In rapid succession, our quiz team defeats quiz teams representing two nearby bomb groups. They are easy wins. If other bomb groups don't have stronger teams, we are going to have a bunch of victories. We have a good team. I notice a curious thing. I am the only combat flyer on any of the quiz teams. From that, I conclude that I shouldn't be flying, but I doubt that I can convince Colonel Reed, the 92nd Bomb Group commander.

In mid-February, I develop fever, aches, chills, sore throat, and trouble breathing. The doctors diagnose influenza, and it grows worse rapidly. I have never felt so awful in my life—shaking with cold, then burning up with fever, aching everywhere, too weak to move, gasping for breath inside an oxygen tent, unable to eat, and out of touch with my surroundings. Where am I? Is it a hospital? I lie with eyes closed and remember that a half million Americans died of influenza in 1919, and children ran around singing, "I had a little bird. Its name was Enza. I opened the window and influEnza." Why did I have to remember that? The ditty runs through my hot brain without letup.

Medical people move silently around me, and I hear soft conversations, but the words are too faint for me to understand them. Influenza is awful. I feel worse by the hour. I'm burning up and lose track of time as I lie with eyes closed. Finally, I hear low voices in conversation about me, and I wish I didn't hear them.

"What's his temp?"

"It's a little above 103 and looks like it's still climbing."

"Damn! There isn't a goddamn thing we can do for this kid."

"What are his chances?"

"No better than fifty-fifty."

While I lie in bed as weak as a limp noodle, my feverish thoughts turn to Jane. She has astonished me by sending so many letters. We were only together one night, but I like her, and her letters indicate that she likes me. I want to see her again, but is she merely being nice to a doomed flyer? I suspect that instant romance only happens in the movies. Yet a new feeling hits me when I looked at her in my room at the Park Lane. She was in an attractive dress, with shining, blond hair drawn back tightly in a bun. As her blue eyes gazed at me through her glasses, I wanted to take her in my arms and hold her forever. Women are wonderful. Influenza is not.

I didn't think that I could feel any worse, but I do. I think it is night, but I'm not certain. I'm burning up and struggling to breathe. My breath comes in gasps. Each gasp hurts terribly. It is becoming too difficult to breathe the oxygen they are giving me. I can't lift my arm. It would be pleasant to just stop breathing. Maybe I should. Medics around me speak in low voices, but I hear enough. They don't think that I will live through the night. The Germans haven't killed me yet. Influenza just might.

CHAPTER 13

Secret Mission

Influenza does not kill me, but it was a close call. I survive the terrible night. The next day begins a slow recovery that has the medics smiling. By February 20, influenza is gone, although I'm too weak to fly. Squadron operations pulls an unlucky radio operator away from a day's rest to go with my crew to Leipzig to bomb a factory making ME-109 fighters. They return to tell of vicious attacks by German fighters and the flaming loss of another bomber from the 92nd Group. Ten more men are gone. I knew one of them. He never expected to die. The chaplains must keep busy writing to families.

The next day, the 92nd Group thunders into the air on its way to Germany to bomb an airbase at Hopsten, but my crew does not go. While I snuggle under blankets, I listen to our bombers take off. Thus, it's a surprise later in the morning when the first sergeant hurries in to tell me to get to the flight line fast. A jeep is waiting to take me. While I wonder why insignificant me rates a jeep and driver, we speed to the airfield and stop at an ancient B-17E. Colonel Andre Brousseau, the 92nd Group's executive officer, and two lieutenants stand beside it. Colonel Brousseau, the most gung-ho flyer in the group, fixes me with piercing eyes and questions me for several minutes about radio procedures. This is surprising, but I have no trouble with his questions. When he seems satisfied, we climb into the B-17E and take off, with me alone in the rear of the plane.

We have not been in the air for long when I get a message sent with real speed. The message for the colonel may be important, so I take it to him. It was nice to get a message for a change, especially one where the operator sent it fast and made my pencil race to copy it.

We land at an airbase, where Colonel Brousseau and the lieutenants go off to conduct business. I sit quietly under the bomber's wing. A chilly wind whips across the airfield, but I'm not flying a mission, so I can put up with a cold wind. A friendly lieutenant stops his jeep to look at the old B-17E. He says that he is a communications officer at this base, so we chat about radio communications. He asks a number of questions to which I'm sure he knows the answers. It's almost as if he is trying to test how much I know, but he is so friendly that I'm not concerned. This must be test day. Soon, Colonel Brousseau and the lieutenants return. We roar into the air again and return to our base.

"Where you been?" Ken Tasker asks.

"I had to fly to another base with Colonel Brousseau. I don't know why he needed a radio operator, although he did get an urgent message."

When Sam Smith from group communications comes into our building that night, he gives me a wry smile.

"I heard you flew with Colonel Brousseau today," he says.

I nod and give Sam a weak smile. Sam is the person I convinced that I could not handle Morse code fast enough to be a lead radio operator.

"You handled a message today, didn't you?' he says with a smirk as he walks away. He knows that I bamboozled him. Woe is me. What happens next?

February 22, 1944. I still can't fly with my crew because the doctors are worried that I may have trouble if I'm at high altitude for many hours. Thus, I'm puzzled when the first sergeant again hurries into my building to tell me that I have to get to the flight line fast. A cold feeling grabs me. I bet someone can't fly on the mission scheduled for today, and I'm a last-minute replacement. The first sergeant shakes his head. The bombers have gone. I never heard them take off.

I grab a Cadbury chocolate bar and go outside just as a jeep pulls up. This business of having my own jeep and driver is going to turn my head. We speed away and stop at the operations building.

"Get your flying gear and oxygen mask," a sergeant says. "I was told to tell you it's a short flight, but it's at altitude."

"Where did the group go today?" I ask.

"Aalborg in Denmark," he says. "They're a decoy, so they won't have any fighter escort. Ain't you lucky you ain't with them?"

I nod, get my gear, and run for the jeep. As it races around the perimeter track, past empty parking pads, I wonder if luck is with me. The group's twenty bombers flying alone will certainly have trouble with German fighters on the way to Aalborg. Some of our planes will go down today, and more of our guys will die. But where am I going on a short flight at high altitude? Maybe someone is going on a training flight and needs a radio operator. It can't be another errand—not at high altitude.

The jeep skids to a halt next to a patched B-17F. A captain and two lieutenants stand beneath the bomber's nose. I have never seen them before. The captain grins and shakes hands. I note that he knows my name, but he doesn't mention his or those of the officers with him.

"We're from another group," he says. "We're borrowing the plane and you. I hear you're a hot shot on the radio."

"I'm no hot shot," I say, "but I can operate a radio."

"We're going to depend on you. Get aboard. The four of us are the crew." He points to each of the lieutenants. "Copilot and navigator, and you'll have the rear of the plane to yourself. Let's go."

He hands me a transparent plastic case holding a sheet of rice paper with secret codes and communications information. This is like a combat mission. A chill shoots through me. Where are we going?

"Dial into that frequency and listen for messages, especially the abort message on the sheet," the captain says. "If you hear it, tell me quick."

I climb aboard, and the engines start. It's an eerie feeling to be the only person in the rear section of the big bomber. We taxi out, roar off the runway, and head southeast while we climb toward 15,000 feet.

As we drone along in frosty sunshine, I admire green hills and valleys, towns and villages, and fields and forests of the English countryside, while I listen for a message on the radio. A train below us races along a track and leaves a long trail of smoke. We fly on. I continue to gaze at the countryside, but I'm still weak from the influenza, so my eyes close. I awake with a start. My watch says that I dozed for ten minutes. While I shake my head to wake up, a squadron of British Spitfire fighters sails overhead, heading north. We must be in the far south of England. Where are we going?

"Time to go on oxygen," someone calls. "You OK back there?"

"I'm fine, thanks."

To my surprise as I buckle on my oxygen mask, we roar across the white cliffs on the south coast. The gray water of the English Channel is below us. What are we doing out here? We continue to fly southeast. My heart suddenly beats rapidly and my mouth is dry. Where is this guy going? We're in an unarmed plane over the Channel. The English coast fades behind us. German fighters patrol out here. One could shoot us down in seconds. The Germans had a fix on us the minute we left the coast, and their fighter controllers are watching our flight path now. My heart beats like a trip hammer. Am I scared stiff? You better believe it!

"Listen for that message and keep a sharp eye out for German fighters," the captain calls.

The French coast approaches. No! No! Stay away from it! The French countryside is pretty, but today I regard it as I would a rattlesnake. As we near the coast, I am in a panic. It's bad enough to go over enemy territory in a bomber formation with fighter escort, but this flight is suicide. I'm flying with lunatics, but I can't get out and walk, so I watch fearfully for German fighter planes that will certainly appear. We sweep over the French coast and soon turn east. The countryside below us has the pale-green fields of winter, dotted by lakes and ponds. Narrow rivers run through it. I see a network of roads and an empty railroad track.

"Would you mind telling me where we are?" I croak to the captain.

"Pas de Calais."

The officers discuss the relative merits of music by Glenn Miller and Benny Goodman while I listen for the coded message and scan the sky for German fighters. I'm sure they will appear any second. After what seems like an eternity, the big bomber turns and flies north over the French coast and the English Channel. I breathe a sigh of relief.

"I'm going to turn on the IFF," I call.

"Oh, yeah, good," the captain says. "No sense in stirring up the RAF."

After crossing the Channel, we fly low over English countryside, and I engage in my favorite pastime of gazing at England's fields, forests, lakes and villages. I see another passenger train racing along a track, leaving its trail of smoke. A convoy of thirty (I count them) army trucks moves down a road toward a field where dozens of military tanks park. Hundreds of artillery guns line another road.

We descend and land at my base. I'm still unglued as I climb from the bomber. The captain grins and shakes hands.

"That wasn't so bad was it? Just think, you were over enemy territory, so you get credit for a combat mission."

I hadn't thought of that. I grin and nod. His face becomes stern.

"There's one thing that I want you to remember. This flight is classified as secret. Do you understand? It's secret. You don't discuss it with anyone, and I mean anyone, including your crew. If anybody asks, you were on an errand to another base like you were yesterday."

How did he know about yesterday? He told me that he is from another group. Understanding begins to come like the dawn breaking.

"Don't forget—no talking," he calls as he walks toward a waiting jeep. "I'll know if you do, and you'll be in a shit pot of trouble." He grins and waves. "See you soon."

I manage a sick smile as I wave. See you soon? We're going again? I would rather do anything than fly alone over enemy territory in an unarmed plane. I'm still trembling. What kind of a crazy flight was that? Obviously, other people know a lot more about it than I do. We were so lucky not to be shot down. Still, I get credit for a combat mission.

When the group returns from Aalborg, I hear that German fighters made vicious attacks and shot down two of our bombers. They say that a B-17 from our squadron went down when an ME-109 fighter smashed head-on into it. Another acquaintance is gone. At least I missed the Aalborg mission, but the flight with the captain was scary enough.

"Where you been?" Tasker asks.

"I was off on another errand."

He grins.

"Somebody's sure got it in for you," he says.

I settle down to read a letter from Jane. Each letter seems more affectionate than the last. Could she truly like me? She again asks when I can come to London, and I realize that I am as anxious to see her as she seems eager to see me. We have written dozens of increasingly affectionate letters, and we are both panting to meet again. What is happening with us? I never had a girl act this way with me before.

When I see Jane, I will have plenty of money to spend. Before we left the United States, the air force promoted me to staff sergeant (four stripes on my arm), and at the beginning of February, the 92nd Bomb Group promoted me to technical sergeant (five stripes), each time with a boost in pay. In addition to regular pay for five stripes, I get 50 percent additional pay for flying and 20 percent additional pay for being overseas. There's more. I make an amazing amount of money on my cigarette ration. I never smoked (not even once), but I get a carton each week from the British girls at the post exchange and sell the cigarettes to the highest bidder. Among my bidders, Lucky Strike is the favorite, with Chesterfield a close second. The more nervous that smokers get about missions, the more they want cigarettes. A carton per week is not enough for them under the tense conditions in which we live, so they offer astonishing amounts of cash for cigarettes, and the bids get higher every week.

But one terrible thought won't leave me for long. The instructors at Bovingdon were not trying to scare us by saying that the average life of a bomber over Germany is only eleven missions. They stated a fact. I'm nineteen, and the probability is good that I won't live to see my twentieth birthday next summer.

CHAPTER 14

Hell over Schweinfurt

February 24, 1944. The intelligence captain pulls back the curtain covering a map of Europe. The crowd of flyers gasps and groans. I see faces go pale. A nearby flight engineer bows his head and begins to pray. The red line goes deep into central Germany to the city of Schweinfurt, a name that strikes fear in the flyers of the Eighth Air Force. The target is crucial because factories at Schweinfurt manufacture ball bearings that are vital to German military production. If we knock out ball bearings, we deal a big blow to production of planes, tanks, trucks, and machinery. The Germans know it and are ready to defend the city furiously.

The Eighth Air Force fought its way to Schweinfurt twice before. In August of 1943, our bombers smashed the ball bearing plants, but the Germans' shot down thirty-six of our bombers. Germany rebuilt the plants in record time, requiring a mission in October of 1943. Our bombers again destroyed the ball-bearing factories, but at a cost of an astounding sixty of our bombers destroyed. That is equal to three bomb groups. Six B-17s from the 92nd Group were lost in that raid, so combat veterans fear a Schweinfurt mission. It's a death sentence for some of us. Everyone looks grim. Some are obviously frightened. A fellow next to me covers his face and mumbles that he wishes he'd written to his wife last night.

The only good thing about the mission is that we will fly in a new B-17G, and I will have a lovely Plexiglas roof over my head. It's still bitter cold in the plane, but the absence of a below-zero blast coming in through an open roof makes a huge difference. I won't have the wind chill taking the temperature to 100 degrees below zero. I'm not as likely to freeze accidentally, and I won't have to clear ice from my oxygen mask as often. But Schweinfurt shapes up to be a scary flight. It's the worst that I have faced thus far.

After takeoff around 9 A.M., we do the usual climbing and circling to get into formation, while the temperature in the radio
room drops. Still climbing, our armada of several hundred four-
engine bombers crosses the North Sea. It is always an impressive
sight. Tense and fully alert, we speed across Belgium, and enter Germany. Each time we fly over Germany, I think of German civilians
ready to beat me to death if I parachute from our plane.

The gray and white landscape 21,000 feet below looks cold and
wintry. It seems quiet down there, but I know that air raid sirens
blare in towns, and people hurry to hide in underground shelters. I
see a countryside of dark forests and white fields dotted with cities
and villages, all connected by roads and rail lines. While I fill my log
with everything that I see, I gaze at the Rhine River, spanned by
dozens of bridges, and lined with cities pouring smoke into the air
from factories. The sky is brilliant blue, but it is filled with myriad
white trails high overhead. They twist and circle as our fighters battle
what looks like an immense number of German attackers. I tremble
from cold and fright. My headache is back, and it's killing me.

"Fighters!" Lloyd yells.

A swarm of silver fighters dives toward us. They hit a bomber
formation on our right. The bombers shoot strings of red tracers
toward the fighters. The fighters' wings blink as their many guns
fire. Orange streams shoot toward the bombers like fire from hoses
and smash into a B-17. Pieces of the unlucky bomber fly off in a
cloud of smoke. Gunfire hits the Plexiglas dome of a bomber's top
turret, and it explodes in a white cloud that turns red with blood
from the gunner's head. The first bomber catches fire, then the second, each trailing a long stream of orange flame. Both B-17s wobble
as blazes engulf them in seconds. No one gets out. The men are
burning alive in there. In thirty seconds, the bombers are flaming
torches, totally enveloped in fire. The blazing planes tip over and
fall, trailing long tails of flame. Fighters wheel around and race
back from the rear toward the hapless formation of bombers. Red
tracers from bombers spray out toward the fighters. Orange fire
spews from the fighters' wings. It hammers a B-17, hitting wings and
engines. Smoke and fragments erupt from the bomber. Fire spurts
from its engines, and the big plane dissolves in a mass of flames.

Two men jump from the bomber's nose, but there's an inferno in the rest of the B-17. A gunner jumps through fire from the rear door. Trailing smoke and sparks, he opens his smoldering parachute, but the silk ignites as it opens. It burns in seconds, and he falls toward the earth far below. His arms wave frantically, and I think with horror of how he must feel, knowing that he is doomed. With the rest of the crew burning inside, the big bomber flips over, drops several hundred feet, and explodes in a boiling, orange ball. The guns of several bombers spray fire toward a speeding fighter. Their red tracers explode its windshield in a red cloud. The FW-190 gushes smoke and leaves a fiery trail as it spins like a wounded bird toward the earth.

The sky around us fills with fighters slashing through bomber formations, and bomber gunfire spurting toward fighters. Bombers catch fire, and fighters trail smoke as they fall toward the earth. A fighter pilot jumps from his stricken fighter and opens his parachute. A bomber's tail gunner fires a long burst at him. The pilot's body jerks and hangs limply from his parachute. Fighter pilots must have seen the killing, because two FW-190s attack the tail gunner's bomber. Their guns smash the tail gunner's position to shreds and hit the engines until the B-17 explodes in another ball of fire.

"Look out!" Lloyd shouts.

Terror grips me as fighters head for us. Rex dodges and weaves our B-17 to spoil their aim. Lloyd's twin guns fire, joined quickly by Ralph Ballmer's new, twin machine guns. Guns on other bombers hammer frantically, sending tracer bullets toward incoming FW-190s. The fighters blast through our Group, spraying orange streams of cannon and machine gun fire. They hit a nearby B-17, and it blazes from nose to tail before it slides into a downward dive. There is a brilliant flash behind me. I whirl and see a huge, orange ball of fire hanging in the air behind us. Another B-17 has exploded. I duck when a fighter sprays orange fire five feet above me, and I duck again as gunfire blasts past just outside my right window. Every gun on our plane seems to be firing. Even through my oxygen mask, the pungent smell of burned gunpowder is strong.

We turn into the target to face an immense, black cloud of smoke from hundreds of bursting antiaircraft shells. The Germans are putting up an awesome barrage of fire to protect the Schweinfurt factories. The black cloud stretches across the sky ahead of us. I look at stuttering flashes of exploding shells and wonder how we can get through it alive. We plunge into the cloud amid a blizzard of explosions. The bomber rocks and bounces from blasts around us. I hear loud snaps as shrapnel rips through our B-17. Clusters of fragments sound like sleet hitting a tin roof, but there are loud bangs as big pieces slash through our plane. There is no place to hide, and a piece is bound to hit someone soon.

"Bomb bay doors coming open," Ralph Ballmer calls.

I open the door to the bomb bay and crouch down to see the bomb bay doors opening below me. A blast sends another piece of shrapnel through the plane. It sounded like a big one.

"Doors open," I gasp.

I look down through the bomb bay at Schweinfurt 21,000 feet below. It's a large city tucked into the curve of a river. Our plane rocks and bounces from hundreds of antiaircraft blasts while Ballmer tries to focus his bombsight on the ball bearing plants. Smoke rises from fires burning fiercely down there.

"Bombs away," Ballmer calls as the heavy load of bombs drops from the bomb bay. I watch them plummet down and burst with multiple flashes in the burning factories. Bombs from other planes coat the factory area. Nothing could live in the hell of fire and explosions down there. The destruction is awesome.

Our armada turns from the target, but there is no respite. FW-190 and ME-109 fighters wait, and they attack again and again, slicing through our group and those nearby. Between fifty and a hundred fighters buzz around the bomber fleet like angry wasps, firing continuously and destroying one plane after another. Tracers from bombers and fighters crisscross the sky around our B-17s. Our gunners must have used up most of their ammunition. The fight seems to go on forever, and our guns never stop firing.

Just as I am certain that the gunners will run out of ammunition, the battle eases. German fighters, probably low on fuel, dive away. Soon, a flight of American P-38 fighters sweeps overhead. The sight is fantastic. We fly on northward for a time, and I see a whole squadron of P-47 fighters above us. We're over Belgium. Soon, our battered formation crosses the coastline and drones out over the North Sea. We survived, but I can't stop trembling.

After a bumpy ride 3,000 feet above the English countryside, we reach our airbase at Podington, and Rex Townsend makes a nice landing, despite piloting the bomber for more than seven hours through a terrible mêlée. I crawl unsteadily from the plane and lean against the battered B-17 to keep from falling. Shrapnel tore holes all over the plane. It's a miracle that someone wasn't killed. More than seven hours in the cold at high altitude is bad enough, but facing death for much of the time is pure horror. The crew's smudged faces are pale, and their eyes have a haunted look. We can't survive these fights much longer. Some of us are going to die.

"I think they better pay us more," Ralph Ballmer says, trying to bring some lightness to a bunch of shaken flyers.

Ken Tasker looks at me.

"How you doing?" he asks.

"I've never been so scared," I say.

At interrogation by intelligence officers, I hear that the 92nd Group lost three bombers today. At dinner, I stare at empty seats at tables. Thirty guys were lost. They gave their lives so we could destroy the ball bearing factories. For me, it was mission number eight. Seventeen remain.

"We're alerted for another mission tomorrow," Greg calls as I reach the door to my building. I sag. After today's mission to Schweinfurt, I'm exhausted. A mission early tomorrow morning is awful news.

A letter from Jane lies on my bed. I grab it like a drowning man grasping a rope and lie down to read her calm words. The Armed Forces Radio plays music by Glenn Miller and Tommy Dorsey. After reading the letter, I surrender to exhaustion.

During the night I have a terrible nightmare. I'm in a burning B-17. Fire is everywhere. Before I can buckle on my parachute, an explosion blows me from the B-17, and I fall toward the ground thousands of feet below, just like the fellow that I saw on the mission to Schweinfurt. I wake up terrified and gasping for breath. The nightmare was so real. I lie in bed for an hour before I calm down enough to get back to sleep. The nightmare returns with startling clarity. I wake up shaking and drenched with sweat. After another period awake, I drop off and face the nightmare again. For the rest of the night, I sit up and force myself to stay awake until a voice from the darkness tells me that it's time to get up and prepare for another mission.

The original bomber crew. Front row, from left: John Kindred, tail gunner; Greg Araujo, ball turret gunner; Ken Tasker, waist gunner; the author, radio operator; Ed Norton, waist gunner; and Lloyd Lyons, flight engineer. Back row, from left: Ken Kinsella, navigator; Ralph Ballmer, bombardier; Gunnar Swanson, copilot; and Rex Townsend, pilot. Kinsella, Ballmer, Swanson, and Townsend were killed in March 1944. Kindred was killed in April 1944. The author was wounded in May 1944. U.S. AIR FORCE

The author dressed for flight.
AUTHOR'S COLLECTION

The author made up as a European for identification papers to help escape from Europe in case his bomber was shot down. U.S. AIR FORCE

Boeing B-17F bombers. New crews flew the oldest planes. There was no roof on the radio room of the B-17F, and the waist compartment had open gun ports. A subzero wind blew through the radio room and waist at 170 miles per hour. It was incredibly cold. U.S. AIR FORCE

Spectacular contrails from 92nd Bomb Group planes heading into Germany on a winter morning. Gunners hated contrails because German fighter planes could hide in them to sneak in close behind the bombers. U.S. AIR FORCE

Swirling contrails of fighter planes ahead mean trouble.

U.S. AIR FORCE

A German fighter plane speeds past after firing its guns into a bomber formation. U.S. AIR FORCE

A B-17F on fire as it falls toward the earth below. U.S. AIR FORCE

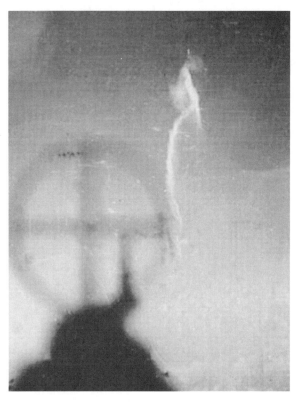

Bomber explodes in midair, leaving a trail of falling debris. U.S. AIR FORCE

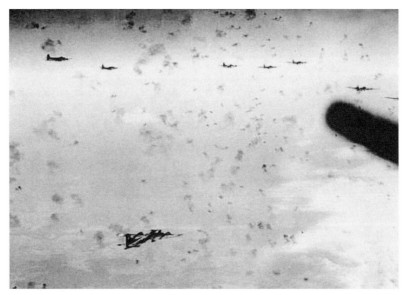

Antiaircraft fire above a German city. The barrage usually destroyed many bombers while they flew through it. U.S. AIR FORCE

Bombers heading home after hitting a target and surviving fighter attacks and antiaircraft fire. U.S. AIR FORCE

Our crew with four replacements for the crew members killed in March. Front row, from left: the author, Ken Tasker, Lloyd Lyons, and Ed Norton. Back row, from left: John Kindred, temporary navigator, temporary bombardier, Virgil Hill, new pilot, and temporary copilot. John Kindred was killed soon after this picture was taken. U.S. AIR FORCE

New B-17G bombers of the 92nd Bomb Group drop bombs after fighting their way to a target in Germany. The "B" inside the triangle on the rudder identifies the plane as being from the 92nd. U.S. AIR FORCE

Bombs dropping, as seen from the bomb bay. U.S. AIR FORCE

Bomb pattern of destruction on factories in a German city. U.S. AIR FORCE

Final crew with which the author flew as a replacement for an injured radio operator. Front row, from left: Sam Johnson, ball turret gunner; Joe Topolosky, bombardier; George Keith, tail gunner; injured radio operator; and unknown waist gunner not used on final missions. Back row, from left: Milt Powell, waist gunner; Richard Funk, copilot; Victor Trost, pilot; Franklin Burks, navigator; and Bill Honaker, flight engineer. U.S. AIR FORCE

The new B-17G, named *Pop*, on which the author flew his last two missions. U.S. AIR FORCE

A B-17G on fire after an attack by German fighters. It is an identical scene to that which occurred on the author's final mission, as German fighters destroyed an adjacent B-17G in a head-on attack. Then they turned to attack the author's plane from the rear, wounding him and Milt Powell and setting the plane on fire.

Pop after a crash landing on a field at Bulltofta, near Malmö in southern Sweden. Note the damage to the plane. FROM *MAKING FOR SWEDEN, PART 2*
BY BO WIDFELDT AND ROLPH WEGMANN. USED WITH PERMISSION.

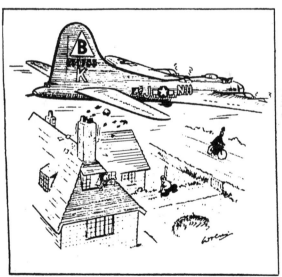

**HÖRT PÅ BULLTOFTA: — Ta noumeret pou
han, kounstabelen!**

Shortly after the author's arrival in Sweden, this cartoon appeared in a
Swedish newspaper. The "B" in a triangle on the plane and its low-alti-
tude crossing to the Swedish coast put the finger in his crew's plane.
AUTHOR'S COLLECTION

The author, wounded in his left leg, stands in front of his Loka Brunn home, Villa von Essen, where he was interned in Sweden.

CHAPTER 15

Barbiturates and Amphetamine

Drained by lack of sleep from nightmares, I sit through a briefing for a long mission to bomb Augsburg in southern Germany. A sense of doom hangs over me like a shroud. We will not survive it. But after my headache and I climb aboard our B-17G, mechanical trouble stops our plane from going.

It's a surprise several hours later when I get a call to hurry to the flight line. A jeep arrives to pick me up. I can't get accustomed to this kind of service. After a fast ride to pick up my flying gear, the jeep deposits me beside a new, silver B-17G that gleams in the sunlight. It's so new that it doesn't yet have a giant "B" inside a triangle, the insignia of the 92nd Bomb Group, on its rudder. I see the captain from the other group standing next to it with three lieutenants. Oh, no, we couldn't be going over to the Pas de Calais again in an unarmed plane. Or could we? The captain grins and waves.

"Hop aboard," he says, handing me the secret codes. "We're going to take a little trip. We won't be gone very long." He cocks his head at me. "You look kind of peaked. Are you all right?"

I nod.

"We had a rough mission to Schweinfurt yesterday," I say. "There were German fighters all over us. It wore me out."

I don't tell him about my nightmares.

"I heard about the mission," he says. "Well, let's go for a ride. Don't go to sleep on me. I'm depending on you to watch our back for fighters."

That means we are going back to the Pas de Calais. What did I do to deserve this? I climb aboard and settle into the sparkling-new radio room with my secret codes. Away we go. The captain knows how to fly. He handles the big, four-engine B-17G as if was a fighter plane. We head south while we climb slowly toward 15,000 feet. I'm not happy with another foray into France in an unarmed plane, but no one asked me.

The English countryside gives me plenty to watch. England is so pretty, and I gaze down at towns, villages, hills, forests, trains, and a long convoy of military trucks. We pass near an honest-to-goodness castle. I bet its original occupants never dreamed of people flying above it. Soon, we are over the English Channel, and I get tense. At this point, the channel is narrow, so the French coast is in view immediately, and it approaches quickly. We cross the French coast and fly over the Pas de Calais again. Now I'm really tense.

"Keep alert back there," the captain calls.

"I'm all eyes and ears."

This gets a chuckle from him. Actually, I'm worn out from lack of sleep, but fear keeps me wide-eyed with a racing heart. While I listen for a radio message, I scan the sky. The Germans aren't going to let us get away with this again. I see planes far off, southwest of us, but they have not yet turned toward us.

"Keep alert for fighters," the navigator calls.

He sounds tense. Ha, it's not just me.

"I'm watching," I say.

"Hey, what's that down there!" the copilot yells.

"Holy shit!" the captain says.

I peer at the ground. Smoke rises from a fire in some kind of structure on the ground. German military vehicles surround it. The captain says that the fire must have burned away the camouflage covering the site. Is this one of the V-2 rocket positions? While I peer at it, I suddenly feel that German fighters are diving toward us. In terror, I gaze upward, but the sky is clear. Heart racing, I keep my attention on the sky.

"That's a real surprise," the navigator says. The pilot, copilot, and navigator must still be looking at the fire on the ground. "Do you want pictures?"

"Hell, yes," The captain says. "This could be important. It's worth taking a chance. You got its location?"

"Got it."

"Get the camera ready," the navigator calls to me.

Does this new plane have a camera? I open the hatch in the floor, and sure enough, a sparkling new camera is embedded in the bottom of the fuselage.

"We got to get in, get the pictures, and get out, because they sure as hell don't want us to get pictures," the pilot says. "They're probably scrambling fighters already."

Fear clutches me as the plane banks sharply and heads for the fire. I hurry to lie on the floor by the hatch and check the camera. It seems to be in good shape and ready to take pictures. The floor tilts steeply downward. The captain must want to get closer to the ground for the pictures.

"Are you set?" the navigator calls. "We're almost there."

"I'm ready."

I take a worried glance upward, but the blue sky is empty.

"Almost there," the navigator calls.

The intercom is silent. The plane bounces a little at the lower altitude.

"OK, start camera!"

The camera whirrs as it takes a series of pictures.

"OK, stop."

The bomber banks sharply as it turns around.

"Get ready,"

They're crazy! They obviously want to take another set of pictures.

"All ready."

"Start!" the navigator says.

The camera runs again.

"Stop!"

"Let's go home," the captain says. "Keep an eye out for fighters. They're going to be very sensitive about us taking pictures of that site."

The plane banks and heads north. I search the sky for fighters. Four planes are low on the horizon. They quickly become fighters, and they race toward us.

"Fighters are coming from 260 degrees!" I call.

"OK, I see them."

The captain puts our bomber in a steep dive at full power. The French coast is still ahead, and the German fighters are coming fast. Just off the coast, three boats speed west, leaving long, white wakes. They must be German E-boats, small, fast boats with guns and torpedoes, similar to American PT boats.

Still in a dive, we roar across the French coast and out over the gray water of the English Channel. The four fighters are closing in on us. My heart races. The fighters are so close that I can identify them as FW-190s. The captain pulls out of the dive about fifty feet above the water. The fighters are closer, but we are crossing the Channel at its narrowest part. The English coast is coming at us like a speeding train. Dover is just ahead. The German fighters turn back. The captain cackles with glee as we sweep over England just above the famous white cliffs of Dover.

"They really didn't want us to bring those pictures back," he says.

His voice is light, as though nothing happened. In contrast, I'm in a panic. That was too darn close! My heart slows down while we head north above the English landscape. This time, I'm too shaken to admire it. We land at an unfamiliar base for a photo technician to remove the film, and then take off again to land at the 92nd Group's base at Podington.

"See you later," the captain says with a grin as he and the officers get into a staff car. "Remember, absolutely no talking about this."

See you later? Does that mean another flight? Isn't that just wonderful? I smile and wave to the officers before I get into a waiting jeep. I don't like these flights, and I don't like having to keep information about the flights from my crew and all of my friends at Podington. Still, I have credit for another combat mission, my ninth.

But going with the captain on a scary mission is no worse than it would have been to go on the mission to Augsburg with the 92nd Group. The Eighth Air Force lost thirty-one bombers on the Augsburg mission. Two are from the 92nd Group. Charles Nashold is the pilot on one of them. His crew came to Podington with us at the end of December. Returning crews don't think that any of them survived. Thus, after only a month of combat, two of the three crews that arrived with us are gone. Our crew and the Parramore crew are the two that remain.

We end the month of February with a mission to bomb a Crossbow (V-1) site at Heroubville on the French coast. We are only at 14,000 feet, but the mission turns perilous. As our armada of bombers reaches 14,000 feet and heads for the English coast, I find that my right foot is cold—really cold. Soon, it tingles. I pull off my boot and examine the electric shoe. The plug that connects the shoe to my electric suit is charred. The connection must have shorted out and failed. I replace my boot and feel my foot go from tingling to numb. I stomp it while I worry about losing the foot if it freezes.

When we land, I show my foot to a doctor at interrogation. It is dead white and then turns bright red and burns. The doctor examines it carefully. He thinks that it will be all right, but I must let him see it tomorrow.

As February ends, I have survived ten of the required twenty-five missions. I'm a veteran, but at the cost of a nonstop headache and nightmares that keep me from sleeping. When I go to see the doctor, I describe the headache and nightmares. The flight surgeon nods.

"Some of your buddies have headaches. They probably are what we call tension headaches. You get tense during combat, and your neck muscles contract to cause the headache. I'll give you an envelope of aspirin to control them. Take two and repeat in three hours until the headache is gone."

He stares at me with a serious look.

"Now, your nightmares are a different matter. You can't fly missions without sleep, so I'll get you some sleep."

He pulls a blue capsule from an envelope.

"This is sodium barbiturate to make you sleep. One capsule should knock you out enough to keep the nightmares away and get you the rest you need. These are powerful, so only take one capsule each night. I'm pretty sure that one will be effective."

He pulls a big, white pill from another envelope.

"You probably recognize these amphetamine pills. Sometimes the label will say Benzedrine, but that's just another term for amphetamine. When they wake you in the morning, after you take this barbiturate, you will have to take the amphetamine in order to get going."

He gazes at me seriously.

"Both of these substances are addictive, so I don't want you taking them any longer than necessary, but we have to keep you flying."

The sleeping capsules do a good job. I sleep through the night without a nightmare, but I certainly have to take amphetamine in the morning to wake up enough to function. This is not good. I'm as bad as the veterans. Of course, ten missions make me a veteran, too. It's interesting to see that radio operators on new crews come to me for advice. All I can do is tell them the truth. Unlike the movies, there is nothing glamorous about combat in the air. It's deadly and savage. It kills your friends. How soon before it kills you?

CHAPTER 16

Wonderful Respite

March begins as gloomy as February. Rain and cold wind sweep across a sodden airbase. Water pelts my face while I peer from the hood of my green poncho and trudge down the road to the combat mess. Around me, low buildings huddle beneath rolling masses of gray clouds. Winter is not going to give way readily, and that means hazardous flying before the Germans even get a shot at us. Still, the combat mess is warm and bright and filled with the aroma of food. I'm amazed at the ways the cooks devise to serve Spam.

On the first of March, I see good news and bad news. On the good side, I'm alive. Of the ten missions on which I flew, we destroyed ball-bearing plants at Schweinfurt, factories at Brunswick, and the German airbase at Chateaudun, and we tore up the submarine base at Wilhelmshaven. I guess the two missions with the captain to the Pas de Calais were also useful, whatever it was that we did. The other missions ran afoul of bad weather. On the bad side, my friends are being killed, one after another, and I know that my probability of dying is increasing with each mission. I take barbiturate capsules and amphetamine for nightmares, paregoric for chronic diarrhea, and I have a headache so bad that it makes me sick.

The Eighth Air Force has a new commander, Major General James Doolittle, called Jimmy in the press. He was a stunt flyer and air racer during the 1930s. He returned to the air force as a colonel and shocked the Japanese in April 1942, by leading a group of B-25 bombers from an aircraft carrier to bomb Tokyo and fly on to China. Most of the bombers were lost, but Doolittle survived, and now he will lead us.

More fliers in my building have jitters. Many go out and get drunk as often as they can. I understand. Some scream or cry out during the night. I notice that more take sleeping capsules at night and amphetamine in the morning, so I don't feel that I'm the only flyer having trouble.

Group headquarters calls a dozen flyers, including me, to a ceremony where Colonel Brousseau shakes my hand and gives me an Air Medal with an Oak Leaf Cluster. The Air Medal is pretty, with a royal blue and gold ribbon, but I would trade it in a flash for something to stop my splitting headache. Except for the time with Jane, I've had it for more than three weeks. Aspirin doesn't help.

I go back to the medics. A doctor agrees that it needs treatment. He gives me an envelope of white capsules. They stop the headache wonderfully, but they put me to sleep. I can't keep my eyes open after I take one. When I return and tell the doctor, he frowns and nods his head.

"I hoped the medication wouldn't affect you that way, but drowsiness is a frequent side-effect. I wish we had better drugs than aspirin to treat headache." He sighs and stares at me. "You're pale and trembling, and your skin is clammy. I can tell that you're hurting. Have you had any relief, except when you took the capsules?"

"Just once, while I was with a girl I met in London. It was wonderful to be free of the headache, but it was probably a fluke."

"It may have been real. You have a tension headache. You describe how it comes from the back of your neck upward through your head. Combat causes varying degrees of tension in different people. From what you have told me, your scientific background has allowed you to see the lousy odds you have of flying twenty-five missions successfully. We really should restrict combat to dumb guys who think they're invincible. In your case, you think too much, and it has caused the tension to be severe enough to be debilitating, like a migraine. We need you on flying status, but maybe I can work out a way for you to handle the pain and keep flying."

He paces back and forth as his thoughts seem to crystallize.

"Take a capsule on days that you are certain you won't be flying. It'll put you to sleep, but who cares? When you fly, take aspirin. You'll be in pain, but it should get you through the mission. Don't take it too often. It can make your stomach bleed, and if you're on a mission, you could bleed to death."

He smiles.

"If you can keep flying by using the medications this way, let's see if you get periodic relief with forty-eight hours of medical leave in London. I'm going to give you forty-eight hours now. See if it gives you respite from the pain."

As I leave the medical building, excitement surges through me. Maybe I can see Jane. Her letters say she wants to see me. I pack, grab my gas mask, and take the shuttle truck to the railroad station at Wellingboro for a fast ride on the train to London.

The day seems brighter as I watch the changing panorama of fields, forests, and villages pass by outside the window of the first-class compartment that I share with a rotund gentleman dressed in tweeds, two elderly ladies, and a pretty girl in a blue dress.

We stop at Bedford, and I gaze at two dozen British tanks sitting on flat cars on a railroad siding. We race southward again. These British trains really fly. When we stop at Luton, I see a dozen C-47 transport planes (the military version of the DC-3) fly low across the countryside. They will carry paratroopers when the allies invade France. When will the invasion occur? Speculation on the BBC is that it will come as soon as weather is good, probably late May. I think about it while we stop briefly at St. Albans and roll on into London.

When I get off the train at St. Pancras station, I wonder if Jane will be as happy to see me as her letters suggest—or is she only being kind to a fellow who is likely to be dead soon? My anxiety grows while a taxi takes me past crowds on London's bustling streets to Jane's upstairs flat off Baker Street. My mouth is dry, and my heart races when I knock on the door of her flat. I hope she doesn't have a guy in there. There's no answer, and I hear no noise inside, so I knock louder. Suddenly, the door opens to reveal a disheveled Jane in a thin wrapper, just out of bed. Her sleepy eyes pop open. She screams, rushes into my arms, and kisses me repeatedly.

"Oh, love, it's simply fabulous to see you here," she bubbles. "Your letters have been so sweet, but I wasn't certain that I would ever see you again. I've heard often enough that the favorite expression of you Yanks is love them and leave them."

"I guess I'm too serious a guy to do that. I've thought of you every minute, and I wanted so much to see you."

She cups my face in her hands.

"My dear, dear fellow," she says with a quizzical grin. "I don't find you too serious at all. I find you quite nice."

Her eyes sparkle as she pulls me into the flat and kicks the door closed. She brushes her blond hair away from her face and throws aside her wrapper. There's nothing like a nude blonde to get your complete attention.

"I've been dreaming about us," she says, putting her arms around me, "and I hope you are simply bursting with energy and all manner of manly things."

I smile uncertainly, but she kisses me and grins impishly as she pulls me into the bedroom.

Later, her chatter about the theater and London takes me away from burning bombers and dead friends. For the first time since I last saw her, it has happened again. My headache is gone. I feel totally relaxed with her. My neck is sore, but Jane straddles my back and massages my neck until it feels better.

She arranges time off from work, and we dine on black market veal with truffles at a French café in Soho. In the café, Jane is a picture of primness, with glasses and her blond hair drawn back to a bun. Later, she clings to my arm while we walk along crowded sidewalks in the blackout. She is the first woman to ever hold my arm that way, and I like it. Pearleen never did. I wonder if there is a message in that.

We reach the big Odeon Cinema in Leicester Square and go inside to see *The Lodger* starring Laird Cregar, Merle Oberon, and George Sanders. It's a scary movie about Jack the Ripper. After it ends, I want to take a taxi ride through the Whitechapel district where Jack the Ripper operated.

"You're daft!" Jane says. The taxi driver looks unhappy.

But Jane relents, and we drive to Whitechapel. It is probably the blackout and the fog, but the neighborhood looks downright scary, and we are all happy to leave.

When we are back at Jane's flat and finally ready to sleep, I luxuriate in being pain free. The doctor was right. What a way to treat a headache! I lie back with a contented smile.

During the night, I am asleep next to Jane when the mournful wail of the air raid siren rolls over the moonlit roofs of sleeping London. Despite my sleeping pill, I awaken and stare groggily into the darkness. Jane stirs.

"Damn those bloody bombers," she says. "What time is it, love?"

"It's a little after 2 A.M. Do you want to go to an air raid shelter?"

Antiaircraft fire begins to bang in the distance.

"And lose a chance to snuggle with you? Are you daft?"

"I guess that means you don't want to go."

"Darling, if you would feel better about it, we shall go, but the underground is cold and drafty, and all this bare skin under the covers is so warm and nice."

"Let's stay here."

"Bully for you. Hold me and go back to sleep."

Next morning, I wake up feeling marvelously rested and happy. At breakfast, I gaze with distaste at Jane'a kipper.

"That fish is staring at me again."

"Oh, you silly goose, it is not!"

During a clear, chilly day, we walk, arm in arm, along the embankment, and it is restful to gaze up and down the river and watch the broad Thames flow, even though silver barrage balloons fill the sky above it. Boats and barges move along the river with a subdued hum. Large buildings of all shapes and colors line the Thames, and I wonder what they contain. Cars, trucks, and red, double-deck busses cross the many bridges that span it. Down the river, the distinctive structure of Tower Bridge looms to remind me that this is London. Jane's eyes glow through her glasses, and I sense that she is as happy as I am. Near Parliament, people move briskly. It's a different crowd from those at night. I see colorful uniforms from a dozen nations. Men in black suits, white shirts, and black derby hats stride briskly, carrying brief cases or tightly-rolled, black umbrellas. Women in expensive furs stroll past.

We take a taxi to Harrod's famous department store in Knightsbridge. I get great pleasure at Jane's squeals of delight with each item that I buy for her. I am also astounded at the black market things that we can buy in little shops all over London. Jane knows about a seeming endless number of such places, so we outfit her in all manner of finery.

"Love, you really must not spend so much money on me," she protests.

"You deserve them. You've given my life back to me for these two days. Also, I want you to be in beautiful clothing and jewelry if you will let me take you to elegant restaurants and other places here in London."

She rewards me with an adoring smile. Somehow, she seems prettier than the first time we met. We spend hours holding each other closely and talking. She even goes with me on another visit to the British Museum. On the way, we pass blocks of buildings bombed into piles of rubble. Other blocks have skeletons of one or two buildings standing windowless in a flattened block. The ferocity of destruction is beyond imagination. Rubble and broken glass are piled everywhere.

That night, Jane dons some of her new clothing and jewelry. She looks every bit the aristocrat while we dine at the Café Royal and go to a sparkling musical at a Leicester Square theater.

The forty-eight hours with Jane are a wonderland, but I know that the hours are counting down until I must return to the base. We treasure every minute, but it comes to an end. At St. Pancras Station, I hold her while her tears wet my cheeks.

"I don't want to leave you," I say. "It's crazy. We've spent so little time together, but I care so much for you."

"You forget all the letters we've written," she chokes. "You said you read my letters over and over. I do the same with yours, and I hold them next to my heart and dream about you. We've actually been together since the night we met."

"I guess you're right."

"You are very precious to me," she quavers. "Please be careful and never forget that I truly believe you will come through your missions and come back to me. I will wait for you."

On the train, sadness at leaving Jane mixes with optimism from her firm belief that I will survive my missions. What is happening between us? Although I dated girls during high school, I never had a real girlfriend. Pearleen is a wonderful friend, but I don't think that we ever thought of each other as girlfriend and boyfriend. I don't know how it feels to be in love, but my feelings about Jane are different from anything that I have felt before. I want to be with her all the time. I want to do things to make her happy. I would be happiest if I could look forward to being with her forever. Am I falling in love with her? How could it happen after such a brief time together? Am I making a fool of myself over a woman who stands on stage naked? Am I ready to take her home and say, "Hey, Mom, this is Jane, she's English, she eats smoked fish for breakfast, and you don't want to know how she earns money." I'm thoroughly confused, but since I put on a uniform, my only happy times have been with Jane, and she acts like she's nuts about me. I think of nothing but her while the train speeds me back to Wellingboro, and I return to the airbase.

The airbase, with its four-engine bombers scattered all around the airfield, brings me back to harsh reality. Now I face more missions into that cold sky above Germany. Will I see Jane again, or will I end up trapped inside a blazing bomber as it falls to earth?

CHAPTER 17

Death Pays a Visit

While I had two, blissful, headache-free days in London, the 92nd Group bombed Frankfurt on March 2 and lost two more B-17s with twenty more men. Another friend is dead. I can't get accustomed to all this death.

The stunning news is that the 92nd Group set off for Berlin on March 3. Berlin has been the giant fear for combat crews since the Eighth Air Force began bombing German targets. It is deep inside Germany, and the German Air Force will defend it savagely, even more so than Schweinfurt. Until now, estimated losses made the mission too costly to attempt, but on March 3, General Doolittle decided that the Eighth Air Force, with more bombers and more fighter planes, was strong enough to try it, so its bombers headed for Berlin. Unfortunately, the weather was terrible, and Eighth Air Force called the armada back, but not before German fighters shot down eleven bombers, including still another from the 92nd Group. Ten more fellows gone and nothing accomplished.

The next day, my crew is not on the alert list for a scheduled mission. This is good, because I suspect that General Doolittle will keep the Eighth Air Force going to Berlin until it succeeds, regardless of losses. While we have another day off, Rex Townsend and I congratulate each other. The air force promoted him to first lieutenant, and it had already promoted me to technical sergeant (five stripes). We grin and shake hands.

"Keep it up, and you'll be a colonel," I say.

"You'll be a lieutenant before I'm a colonel," he chuckles.

That reminds me of my misplaced chance at officer candidate school. If it hadn't been for the drunken sergeant, I might be a first lieutenant now, but officer candidate school will have to wait until I finish what Jane calls "those bloody missions."

By a miracle, the group passes up our crew when it again flies toward Berlin, but bad weather causes it to turn back again and bomb Bonn instead. It's obvious to everyone, including the Germans, I bet, that General Doolittle is determined to hit Berlin. The story is that the Eighth and Ninth Air Forces now have a total of 800 fighters to escort 700 bombers. General Doolittle wants to wipe out the German Air Force, and the most likely way to get it to come up and face our fighters is to offer German fighters the challenge of our bombers going to rain destruction on the German capital.

I have a bad feeling that our crew won't be passed over forever. We will likely go when they try again. But to my surprise, we are not alerted on the night of March 5 for a maximum-effort mission scheduled for early tomorrow. I bet it's to Berlin again. Talk about luck! I wish the best to fellows on other crews that are scheduled to fly.

I awaken slightly from a drugged sleep to hear the thunder of bombers taking off at dawn, but I turn over, snuggle down under my blankets, and sink into blessed sleep.

The combat mess is almost empty when I go to breakfast. The group certainly put up a maximum effort. It looks as if almost everyone went. Sure enough, they were briefed to go to Berlin. How did our crew miss that?

The first hint I have that something is wrong comes when I walk back to my building after lunch. I meet a sergeant from group operations who lives in my building.

"Have you heard any news about the Berlin mission?" I say. "Someone at breakfast told me that they were briefed to try again to go there."

"Yes, they did, and they've gone all the way this time. We got a strike message from the lead plane that they bombed Berlin." He stares at me for a minute. "Do you know that four members of your crew are on the mission?"

I gape.

"No! Who went?"

"Townsend, Swanson, Kinsella, and Ballmer had to go at the last minute. The pilot, copilot, navigator, and bombardier on one of the old crews had finished twenty-four missions, but the rest of the crew only had twenty-three. You know the drill. You get to pick your last mission so you can get an easy one, but someone screwed up and put the whole crew on the Berlin mission. When the four found out that they were scheduled for Berlin, they bitched plenty loud, so your guys got routed out of bed to replace them and fly with the rest of that crew."

"I hope they don't have a tough time," I say, but worry gnaws at me.

"The group's on its way back now," he says as he waves and hurries off.

I write a letter to Jane and am deep in study on my latest university lesson when I hear the 92nd Group's formation thunder over the airfield and begin to land. By the time I finish the lesson, the bombers have landed. As I stroll back to my building after mailing Jane's letter, I hear someone call to me. It's the sergeant from group operations. He is pale and excited.

"Have you heard? Your guys were killed."

Stunned, I stare at him. He sees that I am having trouble comprehending what he said, so he speaks very slowly.

"They didn't make it," he says. "They got hit by an antiaircraft shell somewhere near Dummer Lake on the way to Berlin. It blew up the plane. A gunner on a nearby bomber thinks the tail gunner might have been blown free, but the rest died in a big fireball. I guess the plane really exploded big-time. Your guys are already listed as killed in action."

I'm numb. Rex Townsend, Gunnar Swanson, Ken Kinsella, and Ralph Ballmer are all dead. They were wonderful guys. We had so many good times together. They were almost like family. They watched over my nineteen-year-old innocence. They talked with me and joked with me. They were concerned that I was comfortable and treated well. They asked about my family and insisted that Pearleen was my girlfriend, but I was too dumb to know it. They even listened, without laughing, when I talked about how much I loved my cat, Ginny. Rex knew about my aborted chance at officer candidate school and said that I would get a direct commission as a lieutenant when we returned to the United States. You couldn't ask for better men, and now they're dead. But the shock is not finished. The sergeant gives me a strange look.

"At first, the operations officer was going to replace the whole crew with your crew. If he had, you wouldn't be standing here alive now. You're damn lucky that he decided to take just four of your crew. You sure as hell had a close call."

A cold fist grips my heart, and I shiver. My headache returns like an axe hitting the back of my neck. I thank my friend for giving me the news and hurry off to tell Lloyd, Greg, Ken, Ed, and John, but they have already heard. We sit and sadly discuss our dead friends. I think of how this took away the rest of their lives. All their dreams and plans are gone. No chance for college, or career, or wife, or children, or just seeing the beauty of the sun rising each morning on a new day. We go to their quarters to find home addresses so we can write, but a lieutenant there says that he is already doing it.

Townsend, Swanson, Kinsella, and Ballmer lost their lives during fierce combat while our planes forced their way to Berlin. The cost was the loss of sixty-nine bombers, the greatest loss in Eighth Air Force history. Of the sixty-nine bombers, four are from the 92nd Group, so forty more flyers are gone and hundreds of family and friends will grieve.

Our fighters shot down eighty-six German fighters while losing eleven. Thus, we lost eighty planes, and the Germans lost eighty-six. It was pretty much a toss up.

I knew that our crew couldn't go through these battles without someone getting killed, and the deaths of Townsend, Swanson, Kinsella, and Ballmer prove it. Except for a snap decision by an operations officer early this morning, I would be dead also. I've had too many close calls and fear my luck is running out.

CHAPTER 18

The New Guys

Life goes on. Our squadron operations officer talks to the remaining six of us on the crew and promises to have four replacements for our crew as quickly as he can find them. He confirms that we were originally scheduled to go on the mission, but they decided at the last minute to take only four of our crew members. A chill spreads through me again when I think of how I could so easily be dead. Only a snap decision by a busy operations officer meant the difference between life and death. That realization and the deaths of my friends shake me like nothing has yet. All the optimism that I got from Jane is gone. I must face the grim fact: I'm not going to survive twenty-five missions. The only question is which mission will kill me?

In the meantime, the squadron operations officer gives the six of us a forty-eight-hour leave. With thoughts of Jane filling my head, I pack and sprint for the truck to Wellingboro while the rest of my crew is talking about what they will do in London. At Wellingboro, a train to London rolls in just as I reach the station platform. I find an empty first-class compartment and ride off alone on the London, Midland, and Scotland Railroad's train. While it speeds southward, happiness at seeing Jane again mixes with melancholy at the deaths of my friends and fear of the future.

When I reach the door of Jane's flat near Baker Street, she is dressed and ready to go out. We embrace fervently and mix talk with kisses, but she pulls back to stare anxiously at me.

"Something is wrong, love, I can see it in your face."

"Four members of my crew were just killed. They had to fly in place of some other flyers, and their bomber blew up. The group almost sent the rest of us. If it had, I wouldn't be here. It has knocked the wind out of me."

"Oh, dear God! I am so sorry for your friends and their families, but I thank heaven that you are all right."

Her eyes fill with tears.

"I don't want anything to happen to you," she wails. "I must not lose you."

We hold each other tightly. After a time, she gazes at me.

"I want this horrible business to be over."

She turns away for a minute, and then turns back to me with a smile. She pulls me to the sofa and takes me in her arms.

"I will do everything I can to take away your pain, but you must press on and finish the bloody missions. You will complete them. Remember that. Then, I can stop my daily worry about you."

"We've known each other for such a short time, but I feel so close to you," I say.

"Mum says things can happen fast when the right person meets the right person."

"I wish I could tell you how much I care for you, but I don't want to make a fool of myself."

She kisses me.

"You couldn't do that. Tell me when you are ready, and I may surprise you. If it helps for me to tell you, then I will tell you now that you are the only man in my life."

I'm falling in love with her. I'm sure that is it. I'm crazy about her, but I'm tongue-tied about how to tell her. We settle into two days of happiness together. The war seems so different with this wonderful girl in my life. My headache is gone, the sense of doom is gone, and I wonder if I may make it through the fifteen remaining missions. This is the effect that she has on me. It's a wonderful feeling.

We try different restaurants. Jane knows the location of good ones. We go to movies and stage shows. We shop at the Harrod and Selfridge department stores. These are large, magnificent places, equivalent to the best department stores in the United States. We walk through parks and along London's streets. London seems to go on forever. We talk endlessly about our lives before we met, about our likes and dislikes, and tentatively about the future. Some of the time, we simply relax in Jane's flat. Her friends at the theater now refer to me as Jane's Yank.

But much too soon, forty-eight hours pass. We have another tearful farewell. This time, she clings to me.

"I can't let you go," she says through tears, but sadly I board the train and return to the airbase at Podington.

While I rested in London, the 92nd Group went to Berlin twice, losing two more bombers and twenty more men. Along with that sad news is news that we have replacements for the four members of our crew that we lost. The new pilot is Virgil Hill, a veteran of many missions. He is a tall, brown-haired man with a mustache. Soft-spoken, he exudes quiet confidence—just the thing that we need. He has seen much combat and has only a few missions left.

On March 11, we climb aboard a B-17G and fly around England to get accustomed to each other. As soon as he begins to fly, I know that we have the right man. Our new bombardier is Jerome Charbonneau, a sergeant with more knowledge of bombs than most lieutenant bombardiers in our group. Rotated in to join Hill and Charbonneau will be a temporary copilot and navigator.

Two days later, I stroll to group headquarters to chat with Dick Shaw. While we talk, I hear the sound of two fighter planes cavorting overhead and swooping down to buzz the base at treetop level. Suddenly, one dives, and the roar of its engine gets louder and louder. Clerks and officers look up in alarm. It thunders just above the roof, and an enormous explosion rocks the building. We run outside to confront a fiery hole in the ground about 100 feet from headquarters. Nearby haystacks blaze furiously, and gasoline fires burn around the hole. A corporal lies face-down on the ground outside the door to headquarters. One of the P-47 fighters buzzing the field slammed full speed into the ground. Fire trucks arrive and extinguish the flames. A big clod of flying dirt hit the corporal in the back and knocked him unconscious, but a medical crew revives him. Dick and I walk over and peer into the smoking hole. It is deep, and there is no sign of plane or pilot. The biggest piece of debris that I see is two inches across.

"What a way to go," Dick says.

"It's bad enough to get killed over Germany, but to have it happen right here seems somehow worse. It could easily have hit us."

"That was a close call," Dick says, his face pale.

I nod and shiver. Another close call.

Beware the Ides of March. On March 15, we get bad news. Eighth Air Force raises to thirty the number of missions that we must fly. It wipes out five missions that I have survived and moves the goal farther ahead. Will I ever finish?

Our quiz team storms across Eighth Air Force bases, defeating every team that comes against us from bomb groups and all manner of units. I love the competition, and our team members seem to complement each other in the areas of knowledge that we have. During competition, questions on science are a breeze for me, but I also recite the Declaration of Independence on and on until told to stop, identify hemidemisemiquaver as a sixty-fourth note in music, and identify the American vice president under Calvin Coolidge as Charles Dawes. The rest of the time, I sit back and listen to the other team members amaze me with their knowledge. As we win contest after contest, I decide that the four good things in my life are Jane, letters from home, the quiz team, and university study. The four bad things are missions, missions, missions, and missions.

The sun makes a rare appearance, so I decide to take a walk outside the base. After I pass through the gate and saunter slowly down the tree-lined road, I soon come upon Hinwick House. It is an impressive place and reminds me of a castle. I stare at it like the wide-eyed tourist that I am. Far off is the roar of B-17 engines, as mechanics at the base test them, but standing here, I feel that I'm in a different world—a normal world of homes and trees and peace. It's similar to the feeling that I have with Jane at her flat, a feeling that there is a life for us, instead of explosions and fire and death.

"It's a fine house," a voice says behind me.

Startled, I turn to face a middle-aged gentleman in gray tweeds. He wears knickers, leather boots, and a brown, felt hat. He carries a beautifully-carved walking stick.

"Do you like Queen Anne architecture?" he says.

"Oh, ah, yes," I say.

I don't have the foggiest notion of what Queen Anne architecture is, but I assume that Hinwick House must be Queen Anne style.

"I find it quite attractive," the man says. "Of course, today, the trend is all toward simple lines with no bloody personality whatever.

One of your chaps told me that you are building what he called cracker boxes in America, with every house the same in some neighborhoods. I find that dreadful. Look at the character of a Queen Anne house, with its turrets and gables and intricate exterior."

"I see what you mean. It's an attractive place. It's also well-kept, but it looks like it dates back quite a few years. Do you know how old it is?"

"It was built in the early eighteenth century. The date that I have heard most often is 1710."

"That's long before the United States was an independent nation."

"Yes," he says with a chuckle, "you were a colony of the British Crown."

"Being built in 1710 makes it more than 200 years old," I say as we gaze at the castle-like house, framed by trees and green foliage.

"It was built by Richard Orlebar," the gentleman says, "a man involved in the legal profession. He did not have the funds to build it, but his new wife, Diana, had a large inheritance, so he was able to have it constructed. The house has remained in the Orlebar family continuously since then, passing from one generation to the next. August Orlebar held the 1929 speed record in the air."

"A home passing through that many generations is impressive. I can only imagine the history that those generations witnessed. I grew up in a house that was built around 1880, and I considered it old, but the ages of buildings here are amazing."

"If you would like to see some very old buildings, come along with me to Podington. Some go back to 1400 or 1500."

We stroll down the road together while the gentleman uses his walking stick to point out all manner of things about cottages, fields, roads, and people that we pass. At the village of Podington, I see a street lined with stone cottages and buildings. It looks like it might have appeared in the Middle Ages. Ahead, the spire of an ancient church rises above the village. I can imagine a knight in a suit of armor riding a white horse up the road toward us. The gentleman tells me that the buildings date from the seventeenth and eighteenth centuries. The church, he says, has some Norman and fourteenth-century work.

"This is a fascinating village," I say.

"I don't believe that many of your chaps think so. It does not have a pub—not a one."

This causes us both to laugh. I thank him and saunter back to the airbase feeling relaxed. I had a comforting walk. I learned a lot, and I reassured myself that there is a normal world outside the airbase.

But once I return, the knowledge comes back with a rush that killers are waiting in the sky over Germany, and I will be back there soon.

CHAPTER 19

Bad Day at Augsburg

March 16, 1944. When the intelligence captain draws back the curtain, the red line runs far to the south in Germany. A groan rises from the audience. Flyers shake their heads and curse their luck for drawing this mission. The target is the Dornier aircraft factory at Oberpfaffenhoffen in high country almost to the Swiss border. It is good for us to wipe out as many aircraft plants as possible, but he says that this is an especially important target, and the Germans will defend it strongly. Hundreds German fighters are based along our route, so we should expect fierce opposition.

We are off the runway at 8 A.M. with our new crew and a new, silver B-17G that climbs to 19,000 feet. Despite the Plexiglas roof on the radio room, I am freezing, although it is far better than having the wind blast in through an open roof. I note that there is no more sheen of frost covering the walls, but rubber-tainted oxygen freezes my lungs and makes me shiver with each breath. Ice accumulates in my oxygen mask, although the build-up is slower, and the heavy armor still makes movement exhausting. I'm jittery. I guess this is the way you are after ten missions. I check and recheck that my parachute pack is within reach on the floor. Thick cloud hides Germany, but around us, silver bombers glisten in sunshine beneath an intense, blue sky.

My radio is silent, so I record in my log everything that I see in the air. In the waist compartment, Ken and Ed stand by their guns and peer in all directions to search the sky. Back in the tail, John kneels behind his twin machine guns. Outside, an armada of hundreds of bombers stretches away as far as I can see.

"Look out!" Lloyd yells.

German fighters slash through our fleet, like sharks tearing through swimmers. Where did they come from? There must be fifty of them, and they leave fire and death in their wake. Their silver bodies glint in the sunshine as fire shoots from their wings. It hits a B-17 above us, and the bomber explodes into a boiling, orange ball that rains fire onto planes below it. Another B-17 trails a stream of flame from its left wing. It flips upside down and falls, while fire engulfs the fuselage. Two fighters attack a B-17 from two o'clock. While the gunners concentrate on them, four attack from ten o'clock. The B-17 explodes. More fighters curve around toward our formation. A cold fist tightens inside me.

"Watch out!" Lloyd shouts.

His guns hammer. I hear Charbonneau firing the nose guns. German fighters flash past. One streaks by a few feet above me, and our B-17 bounces violently from its passage. Frantic firing blasts out in long bursts from our guns. Our bomber rocks as fighters dash past spewing gunfire. Around me is an inferno of burning bombers and flaming fragments of planes. Careening fighter planes slash through the bomber fleet. The sky is a confusion of hammering guns and fighters zipping around like silver hornets. Two more bombers trail long streams of fire.

"Get out," I yell helplessly to their crews.

Figures topple head over heels from one plane, but fire spreads too fast on the other, and it carries its doomed crew down to a fiery death. Another B-17 catches fire. Three men jump from the rear door, but they fall through the fire and become three twisting, blazing torches falling toward the ground. Abruptly, the fighters leave.

"They're hitting a formation behind us," John reports from his tiny compartment in the tail.

"Oberpfaffenhoffen is socked in with clouds," Hill calls. "We're going to try to bomb Augsburg."

Wonderful.

As we continue southward, the awesome, snow-topped peaks of the Alps rise ahead of us. We are at 19,000 feet, but they seem to be a jagged wall facing us. Their white caps glisten in the sun like a million diamonds.

The sharp peaks are a breathtaking sight, but I can't appreciate them because—I can't help it—I'm terrified and trembling badly. We turn toward the target to face a black cloud over Augsburg that is filled with exploding shells of an antiaircraft barrage. We plunge into it, and our bomber rocks and bounces violently from explosions. Loud snaps tell me of shrapnel ripping through our bomber's skin. The bomb bay doors open. While we pitch and rock from the force of nearby blasts, I crouch in the doorway to the bomb bay, but I don't look down. I'm afraid that I may see shrapnel coming right up toward me. Our bombs drop, and we turn to leave the antiaircraft barrage.

Ahead is the long trip home. German fighters are waiting. While I nervously hope that they won't attack our B-17, they slash through the fleet of bombers, setting fire to plane after plane in an endless nightmare. After an eternity of gunfire and blazing planes, the sky empties of German fighters, but I tremble on the flight north over Germany, waiting for another attack.

When we finally leave Europe and land at our base in England, everyone's face is pale, but it's the eyes that frighten me. They are haunted. They've seen death, and they know that it is coming closer.

The mission kept us in the air for nine hours. Most of this time, we were on oxygen at high altitude in below-zero temperature. I am exhausted, trembling, and almost crazy with the pain of my headache. I rush through interrogation and gulp dinner so that I can get back to my quarters and swallow one of those precious, white capsules. I lie down while numbness creeps through me. This was my eleventh mission, the average life of a bomber over Germany. From now on, I will live on borrowed time. With the raised requirement for thirty missions, I have nineteen missions ahead. Please, no more like Brunswick or Schweinfurt or Augsburg.

The Eighth Air Force lost twenty-three bombers and ten fighters on the flight to Augsburg. One of the bombers is from the 92nd Group. Ten more of our guys are gone. American fighters shot down seventy-eight German fighters, so the savage warfare continues.

One sleeping capsule no longer takes my nightmare away, so I decide to begin taking two. The doctors warned me not to take more than one barbiturate capsule, but I can't face the possibility that the nightmare will repeat tonight.

Two barbiturates knock me out so thoroughly that I can hardly wake up in the morning, and I must swallow two amphetamine pills in order to function. I know that it is dangerous and addictive, but I have to be ready to fly. I guess I look awful to the doctor at interrogation after the Augsburg mission. A few days later, he calls me in and promises another forty-eight-hour medical leave in London as soon as he can arrange it.

Our crew does not go, but the 92nd Group goes to Lechfeld and loses a bomber. Without us, it goes to Hamm and loses five bombers. Sixty men are gone that quickly, and hundreds of people in sixty families are devastated. I think that it must be especially hard on children to know that they will never see their father again. But I mustn't think of these things. By now, so many of my friends and acquaintances have been killed that I don't want to make new friends. It hurts too much when they die.

Jane has become the saving factor for me. We have only been together briefly, but letters now speed back and forth between us every day. Dreaming of her keeps me from thinking of how bad my chances are of living much longer.

March draws to a close with a stormy mission to dreaded Schweinfurt, a long flight to bomb an airbase at LaRochelle, France, and another brief flight over the Pas de Calais with the jovial captain.

I have now survived fourteen frightening, sometimes terrifying, missions, but sixteen lie ahead. I can hardly face them.

CHAPTER 20

Air Raid

The first day of April 1944 finds me alive, but I can't get it out of my mind that more than thirty of my friends and acquaintances are dead, especially Townsend, Swanson, Ballmer, and Kinsella. I miss them. Chance decreed that they would die and I would live. It still sends a chill down my spine.

Dick Shaw jokes that I'm beyond the eleven missions that are the average life of a crew in combat, so I'm living on borrowed time. He doesn't know how much that bothers me, but I laugh with him.

The fourteen missions that I've completed have only been possible with the help of aspirin, narcotics and medical leaves for my headache, paregoric for unending diarrhea, barbiturate to stop nightmares, and amphetamine to counteract the barbiturate. I'm a walking pharmacy customer. I hope that I'm not a walking drug addict. From the doctors' questions, I suspect that I have "combat fatigue." I think this means that the missions have driven me slightly nuts. I hope they don't do any more than that. I don't want to be one of the flyers that I have heard are in mental hospitals. They sit and stare at a wall all day. I guess the terror up there just overwhelmed them. Will they ever recover after this war is finally over?

One thing that helped me have credit for fourteen missions is the smiling captain and his brief, but scary, flights over the Pas de Calais. I could be wrong, but I have a theory about why we fly there. Allied forces will invade France soon, and I bet they land on the Pas de Calais. It's only twenty miles from Dover to Calais, so it's the shortest route for troops to cross the English Channel. I figure that the captain and his officers are scouting for the invasion. No wonder it's so secret. Will the captain take me on more flights? Can we keep going over there without German fighters catching us? We won't last long if they do, but we have made it thus far, and each flight is short and gives me credit for another mission.

The executive officer calls me in to tell me that I have a forty-eight-hour medical leave. The doctor came through. My heart leaps: I can be with Jane again! I pack a bag and smile all the way to the railroad station in Wellingboro. Six black soldiers are on the station platform waiting for the train. They see me smiling (I'm still thinking of Jane), and they grin and wave to me. When I wave back, they amble over to where I'm standing.

"You've been in combat," one says. "Look at that Air Medal ribbon."

"Yeah," I say, "but I'd trade the medal for a ticket home."

They laugh.

"We're going to London," a short fellow with glasses says. "It's our first time, and we're a little worried. Most of our guys are afraid to go. You know how some whites are, especially from the South."

"I don't think you'll have any trouble if you stick together and stay away from white girls. That's what gets the southerners riled up."

"Are there any dark girls in London?"

"Yes. My girlfriend says that some come directly from African countries. The ones I've seen are very pretty."

"That's for me!"

The London train rolls to a smooth stop at the station platform, stopping further conversation. Along with British civilians, British soldiers, and American airmen, we board the crowded train. The black soldiers fill a compartment, so I find a vacant seat in a compartment with a British family. Away we go, and I smile at passing towns and countryside in pale sunshine while the train speeds down the track toward London. By now, I know every fencepost along the railroad from Wellingboro to London, but the scenery is changing. Tanks, artillery, trucks, and other military equipment park in fields near the tracks. In some places, rows of tents stretch off as far as I can see. Preparations for the invasion are showing up in place after place, but my thoughts are on Jane, and it gives me a warm glow inside.

As I jump from a taxi in front of Jane's building near Baker Street, she pops from the door with her shopping basket. She sees me. My heart leaps. She screams, flings the basket and British restraint aside, and runs to hug me, while we get smiles from people passing on the street. We hold each other and kiss a dozen times.

"Now that I'm holding you again, I don't want to let you go," I say.

"Oh, I jolly well like to hear that," she says. "I don't want you to let me go—not ever. Oops, I guess I'm being too bloody forward, but I can't help myself. Now don't give me a lecture about not getting serious because you're not going to survive. Your letters tell me that you worry over it, but I have it on good authority that you will."

"What authority?" I say as I think of the Augsburg mission.

"My own, and you can laugh if you wish," she says, blinking rapidly at me through her glasses and pretending to be miffed, "but the day will arrive when you shall come and tell me that you just flew the last of the lot, and I will jump on you and never let you go."

"If that happens, I will just lie back and enjoy it."

"You will. I promise."

In her flat, she chatters excitedly between kisses. When many of the men in my building talk about women that they date in Northampton or London, it's nothing but sex. One fellow in our squadron has smoldering good looks that must hypnotize women. From his stories, he only has to look at them, and they hop onto a bed for him. For his part, he calls them pigs. But when I'm with Jane, it's not like that at all. I enjoy talking with her, walking with her, shopping with her, dining with her, and all the little things that we do together. As before, my headache is miraculously gone. When we go to dinner, I am struck by how pretty she looks.

"You are gorgeous tonight," I say.

"What do you expect when you buy such beautiful clothing and jewelry for me? You have purchased so much. And why do you do it?"

"Well, I—"

"You do it because you care as much for me as I do for you, and that is very much indeed."

I sigh. I know when I'm beaten, but I'm very slow in the romance department.

"You're right, I do," I say as her nose tilts up, and she smiles with British smugness.

I take her hands in mine.

"I've never felt the way that I do about you. This is all new to me, and I have trouble putting my feelings into words. I could never make it through these missions without you, and I'm only happy when I'm with you."

She smiles.

"That is what I wanted to hear, love. Now, I believe I've made you uncomfortable enough. Shall we talk of something else? Tell me more about America."

While I talk, she peppers me with questions about life in the United States. She finds some things interesting, some things strange, and some things funny. Finally, I grin at her.

"Do you think you'd like to live in the United States?" I say.

"I should like it very much, as long as I am with you. Tell me, darling, you are nineteen, and I am twenty-four. Do you consider me old?"

"No, I consider you just right. In three months, I'll be twenty."

"You have made me very happy tonight," she says as she squeezes my hands. Her eyes glisten.

From the way she acts and the way I feel, I think we have fallen in love. I don't know how to broach the subject to her. It's the first time that I have been in love, but this pretty blonde has been patient with my fumbling efforts at romance, and she has hinted that she loves me. I worry that it will break her heart if I'm killed, but each time that she peers through her glasses at me like a puppy anxious to please, I want to hold her and tell her that I love her. I just can't get the words out.

Jane loves to visit shops, even if we don't buy anything. I don't understand this. I like to know what I want and then go directly to it and buy it. I don't understand women, but since she enjoys it, I look at endless things in endless shops. We shop at Harrod's in Knightsbridge and at Selfridge's on Oxford Street. These are awesome department stores, even with wartime shortages. We wander through floor after floor of beautiful things. I once went to Marshall Field's tremendous department store in Chicago. The Harrod and Selfridge stores remind me of it. Jane leads me into little boutiques in the West End, especially on Regent, Oxford, and Bond

Streets. The British have rationing, but she manages to get things. Each time that she looks wistfully at something, my heart melts and I buy it for her, despite her protests. When we return to her flat, loaded with gifts, her blue eyes sparkle, and I am happy.

We try a different restaurant for each meal—little, ethnic ones in daytime and fancy ones in the evening, where Jane can wear the finery that we purchased. We go to a concert at Royal Albert Hall the first night. The second night we watch a revival of a Cole Porter musical in a West End theater. Later, Jane wants to go to a sex show that all her friends at the theater have seen. We find it off Meard Street in Soho and stay long enough to satisfy our curiosity.

"Did that entertain you?" Jane says as we leave. She clings to my arm while we make our way through thick fog in the blackout.

"Now I know what businessmen back home meant when they talked about having a dog and pony show. I always wondered."

"I thought it was all deliciously disgusting."

During the night, the moan of the air raid siren wakes me, but I'm too exhausted to care. Jane was very passionate after we got to her flat. Now, I want to sleep.

"Go to sleep, love" she whispers, and I snuggle down happily beside her.

A *BANG* shocks me awake. *BANG, BANG, BANG.* I shake my head, trying to wake up.

"Bloody hell!" Jane says. "Those are the ack-ack guns in the park. Jerry must be close."

A thunderous explosion rocks the building. Then, an earsplitting explosion makes the building jump. Jane screams. I hear glass breaking outside.

"It's too late to go to the shelter," she says. "Please hold me."

I gather her trembling body in my arms. Another blast causes a squeak from Jane. My mouth is dry. This is scary. It's no fun to be on the receiving end of bombs. The British antiaircraft guns fire in a frenzy. I hear a plane drone overhead.

"Is it ours?" Jane gasps.

"No, the RAF wouldn't fly through an antiaircraft barrage. It's a German."

The banging of antiaircraft guns continues for a time but finally ceases. The all clear sounds, but it is a half hour before either of us can get back to sleep.

When we go outside the next morning, the smell of burning buildings fills the air. We follow the stink around a corner and down the street for several blocks to face smashed and gutted buildings. Sections still burn while firemen play hoses on the fires. Huge, concrete chunks, thousands of bricks, and unrecognizable rubble fill the street. I think of people who were probably in the building when the bomb hit. In the next block are more smashed buildings. Jane is pale and trembling while we gaze at the scene. If a bomb had taken a different path and hit our building, we would be dead.

"When will it end?" she quavers. "I so wish this could be over."

I must make her feel better. She is unnerved.

"It will be over eventually, and I promise that we will be happy together."

She turns to me, and a little smile appears.

"Yes, we shall be happy."

Too soon, our brief time together ends. After a tearful farewell from Jane, I run to catch the London, Midland, and Scotland Railway train. As I go through the gate, I hear Jane's voice.

"I love you," she calls.

CHAPTER 21

Death Visits Again

She said she loves me. The thought fills my mind as I take a Sunday flight with the captain and his lieutenants above the Pas de Calais. It's scary, but I'm getting accustomed to it, so I don't worry as much. I see German planes miles away to the south, but they look like transports. Far off, high in the sky to the east is a formation of planes that may be fighters. I watch them with a suddenly racing heart, but they don't turn toward us, and we are soon on our way back to England and on to Podington. After we land, and the captain and lieutenants leave, I note that this was my fifteenth mission. I'm halfway there. Maybe it's worth thirty minutes of fright.

The next day, we bomb an airfield near Brussels, Belgium. Bright sunshine turns the North Sea green and gives an early spring glow to the pale-green, checkerboard panorama of Belgium. We bounce through antiaircraft fire, obliterate the airfield, and return home to end my sixteenth mission.

Beginning with our return from this mission, our flight surgeons give two ounces of Scotch to each of us. It burns going down, but it relaxes me most wonderfully. Two ounces of Scotch make me think that Jane is right. I may get through the missions. Even the news that we have another mission scheduled for tomorrow doesn't dampen my spirits. It will be my third mission in three days. At this rate, I could finish soon. Maybe things are looking up.

April 11, 1944. A groan of dismay greets the sight when the intelligence captain pulls back the curtain covering the map of today's mission. The red line goes all the way across Germany. It passes south of Berlin, and ends in the southeast corner of the country, where our target is an aircraft plant at Sorau. If we can't bomb it, we will try to hit the industrial area of Stettin up on the Baltic. In either case, it will be the longest combat mission that we have flown. You couldn't ask for a worse one. I look at the pale faces of fellows sitting near me and think of their families back home. Which of these fellows will die today?

Intelligence officers estimate that we will be in the air for eleven hours, most of it in freezing cold at high altitude while we breathe oxygen. But the altitude won't be high enough to protect us from antiaircraft shells. In order to have enough fuel to go all the way to Sorau, our bombers will climb to only 15,000 feet. On a clear, sunny day like this, German antiaircraft gunners will be able to see us and have their best chance ever to hit us. The flak officer says that our route across Germany is designed to avoid antiaircraft fire. This gets hoots of disbelief.

One intelligence officer states that we should expect heavy attacks from German fighters. We will pass near airfield after airfield filled with fighters. The men around me look grim as they nod their heads in agreement. The briefing frightens me, but what can I do? I take two aspirins and head for the equipment room.

I tremble, and my headache is agony as I climb aboard the bomber. A radio mechanic waits to assure me that the radios work perfectly. I check everything more carefully than usual—electric suit, oxygen mask, oxygen supply, life jacket, parachute, body armor, pistol, and escape kit. Everything is fine, but before takeoff, I have such a bad feeling about the mission that I want to jump from the bomber and run.

The 92nd Group will lead the 40th Combat Wing. Each squadron has seven B-17s. The 326th is lead squadron. The 407th is high squadron. We in the 327th are low squadron. The 325th is high squadron for a composite group flying nearby. Thus, we have twenty-eight B-17s flying—twenty-one in our group formation and the 325th's seven in the composite group. This includes most of the flyers in the 92nd Bomb Group.

We take off into a clear, blue sky. Wouldn't you know that we would have a beautiful day to fly a terrible mission? Circling to get into formation occupies us for its usual hour, but we don't climb much. On the mission to Wilhelmshaven back in February, I marveled at how high we climbed above the earth. Now, I marvel at how close we are to the ground. Since we are the low squadron, we are at about 14,500 feet.

The first antiaircraft fire shoots up around us when we cross the Dutch coast at Ijmuiden. It is not heavy, but the bursts are close enough to rock our plane—a result of flying so low. The German gunners on the ground are having no trouble seeing us. We must look as big as houseflies to them. I see a B-17 trailing smoke as it turns around to try to make it back to England. Other bombers have jagged holes from shells exploding so close to them. This is not a good start. I thought that our route is supposed to avoid anti-aircraft batteries.

While we cross the greening fields and network of canals of Holland, I see twisting, white trails high in the blue sky that show our fighters in fierce battles with the Germans. I don't like the looks of it. The Germans are sending up masses of fighters, and we have a long way to our target.

We drone across a sunlit Germany of fields, forests, and towns, all connected by roads and rail lines. My pencil flies as I record dozens of observations of objects and happenings on the ground—trains, truck convoys, barges on rivers and canals, factories pouring out smoke, and even a fire in town. We have crossed the broad Rhine. Now the Weser River below us glints in the sun as it snakes from southern Germany toward the North Sea. The intercom is quiet while our gunners watch the sky. From their windows in the waist compartment, Ken and Ed peer up and around. More white trails high above us promise that we will see German fighters soon.

I note the landmark of Dummer Lake sparkling in sunshine. This is where antiaircraft fire destroyed the bomber carrying Townsend, Swanson, Kinsella, and Ballmer. Explosions blast around us. The plane rocks. The flashes are close. Shrapnel tears through our bomber, leaving ugly gashes in its skin. Antiaircraft shells hit three planes in a formation flying on our left. The B-17s explode into boiling, orange fireballs that dissolve into hundreds of smoking fragments that fall toward the ground below. Thirty lives are gone in an instant. Those gunners down there are really good, but why didn't our route avoid Dummer Lake? I note the antiaircraft in my log.

"Flying this low, they can really hit you," someone says.

"They already put holes in us," another voice says.

I remember again the flak officer telling us that our route would avoid antiaircraft guns as much as possible. Either the plan was wrong, or the navigator in the lead plane made a mistake.

We thunder along in clear air. The intercom is eerily quiet. Everyone must be as tense as I am. The gunners nervously search the sky. German fighters lurk nearby. We cross the Leine River. As we pass Hanover, antiaircraft fire hammers us. The plane rocks and bucks as flashes of explosions surround us. We're flying too low. Antiaircraft shells hit more bombers and blast them into fireballs. The guys in those planes don't have a chance to get out.

"What's the lead ship doing, leading us over all the flak sites it can find?" someone yells.

Explosions stop as we get out of range of the guns. The sky behind us has hundreds of black puffs of smoke where the shells burst. As we move on, I have a feeling that something bad is going to happen. My watch shows that it is nearly 11 A.M.

"Look out!" Lloyd yells.

German fighters are all over the sky. There are nearly 100 of them careening in and shooting at groups in our combat wing. Thirty FW-190s come directly at us. They look like an armada. Guns in our group's bombers sound a sharp staccato as they fire, followed by the louder hammer of our B-17's guns. Lloyd in the top turret and Jerome in the chin turret fire furiously. Red tracers spurt toward the fighters. Silver fighters snarl through our formation as multiple streams of orange fire spray from the guns in their wings. A B-17 close behind us explodes in an orange ball of fire, causing our bomber to buck violently. The smashed plane had to be from our squadron and filled with guys that I know. More German fighters slash through our B-17s in frenzied attacks. Their guns blast three bombers above me. One explodes, and I duck as burning fragments rain down in a shower of fire. The second and third B-17s catch fire and slip downward. A half dozen men jump from each. Farther away, bombers blaze as they spin toward the ground in a mêlée of attacking fighters and flaming bombers.

After racing through our formation, the German fighters surprise me by turning back and circling around us counterclockwise until they reach a point about a mile ahead. They turn and streak toward us again. Our guns open up, and I duck as orange strings of German tracer bullets whiz past above me. Our bomber bounces forcefully when a fighter flashes by a few feet overhead. Bombers around us blaze from nose to tail. A burning FW-190 trails fire as it hurtles through our formation before it spins downward as a fiery torch.

Flyers jump from a blazing B-17 above us and hurtle down past our plane, barely missing fatal collisions with our squadron's bombers. One more flyer, probably the pilot, jumps and drops toward a B-17 above us on the right.

"Look out!" I yell helplessly.

He hits the left inboard propeller. Instantly, the plane's nose has a coating of pink soup, the blended remains of the doomed pilot. My stomach reacts, and I desperately try to keep from vomiting into my oxygen mask. If I clog it, I will die from lack of oxygen.

As if fighters are not enough, antiaircraft shells blast us in the Brunswick area. I see another B-17 blown apart. We bounce and rock from blasts. Nearby explosions tear more holes in our plane. How long can it be before a piece of shrapnel kills one of us? When shrapnel shoots through our plane, it's like being a target in a shooting gallery.

We are out of the antiaircraft barrage, but German fighters have circled around to the front of us again. They speed through our bomber formation. Our gunners fire continuously and the world becomes a wild mêlée of gunfire, blazing planes, and terror. After the attack, I look back to see the pack of German FW-190s turning around and circling us. Are they going to keep hitting us until they kill us all? The silver fighters glisten in the sunlight as they race ahead of us. Again, they reach a point about a mile ahead and turn toward us. Here they come. Our guns hammer frantically to a crescendo of firing while the FW-190s dash through our formation. More bombers catch fire and explode. The sight is sickening. How long will this continue?

At last, the guns stop. The fighters have turned away. Trails of descending smoke behind us show the many planes that fell blazing to the earth below. Trembling, I look at my watch. It is 11:30. I know that our squadron lost a B-17 on the first pass by the Germans. I don't know how the other squadrons fared, but I see something puzzling. Our 325th Squadron, flying nearby, seems to have vanished. Then, I see one of the 325th Squadron B-17s flying alone. Where are the rest of them? They couldn't have lost most of the squadron, could they? Ken Tasker's voice on the intercom interrupts my search of the sky.

"John, are you OK back there?" he calls to John Kindred in the bomber's tail compartment.

"Hey, John," Ed Norton calls.

Through the rear door of my compartment, I see Ed and Ken standing by their guns, but they lean over, peering back into the tail gunner's compartment, where John lies face down on the floor behind his guns.

"John!" Ken shouts with concern in his voice.

John doesn't answer and doesn't move. Anxiety spreads through me like a cold fog.

Ed grabs a yellow tank of portable oxygen, snaps his oxygen mask into it, and staggers back to the swaying bomber's tail. He leans over John for what seems like forever before he returns to his gun position.

"Pilot from waist gunner. Our tail gunner is gone. He's dead."

"Oh, God," I whisper.

The intercom is silent. Now, I see a pool of bright-red blood spreading from beneath John Kindred. To my surprise, I smell the distinct odor of blood, even through my oxygen mask. Since a B-17G is closed in, I suppose the odor of all that blood can spread throughout the plane and penetrate around the edges of my mask.

The formation turns southeast toward Sorau. In the vicinity of Wittenberg, blasts of antiaircraft fire pepper us again. A piece snaps through our B-17's fuselage. I see another bomber catch fire, but I'm becoming numb to more tragedy. After we leave the antiaircraft barrage behind, we fly along quietly, each of us probably thinking of John lying dead in the bomber's tail. I gaze again at his still form and get a lump in my throat.

"Fighters!" Lloyd yells.

These are ME-109s, sharp-nosed fighters. Several speed toward us. Our guns bark rapidly. The fighters turn away. More make feints toward us. They are making us use up already-low ammunition. Suddenly, a flight of ME-109s races toward us and doesn't turn away. They speed in as they fire at us and peel off to flash beneath our formation. They harass us for fifteen minutes, sometimes feinting and sometimes attacking. I don't know how many bombers they hit, but our wing formation is a ragged mess, with many planes missing.

As we continue, clouds increasingly cover the ground below. Finally, the land is no longer visible. Dense cloud hides the ground ahead as far as I can see. The formation turns north.

"We're going to Stettin," Virgil Hill says on the intercom. "We won't have any escort, so keep your eyes open."

I know that Stettin is on the Baltic at the Polish border. This means an even longer trip over German territory. A real worry now is the low supply of ammunition. Without escort, if the formation runs out of ammunition, German fighters can simply destroy us, one by one. We drone on while the gunners watch the sky. I look again back to the tail, where John lies face down.

"Fighters!" Lloyd shouts.

These are twin-engine planes and are larger than the FW-190s and ME-109s that have attacked us. They are mostly ME-210s, but there are a few JU-88s. The Germans intend to destroy us today. The enemy fighters dive toward us. The Group's guns open up with sparse bursts. It sounds like all gunners are low on ammunition.

"Look out!" Lloyd yells. "They're shooting rockets."

Projectiles shoot toward us, leaving white trails. They explode with big flashes. Our guns blast at the fighters as they race through our formation. They wheel around and fire more rockets at us from the rear. Our world fills with explosions. There are so many puffy clouds from bursting rockets that I can't see what is happening. Gradually we pull away from the puffs and continue on. I can't tell how many B-17s the rockets destroyed, but our formation is in disarray, scattered all over the sky.

We roar ahead. I keep my fingers crossed while the gunners scan the blue. We are flying from the southeast corner of Germany all the way north to the Baltic coast. The Germans have plenty of time to send more fighters up. How many more attacks can we survive, especially with no escort and ammunition almost gone?

To my surprise and relief, we come up on Stettin. A black cloud, filled with orange flashes of an intense antiaircraft barrage, greets us. I see a B-17 enter it and explode in another orange ball of boiling fire. Now, it's our turn to enter this black hell of explosions. Our plane rocks and pitches from nearby blasts, and more shrapnel rips through the plane. The bomb bay doors come open, and I gaze down on solid clouds. Here comes an opening. Through it, I see what appear to be factories. The bombs drop, the B-17 jumps upward, and we turn northwest. Looking back, I see heavy smoke rising from Stettin to a height of about 10,000 feet. It is one o'clock.

We still have a long way to go over enemy territory to reach home. Everyone is tense while the scattered remnants of the formation drone on to the northwest. Our route takes us along the north German coast and over the Baltic to Denmark. The combat wing commander is trying to avoid more fighter attacks on our decimated and battered Groups. As we cross Denmark, antiaircraft fire slams our bombers again, but I am too exhausted to see if it destroys any of our B-17s. Then, we are over the North Sea. German fighters could fly out to attack us, but it's unlikely. Soon, we are out of sight of land. The gray water stretches away in all directions. The mangled formation descends below 10,000 feet, and our oxygen masks come off. I rub my grooved face and drop the heavy vest of armor.

After what seems like a year, the coast of England appears—far off at first, then steadily nearer. England has never looked more beautiful. When we sweep over the green countryside, I have trouble believing that I survived this mission. I stare numbly at fields, forests, and villages. I watch a train speeding along below us, and smile. I'm still alive and back to being an airborne tourist. Life has never seemed so precious.

Lloyd fires a red flare when we approach our base, indicating that we have trouble aboard, and we join several other B-17s with problems that land first. As we pull up to our parking spot, an ambulance and medical team wait for us. They hurry aboard the plane. A flight surgeon examines John and pronounces him dead. There is a big puddle of blood beneath him. It looks to me that a German fighter came in behind us and fired into our plane's tail, hitting John in the chest. He probably died instantly. At least, the poor guy didn't suffer. Exhausted, we leave the B-17 and stand beside the mechanics outside the bomber to watch sadly as medics carry John's body to an ambulance.

"He was a good guy," I say to Ken Tasker.

"He sure was."

At interrogation, the two ounces of Scotch knock me silly, since I have not eaten for more than twelve hours. The flight lasted eleven hours and ten minutes. I also learn that Lloyd shot down an FW-190 during the frenzied battle early in the mission, and I shake his hand to congratulate him.

The 92nd Group lost eight B-17s on this mission, a terrible loss, including all but one of the bombers of the 325th Squadron. The Group lost almost 40 percent of its planes. Antiaircraft shrapnel and 20mm cannon shells damaged nearly all of the 92nd Group's bombers. Two have such severe damage that it's surprising they managed to get back. They will probably have to be junked.

Thus, I complete my seventeenth mission. I doubt that I can survive another one like it. I thought that they would become easier as we got more fighters to escort us, but this one makes me wonder if they aren't getting harder. The Eighth Air Force lost sixty-four bombers today, one of its heaviest one-day losses of the entire war. It lost sixteen fighters, but our fighters shot down fifty-one German fighters and destroyed sixty-five German planes on the ground. The entire day was a savage battle.

After that long flight, I barely make it to the bathroom, despite a big dose of paregoric before we took off twelve hours earlier. I want to cry out from the pain in my head. Later, I feel like a zombie at dinner. We eat silently, and I note the many empty places at the tables.

Back at our quarters, everyone peppers us with questions about the mission and about how John died. Finally, John Sloan, the group historian, sits down facing me and gently asks me to describe the mission from start to finish, while he takes notes. By the time I do this, my eyes are almost closed from exhaustion. I take two, sleeping capsules and fall into a drugged sleep.

At breakfast, revived by two amphetamine tablets, I look at the four other members of our original crew. We are all that is left of the ten grinning fellows who met nine short months ago to live together, laugh together, and work together. Sadly, we agree that you couldn't ask for a better friend than John Kindred. He was quiet and generous. As with the deaths of the other four members of our crew, I think of the sorrow that his death will cause at home. Who will die next? Will it be wisecracking Lloyd? Will it be fun-loving Greg? Will it be unflappable Ken? Will it be reliable Ed? Will it be me?

John's death was not the only personal tragedy that day. Charles Pettibone was a big, friendly fellow who lived in my building and flew as part of another crew. He watched daily while friends, with everything to live for, went out and died. Other friends went out and came back torn and bleeding. He saw, as I did, that the odds were high against surviving even twenty-five missions. He had plenty of courage, but he also had plenty of intelligence. In fact, he had so much courage that he walked into the 327th Squadron office and stated that he refused to fly anymore.

The air force could not permit someone to quit combat flying without severe punishment. Otherwise, many of us would quit. Who wants to die? The trouble is that the air force can charge us with desertion, which can rate execution by a firing squad or a long term in prison. But our squadron and group commanders are combat flyers. They face the same terror over Germany. Thus, instead of such severe punishment, they took away Charles' sergeant rank and assigned him as a lowly private to permanent kitchen duty in the combat mess. Each morning during the dark days of winter, I would greet him as he served breakfast. He always smiled and wished me luck.

But the coolie work for long hours gave Charles a chance to think of how many years might stretch ahead of him before the war ended. Also, he had to face us each morning before we went out on a mission, wondering which of us would die that day. That was his real punishment. Several stupid guys made remarks to him about being a coward. Maybe the best way to solve everything was to fly the rest of his missions and take a chance on surviving them. He decided to return to combat flying. There was no longer a spot on his old crew, but a crewmember was ill on the bomber piloted by John Harris. Thus, on April 11, 1944, Charles flew with that crew.

Their B-17, flying just behind us, exploded during the first attack on our group by FW-190s, and Charles died.

There was more drama during that mission. James Underwood, a native of Missouri, was a radio operator on a B-17 in the 325th Squadron. He was a thin, serious flyer who worked quietly and looked like he had been through bad times. In fact, he had. I stood in awe of him because he had flown missions against the Japanese in the south Pacific in the first year of the war. Someone said that he had flown seventy-five missions there. He then volunteered to fly against the Germans. On April 8, 1944, the air force awarded him the richly deserved Silver Star, Distinguished Flying Cross, and Air Medal with Oak Leaf Cluster for his bravery in the South Pacific. Three days later, on this terrible mission of April 11, his B-17 exploded during the early attacks on our group. We assumed that he died, but luck was with him, and I saw a report that he survived the explosion and was taken prisoner by the Germans.

So it goes.

CHAPTER 22

Escape to the English Countryside

I am not feeling well. I don't know if it is from depression at John Kindred's death, or from combat fatigue, or from too much barbiturates and amphetamines. I don't want to tell the doctor. I am afraid that he will send me to a mental hospital. The thing I really need is to see Jane again. Before I met her, my life was ever-deeper depression. Now I'm on a roller coaster of ups and downs. I see Jane, and everything becomes bright and wonderful, and I feel hope, even confidence, that I can survive. Then, something bad happens, such as the mission of April 11, and I plunge downward again, convinced that I will die on one of the remaining thirteen missions. Jane is the key to my happiness. In fact, she is the thing that keeps me flying these missions, one after another. Never doubt the power of a woman. Since the group is so short on radio operators that can handle Morse code rapidly, the air force should give Jane a medal for keeping me flying.

But now, I'm about as depressed as I have ever been. Half of my crew has died while I flew the first half of my required thirty missions. If this trend continues, it suggests that the remaining five of us on the crew may not survive the second half. We will be picked off one by one, like western settlers in a wagon train surrounded by attacking Indians. This is a bad thought, but all I have today are bad thoughts.

If I continue to live through future missions, I will be part of a smaller and smaller group of survivors. There are fewer of us on the base who have survived seventeen missions than have survived eleven, the average time that a crew survives, and there are even fewer who have survived twenty, and still fewer who have survived twenty-five. It comes down to an almost vanishing number who have survived twenty-eight or twenty-nine. Each time that I get through a mission, I am part of a smaller group of survivors. Of course, the probabilities are that I will die on one of my remaining missions. Isn't that a miserable thing for a nineteen-year-old to be thinking about on April 12, 1944? I guess it's a heck of a thing for a nineteen-year-old to have to think about on any date.

Still, I must try to believe that I will survive. I could take a white capsule and sleep the rest of the day, until it's time to take two blue capsules to sleep tonight, but I want more from life than that. I lie on my bed and listen to music by Glenn Miller and Tommy Dorsey and Bennie Goodman on the Armed Forces Radio. Jane has kept me going, but I've also had help from sleeping pills, amphetamine, headache capsules, and paregoric. Trying for a positive outlook, I drum into my mind that each time I survive a mission, I'm nearer to the final one. Then, unlike Rex and Gunnar and Ken and Ralph and John and dozens of dead friends, I'll watch the sun rise on each new day in the future. But how do I survive the thirteen remaining missions if any are like the one to Stettin?

A letter arrives from Jane. I am always happy to see them, but today I grasp the pale, blue envelope like a drowning man. Just looking at the envelope makes me feel better. She writes:

> I only have time for a few words today before I go to work. I am frightfully tired. I have spent the day enquiring about a different position. Now that our love has become serious, I do not feel that it is proper for me to be working on stage. Thus, I am seeking a new position as a clerk or something similar. Unfortunately, the positions I found today did not pay wages equivalent to my current salary, so I will continue the search, although a day spent walking the streets of London is dreadfully dull—not at all like our walks together.
>
> You made me happy beyond anything you can imagine by your words in your last letter that you love me. I know how difficult it has been for you to express your feelings in words, but you solved it by writing them. I have read your letter many times and held it to my heart. I hope you will

be able to tell me that you love me when we are together the next time.

Frightful rumors are circulating around London that Hitler is planning to unleash a massive attack of poison gas on us. If such an event comes, I shall don my gas mask and run to the nearest shelter, so you must not worry about me if this happens.

Now, I must run to work. I want you to know that I love you very much.

As I read and reread Jane's note, it sets me back on the old question of why we are attracted to each other, especially why she is attracted to me. I'm not a heroic figure. I'm a nineteen-year-old, frightened-to-death university biochemistry student. Whatever the reason, she is developing in me, despite bouts of depression, an underlying feeling of happiness. She now says, "I love you," in every letter. I have never before had a girl tell me that she loves me, and it has tended to sweep other things, such as fear of dying, from my mind each time that I read it. I am such a simpleton that I supposed it took many months to fall in love. I thought that instant love was fiction that you see in the movies, but Jane and I have known each other for two months and have been together a total of only seven days. Yet, she says she loves me, and I have fallen head over heels in love with her. This gives me plenty to ponder, and a tiny feeling of optimism, even today when I look ahead at the minefield of thirteen more missions.

One thing that helps is that the weather is getting nicer. January, February, and March were cold, rainy, windy, and gloomy. Now, in April, I remember how good I felt after my previous walk in the countryside to Hinwick House and Podington. I decide that I may feel better if I spend more time exploring the countryside around the airbase.

The next day dawns with a nice outlook, so I take a long walk. It feels wonderful to stroll slowly and gaze at trees and shrubs and cottages and everything else along the roads. The airbase is always noisy, and you must jump out of the way of trucks and jeeps speeding along the roads. The countryside outside the airbase is quiet and tranquil. It's also friendly. Farmers smile and wave. People riding past on bicycles smile at me as they nod or wave. A woman sweeping the stoop of her cottage pauses to greet me. It is so quiet that I can hear birds chirping. Small, brownish birds flit about and I watch a flock of large, black birds wheel overhead.

Here is the village of Podington again. My previous visit was brief. This time I gaze down High Street and feel that I am in another world—one that existed many years ago—and it is a very nice feeling. Some villagers walk, and some ride bicycles. I don't see American uniforms. The shops that line High Street have little or no display windows and are in buildings of dark brown stone with steeply gabled roofs. No flat roofs that you see in American store buildings. The structures look to be several hundred years old. The church—someone says that it is called St. Mary's—which I stand and gape at, looks much older. The gentleman that I had accompanied previously to Podington said it dated from the fourteenth century. Now, another gentleman stops and tells me that parts date from the twelfth and parts from the thirteenth centuries.

On my way back to the airbase, I meet a group of birdwatchers and nature lovers, mostly elderly, and they are cordial to this American tourist. They are happy to identify nearby birds for me. One white-haired lady, an amateur botanist, invites me to stroll with her to her cottage, where she gives me watercress sandwiches, tea, and a fascinating description of the local flora.

The news on the radio from the BBC is full of excited talk of the coming invasion of Europe by Allied forces. The rumor is that it will be late May or early June. It's an electrifying feeling, and everyone is talking about it. General Eisenhower just announced that all bombers in the Eighth and Ninth Air Forces are now tactical to support the invasion. That must mean that the invasion is near. If it means more missions to France, I am all for it. I will be happy if it comes tomorrow. My thought is that our ground troops in France will overrun German airbases, pushing the German fighters back, and giving them less time to attack us.

Axis Sally broadcasts on the German radio that "we are waiting for you." She says that German defenses along the French coast are so strong that our troops will die on the beaches. She urges us to desert and hide to avoid being killed. That gets a big yawn from me. Jane would certainly hide me, but I could not live with myself if I let my country down. I just have to hope that I don't suffer the same fate as Townsend, Swanson, Kinsella, Ballmer, and now Kindred.

I heard an interesting rumor. The Germans' V-1 weapons are reported to be unmanned aircraft containing a huge amount of explosive. They are powered by a new kind of engine, a jet, and are very fast. I have never heard of a jet engine, but I learn that jet engines are the coming thing because they are so much faster than propeller-driven engines. The rumor is that the Germans have hundreds of V-1 vehicles ready to come at us. They supposedly have them targeted to hit all of our airbases, as well as army posts and cities. One rumor is that they will carry immense amounts of nerve gas to kill us before we know what is happening. If it isn't one thing, it's another.

That's enough of these scary rumors. Jane loves me. I wish I could see her and hold her in my arms. I'm a hopeless romantic.

But war crushes romance and happiness under its boot.

CHAPTER 23

More Terror

I hang on for dear life as a jeep careens down the road. The driver is a madman. We are on our way to the flight line in response to a hurry-up call. Still woozy from last night's sleeping capsules, I wait for amphetamine to bring me out of my stupor, while I hold on desperately, and buildings, trees, fences and people race past in a blur. We skid to a halt at the equipment building to let me stumble in to get my flight gear. Then, we speed around the perimeter track to a silver B-17G. Oh, boy, back to the Pas de Calais again. I try to stop trembling as I return the wave of the captain grinning at me from the pilot's window.

"Good to see you," he calls. "Get in. We're on a tight schedule."

I lurch to the bomber's door, where a mechanic boosts me inside and slams the door. We taxi out, roar down the runway, and climb past puffy, white clouds above the English countryside. Bleary-eyed, I study the secret codes and instructions. What a life!

As the B-17 roars southeast, it is clear that my guess was correct. We are heading again for the Pas de Calais. I smile. I'm in for a scary half-hour over France, but nothing has happened on these flights, and I'll be one mission closer to finishing.

I put my nose to the window and watch the English countryside pass 5000 feet beneath us. Everything down there has the pale green of early spring. Forests and rolling hills are breathtaking. Far off, across pea-green hills and meadows dotted with thatched-roof cottages, a stone tower rises above a surrounding forest. I suspect that it is part of a castle hidden by the trees. The farther south we go, the more traffic, especially military, seems to be on the roads. The landscape has a network of railroad lines, and I count the smoke from five trains that are in sight. From this altitude, they look like toys.

We fly over vast encampments of hundreds of tents, trucks, tanks, jeeps, and artillery extending across fields that were empty the last time we flew this route. There must be several divisions of troops down there that have just arrived. I heard that troops from all over the British Isles are moving into temporary sites in the southern part of England, prior to boarding ships to take them to France. Everyone says that the date for the invasion is coming fast.

As we drone southward, I gaze at a tiny village of a dozen, stone buildings surrounded by twice that number of cottages. Its main street looks peaceful. Wouldn't it be enjoyable to be down there, to walk along quiet lanes, and to sit in a pub listening while the villagers play darts and tell stories? By the time I finish my reverie, the village is far behind, and our silver B-17G climbs rapidly while it approaches the coast. I see water ahead. We pass 10,000 feet, and it's time to buckle on my oxygen mask. My compartment is getting cold, and I shiver. The bomber's nose points upward toward our usual altitude of 15,000 feet.

We cross the shoreline and roar over the gray water of the English Channel. Six ships sail in formation along the coast, leaving white wakes in the water. They may be destroyers, but they could also be minesweepers. I am not too adept at identifying naval vessels. We are crossing the Channel a mile west of Folkstone. The Channel is so narrow here that I feel I could step across it. I scan the sky, but we are alone over the water. No, a flight of British Spitfire fighters races along parallel to the English coast west of us.

While we fly above the Channel, I begin to search the sky for German planes. Can we continue to poke into France without the Germans trying to shoot us down? It seems like we can, and I'm happy to spend a tense half-hour in exchange for credit for another mission. Still, as we leave England farther behind, I gaze at the sky intently. Thus far, I see nothing but an empty dome of blue.

"We're almost to the French coast," the pilot says. "Heads up, you guys."

I peer ahead at the coastline coming toward us. France looks even prettier with the onset of spring, but it is also loaded with danger from the Germans there. I wish I didn't have to watch for German fighters. Then, I could be an airborne tourist again and admire the landscape. Maybe someday I can visit France during peacetime and enjoy this lovely country.

Startled, I jump a mile when the radio spits out our call letters, followed by a rapid burst of code! I grab a pencil, copy the message, decode it quickly, and call the captain.

"I just got a message. It says 'Abort!'"

He banks the plane sharply to turn the plane around to head north.

"We're going to get the hell out of here. Keep an eye out for fighters."

I gaze up into the sunny sky and gape. My heart skips. A cold fist clutches me. Two, black dots are heading toward us! Before I can call the captain, they materialize into two German fighter planes that grow bigger by the second.

"Bandits are coming at us from high in the southwest!" I call. "It looks like two FW-190s."

"Oh, shit," the captain says. "Hang on, you guys."

The B-17 is already racing northward. I reach out to switch on the IFF transmitter to alert the British defense network that we're coming back. Before I can touch the switch, the floor drops from beneath me. I grab the desk to keep from hitting the roof. The captain has put the B-17 into the steepest dive that I have ever seen. The bomber tilts precipitously downward, and the engines roar as the pilot dives at full throttle. I look back. The Germans fighters are much closer and pointing toward us. I desperately hang onto my desk in the tilted cabin as we reach the coast and dive toward the water of the Channel. The plane whines and vibrates while we move faster than I have ever flown in a B-17. The vibration becomes more violent. I yank off my oxygen mask because it's clear that we are well below 10,000 feet. I glance back. The German fighters are close, and the captain is diving straight toward the water.

I brace myself for us to crash at full power into the water, but he pulls the big bomber out of its dive. The G-force is like a giant boulder crushing me down into my seat. I hear loud cracking all over the B-17. It sounds like it's coming apart. We level off twenty feet above the water and race across the Channel. The water below passes in a blur. The cliffs of Dover come toward us like a speeding wall. With difficulty, I peer back. The German fighters have turned around and headed back to France. I switch on the IFF to tell the British that we are friendly. We climb abruptly and barely clear the chalk cliffs in the Dover area. The crew of an antiaircraft gun emplacement waves to us. They're so close that I feel I could reach out and touch them.

We climb to about 3,000 feet and sail above the English countryside while my heart slows to merely racing. We escaped from the German fighters, but it was terrifying. I'm trembling, and I can't stop. When we land, I realize that the flight, despite scaring the pants off me, was wasted. Since we didn't go over enemy-occupied territory, I get no credit for a combat mission. Instead, they will likely give me credit for a training mission.

Wonderful. Just wonderful.

CHAPTER 24

Berlin Nightmare

April 18, 1944. I cross my fingers when the intelligence captain reaches for the curtain that covers the map of Europe. The curtain opens. Groans fill the room. A chill goes down my spine. The red line tracks straight across northern Germany to Berlin. Wasn't the mission to Stettin last week close enough to getting all of us killed, in addition to John Kindred? Now we'll see if Berlin can kill the rest of us. Our group has lost seven planes and seventy men while fighting its way to Berlin, including the one that exploded and killed Townsend, Swanson, Kinsella, and Ballmer. I had hoped that I would not have to face a mission to Berlin, but that was foolish, so now I will see the famous objective. Our specific target is the railroad yard in Oranienburg, a Berlin suburb. German fighters always rise to defend their capital city, and Berlin has more antiaircraft guns than any city in Europe. I'm frightened as I climb into our B-17G.

It is good that Virgil Hill is our pilot. He is a no-nonsense guy, and he gets us off the ground and climbs into formation with no wasted motion. He was magnificent on the terrible mission to Stettin, but he has almost finished his thirty missions. When he does, will we have a new pilot? We now have a temporary copilot, navigator, and tail gunner. I don't even know their names. The bomber crew is quiet while we get the squadron, then group, then wing, and finally the whole 1st Air Division into proper formation. Unlike the dark days of winter, we now have weather planes at very high altitude already over Germany to send back weather conditions on the way to Berlin. We also have fighters sweeping ahead of us to gauge German fighter activity and call forward additional fighters.

The day is sunny, with scattered clouds, white and puffy, drifting far below us. The armada of hundreds of silver bombers spreads for miles across the sky and drones across the North Sea and Holland at 25,000 feet. The Eighth Air Force seems to have replaced all of the old, brown B-17Fs with new, silver B-17Gs. I am truly grateful that the B-17F, with its open roof and 170-mile-per-hour blast of below-zero air, is gone. Still, despite the Plexiglas roof on the B-17G, it is cold in the radio room. I can't tell whether I'm shivering from cold or fright, and my headache is agony.

I again gaze in fascination at the pretty pattern of rivers and canals that covers the Dutch landscape. The land down there is brilliant green with the coming of spring. Before I began flying over it, I never realized that water covers so much of Holland. There seems to be almost as much water as land. I would love to visit Holland after the war—if I survive it.

Something is wrong! I'm suddenly dizzy and gasping for breath. I don't seem to be getting enough oxygen. I don't think it is cold enough to freeze my breath this fast. Off comes my oxygen mask, but there is hardly any ice in it. I clean out a tiny bit of ice, but it does not help. I'm suffocating! If you want to know how I feel, cover your nose and mouth with your hand and try to breathe.

In a panic, I turn the valve to force oxygen into my mask, but there is no whoosh of oxygen. Now in a big panic, I peer at the red ball in the oxygen indicator that rises and falls with my breathing. It moves only slightly. Something has clogged the tube carrying my oxygen supply. I inhale as hard as I can to take a deep breath. The ball moves a little higher. I strain to take the biggest breath that I am able to pull in, and the ball doesn't even rise halfway up the tube. Struggling to breathe more deeply than ever before, I keep the ball moving less than one-third of the way up the tube. It is exhausting work, but my life depends on it. The plane can't turn around and go back, and it can't descend below 10,000 feet. There is no other oxygen outlet on the plane. Unless I can pull in enough oxygen, I will die. Then, I remember the yellow, low-pressure tank of portable oxygen stored in our B-17G. It does not have nearly enough oxygen to sustain me all the way across Germany and back, but I may be able to stay alive by breathing some oxygen from the portable tank and pulling hard to get some oxygen from the outlet beside my desk. I connect to the yellow tank and take some blissful breaths of oxygen for a few minutes. Then, I go back to taking mighty breaths to pull oxygen from the regular outlet.

While I strain to breathe, we cross the German border, and I look down at the broad Rhine. I read once that a voyage down the Rhine is a beautiful trip. The Lower Rhine below me doesn't look beautiful. It is lined with industries spouting smoke.

As we roar on and travel ever farther to the east, my chest begins to pain from the effort to breathe deeply enough to get oxygen. I rest my chest by breathing oxygen from the yellow tank, but I know that I am rapidly using up precious oxygen.

We cross the Leine, and later the Weser. We are deep inside Germany now. Ahead is the Elbe. All four rivers glisten in sunlight while they snake toward the North Sea. There is a lot of barge traffic on them, and dozens of bridges span the broad waterways, some graceful and some ugly. I would like to record in my log the things that I see, but the effort of breathing takes all of my strength. German farmland beneath us is a patchwork of brown, yellow, and green, bordered by jade forests. Roads and railroad lines are surprisingly empty. Smoke rises from cities along our route. As usual, I picture German people huddling in air raid shelters. I can imagine German military officers plotting our progress and directing their air force against us.

"Look out!" Lloyd shouts.

A dozen, silver fighters are on top of us. Fear clutches at my throat as the bombers' guns hammer and spit strings of red tracers at the fighters. The German planes spew fire as they dive through the combat wing's formation. Their shells blast a B-17. In a minute, it blazes from nose to tail and flops over to dive toward the ground. Nobody got out. My stomach knots at the thought of ten fellows, just like me, burning alive inside the plane. Flames flare from the wings of a second bomber, and it explodes in a giant ball of orange fire. Those fireballs are horrible sights. They boil and twist like some kind of evil thing. No one had a chance to get out of that plane either. Terrified, I watch the fighters, but instead of circling around to attack us again, as fighters did on the Stettin mission, they speed on toward a fleet of bombers behind us.

"All clear for now," Lloyd says.

"They're knocking down planes in the formation following us," the tail gunner says. His voice shakes. "They're moving through that formation, and it looks like they're knocking down bombers."

It's a relief that they are hitting some other poor guys, but I still tremble. When will the next attack come? While I scan the sky, our B-17s roar on in the sunshine, their silver bodies glinting in the sun. The intercom is silent while the gunners search the sky for fighters. The portable tank is getting low on oxygen. I don't know how long I can keep straining this hard to breathe from my regular outlet.

We move deeper into Germany, passing Brunswick and then the ancient city of Magdeburg. I peer at it, hoping to see some of its medieval buildings, but I see wreckage. To keep my mind off of how frightened I am, I watch the Elbe recede behind us. Its water glistens in the sunlight. My chest feels like it is on fire. How long before I can no longer breathe?

"We're coming up on the IP," the navigator says.

I sigh. This means that we made it to Berlin without being killed. An awesome barrage of antiaircraft fire comes up when we turn toward the target. The sky ahead looks like the black clouds of a Kansas thunderstorm, and the blackness forms a fearsome box for hundreds of orange flashes of exploding shells. We plunge into it. The bomber bounces and rocks violently from blasts around us. How long can we avoid being hit? *Crack! Crack!* There's my answer. I duck as pieces of shrapnel rip through our bomber.

The bomb bay doors open, and I look down on Oranienburg. I flinch as shells explode too close. The heavy, bomb load drops, and the railroad yards disappear in a hell of fire and smoke as hundreds of bombs explode in them.

We turn away from the target to face the long ride back across Germany. Surprisingly, we avoid fighter attacks, but I don't care whether they hit us or not. I can't breathe. The portable oxygen supply runs out, and my chest is an agony of pain as I try to breathe deeply enough to keep from passing out.

While I gasp for air, I see dozens of German fighters attacking formations some distance from us. Again, the scene reminds me of movies of herds of African animals circled by hungry lions. The lions pick out a victim, and it is doomed, but the rest of the herd moves on. It is only their great numbers that save the herd. It's the same with our bombers. We have too many bombers for the German fighters to destroy all of them, but those that they pick out are as doomed as the poor African beasts.

The flight becomes a fight to pull even a tiny amount of oxygen into my lungs. I am no longer interested in where we are. Our progress is now marked, not by miles, but by each, painful breath that I take. Time stands still. There is nothing but the oxygen outlet and me.

About the time that I don't think my throbbing chest can breathe any more, we cross the coast and head out over the North Sea. Soon, the sound of the B-17's engines changes, and I know that we are descending. If I can keep up the deep breaths for a little longer, I'll make it back, but it is now torture to take even one breath.

"Navigator, what's our altitude?" I gasp. "I'm having difficulty with my oxygen. I can hardly breathe."

"We're at 19,000 feet and descending."

"Hold on," Hill says. "You should be able to get enough oxygen without your mask when we drop below 15,000. People do it in the mountains."

I continue to gasp, and each breath sends a piercing pain through my chest. The North Sea stretches away to the horizon. It looks pretty today—a turquoise shade instead of its winter gray. As I admire it, the most welcome words in the world come through the intercom.

"We're at 15,000 feet," the navigator says. "You can probably take your mask off, since we'll soon be at 10,000."

"I'll keep an eye on him," Ed Norton says from the waist.

I remove the mask. The air seems thin, but breathing is easier, although my chest pains badly with each breath. When the navigator announces that we have dropped below 10,000 feet, I smile and know that I made it without suffocating. The coast of England appears. We creep toward it until the formation thunders over the shoreline at 5,000 feet. I have never seen England look so lovely.

We land at Podington after eight and a half hours at high altitude in the icy air over Germany, much of it spent waiting for fighters to hit us. It almost killed me—another close call. I wonder if I have nine lives, like a cat.

This was my eighteenth mission. Twelve left. To celebrate, I gulp down my two ounces of Scotch and wonder how I can get ten more. This thought from a guy who never drank anything alcoholic until a few months ago. Lloyd makes his usual joke about getting a quart when Captain Furniss isn't looking. I grin and nod vigorously. I would like anything that would take away the thought of another mission.

My headache is awful, but I can't take more aspirin because I have pains in my stomach as well as my chest. Captain Furniss warned me about pain and bleeding. Fortunately, there are the barbiturate capsules. Maybe I'll skip dinner and go take two now. I'm getting awfully thin. I suspect it's from skipping so many dinners in order to get to the barbiturate. I hope I'm not getting addicted, but I must have them now.

The Eighth Air Force lost nineteen bombers and five fighters on the flight to Berlin, but mercifully none came from the 92nd. The Germans lost thirty-five fighters.

I can't take much more of this.

CHAPTER 25

A Life Preserver,
If It Comes in Time

No rest for the wicked. I happily read a letter from Jane, for the fourth time, when a call comes for me from the flight line. Oh, just wonderful, it's probably the captain again and another scary trip to the Pas de Calais. I leave the rest of my crew lounging in our quarters—the lucky ducks—and go outside just as a jeep skids to a halt to pick me up for another high-speed ride that ends beside an ancient B-17F. It's not the captain. Colonel Brousseau is going on an errand and wants me to go with him. I assume that he wants me along in case he gets an urgent message. Why me? There are lots of radio operators at Podington. Does it have anything to do with the flights with the captain? I tell everyone that I had to fly on an errand when I go with the captain. I never dreamed that I would be involved in something that appears to be so secret that only a few people on the base know about it. And what is it, anyway? No one tells me anything.

Colonel Brousseau is a no-nonsense pilot. He has us rolling before I hardly have settled in my seat in the familiar sights and smells of the radio room. I am alone, as usual, in the rear section of the bomber. We roar into the air. For the first time in weeks, the wind roars in through the B-17F's open roof, but we're flying low above the English landscape in late April, so the blast is chilly, rather than being downright cold. I gaze at the pretty countryside and dream of Jane. I love her. I'm sure of it now, even though I have never before been in love. Her letters say that she loves me. Merely thinking about her raises my spirits. Maybe we can have a future, if I can survive the rest of these missions.

Since we are flying low and not doing anything dangerous, I can spend my time as an airborne tourist. I gaze down at everything that I can see on the English landscape spread out below me. As usual, I am impressed by how neat and pretty England appears. Of course, they have had hundreds of years to get it this way. The countryside looks like all the movies I have ever seen that were set in England. Our flight is short, and Colonel Brousseau's visit at another airbase is shorter, so we are soon landing back at Podington. After we leave the plane, Colonel Brousseau nods and smiles at me before he climbs into a waiting staff car and leaves. Wow, he never did that before.

"Where you been?" Ken Tasker asks when I get back to our quarters.

"Another flight on an errand with Colonel Brousseau," I say. He grins.

"Boy, you sure get stuck with a lot of them. You're for sure on somebody's shit list."

Maybe he is right, but at least the captain and the colonel smile at me.

Gazing at the English countryside from the air sets me off on another walking trip away from the base. I don't go far before I meet the elderly, botanist lady that I met and had tea with on an earlier walk. I think her name is Mary, but I am embarrassed that I can't remember for certain. I thought that forgetting people's names is a sign of old age, but here I am, only nineteen, and I can't remember names at all. She motions for me to join her. We look at some deep-green mosses and some lichens that resemble pieces of gray paper sticking out an inch from a tree trunk. Then, we stride swiftly across a field while she bewilders me as she points out and names every weed and flower and shrub and grass in sight. When we stop, she apologizes that she can't ask me to tea, but she is off to attend a meeting of nature lovers of some sort. I don't mind a bit. If you have had one watercress sandwich, you have had enough, so I smile, wave, and head down the lane.

The lane and a road take me into the town of Rushden, about six miles from the airbase. Podington was a village of a few hundred persons. Rushden is a real town. High Street (do all of these places have a High Street?) is lined with dozens and dozens of shops and cafes and pubs and tea rooms. High Street is busy. There are bicycles everywhere, but there are also many cars and trucks. There are churches with spires pointing to the heavens, and every church seems to be very old. (Do all of these villages and towns have a church named St. Mary's?) Unlike Podington, most people in Rushden hurry about their business. Since Rushden is near our airbase, its pubs probably attract Americans, so the citizens of Rushden ignore me while I gawk at their town.

I stop at a pub to rest. It looks like all of the pubs that Jane has steered me into in London, with a big bar, tables, dark woods, people talking and laughing, and the aroma of malt. As well as I can understand, English ale comes in three types: mild, which has 3.2 percent alcohol and a faintly sweet taste; bitter, which has a higher alcohol content and is an acquired taste; and half and half ("arf and arf"), which is a popular mixture. With Jane's help, I have sampled all of them. I like some bitters, but not all, so I order half and half.

The English are rather reserved in public, but in the pub, many become downright gregarious.

"I wager you come from one of the flying fields," a man in cap and leather coat says from his place next to me.

I nod.

"I'm at the field near Podington."

"You appear quite young. I suspect it's difficult for you to be so far from home."

"I really like being in England. It's only when we fly over to Germany that I don't like it. Over there, it's just plain unfriendly."

This gets a hoot and laughter along the bar. I ask about Rushden, and the men seem happy to talk. They tell me that Rushden is a fine place to live. They variously estimate its population as 15,000 to 20,000 people, although most agree that the one man's estimate of 20,000 is too high. I learn that the big industry is making shoes and boots. When I ask about the town's age, they agree that it goes back to the twelfth century, and some relics from the Romans are in the area. Again, I shake my head at how so much of England stretches so far back into history.

After I leave the pub, I wander around before I stop to watch trains passing through town. The big, round bumpers on the ends of engines and cars make even the passenger cars look different from American passenger cars. The big difference, however, is in the freight cars, called goods cars by the English, which are little things compared with American freight cars. But they are all fun to watch. I spend the rest of the afternoon wandering through shops along High Street. I imagine Jane being with me, and I buy some things to give to her when I next can go to London.

On April 20, we climb aboard a B-17G and fly to the Pas de Calais to bomb a V-1 launching site near Lingham. I hear that our Generals are very worried about the Germans' V-1 weapon. This mission is the hundredth for the 92nd Bomb Group, so it is a festive occasion. The lead plane taxis out flying an American flag. We join a vast armada heading for many targets along the coast. For the first time, I am not nearly as tense as we wing toward France, and my more relaxed feeling is correct because we see no sign of German fighters. Have the Germans pulled back from the coast? Will missions become easier? When we return after an uneventful flight that plasters the launching site with bombs, I beam at the thought that I now have survived nineteen missions. Only eleven left. Sadly, it's the thirtieth mission for our pilot, Virgil Hill.

"You have been great, and it has been a pleasure to fly with you," I tell him as we shake hands.

"Good luck on the rest of your missions," he says.

For four months, I have been tense, always wondering whether the next mission will be the one that kills me. But now, everything looks brighter. Is it the sunshine of springtime? Is it being in love? Is it the bustle that has taken over England? Fellows who have driven off the base report meeting long convoys of troops, tanks, guns, and supplies. Immense numbers of soldiers and their weapons have arrived from the United States. Jane says that the latest quip by London comedians is that the island is going to sink from the weight of American troops and war material piled on it. Whatever it is, something is having an effect on me. Since late December, I have been convinced that I will soon die. Now I have survived nineteen missions. Only a few fellows have done that, and I wonder if I may sur-

vive the rest. Of course, the killers are still up there in the air over
Germany, waiting for me.

While my crew relaxes, I hang on as a jeep speeds me to the
flight line to get friendly waves from the captain and his lieutenants.
My morning amphetamines have almost cleared my foggy head
while we take off. I eat the only breakfast available, a Cadbury
chocolate bar. I should be terrified to venture over the Pas de Calais
after German fighters nearly destroyed us on the last flight, but the
captain showed that he can escape from them. Thus, I'm not terrified. I'm merely scared stiff.

My confidence in the captain is well grounded. As we fly to the
Pas de Calais, I admire the English landscape, and marvel at all the
fields of parked tanks, trucks, and artillery guns. Over the Pas de
Calais, I see planes in the distance, but they don't turn our way, so I
merely watch them until we are back over the Channel on the way
home.

This time, however, the flight turns out to be not at all routine.
After we land and climb from the bomber, the captain walks over to
me. But he is no longer a captain. He is a major.

"Congratulations on your promotion," I say.

"Thanks," he says, shaking hands. "We won't be borrowing these
B-17s much longer, but I want to transfer you to our group. We
need another communications officer, and I want you. It's a
ground-based job, but I have a feeling that you've put your neck on
the line enough times on combat missions. We can use you, and it'll
be worth your while because you'll get a commission."

I'm stunned. No more combat missions and a direct commission to second lieutenant mean that I would certainly survive. This
changes everything.

"Unless you have a strong objection, we'll do it," the major says
as he strides to a waiting jeep. "I'll be in touch."

As I go back to my quarters, I walk on a cloud about a foot
above the ground. I may survive! Happiness overwhelms me. I
haven't felt so free and relaxed since I entered the military. Because
I can't talk about the flights, I can't tell my friends about it. I will
have to fly missions until I transfer, but if I can get through those,
I'll be home free. Hope blossoms. I will have to stay in England

until the end of the war in Europe, but as long as I am with Jane, I don't care if the war lasts for years. In the meantime, this was my twentieth mission. Only ten to go, no matter what happens, and the operations officers always try to make your last mission an easy one, so that leaves nine potentially tough missions to face, unless the transfer gets me out of here first.

My world is bright. I dream of going back to the university and later settling into a good career as a physician or scientist. Will Jane be willing to live in the United States? From our conversations, I am sure that she will, and I dream of a happy life together.

Of course, there are still ten missions to face.

CHAPTER 26

A New Way to Die

On April 24, the 92nd Group goes to Oberpfaffenhofen in southern Germany to bomb the Dornier aircraft plant there. We no longer have a pilot since Virgil Hill finished his thirty missions and left for home, so we can't go. Gee, too bad, because when the other crews come back from the mission, they tell us that opposition from German fighters was fierce. The 92nd Group lost five planes. The pilot of one is William Parramore. This crew is the last of three that joined the 92nd Group with us four months ago. They were seen trying to reach Switzerland. None of the four crews that came in together will complete thirty missions. When I transfer to my new job, Ken Tasker, Lloyd Lyons, Ed Norton, and Greg Araujo will be the only fellows still flying from a group of forty wisecracking flyers that came to the 92nd Bomb Group at the end of December 1943. That is a 90 percent loss. I hope that my four friends can finish their thirty missions.

April 25, 1944. It's a surprise when squadron operations alerts Greg, Lloyd, Ed, Ken, and me for a mission, but it has cobbled together a crew to join the five of us. The pilot has been working as an administrative officer, and no one remembers him flying, but the copilot flew with Virgil Hill, and he is good. The navigator is a temporary, and I don't recognize his name, but Sergeant Jerome Charbonneau is bombardier, and you can't ask for a better man.

At briefing, I cross my fingers when the intelligence captain reaches for the curtain covering the map. The line runs a long way southeast through France. I've been there before. We're off to bomb the German Air Force base at Nancy. German fighters can still hit us, but it is not as bad as going into Germany.

I fix my mind on Jane's words that I'm going to make it. The thought of her welcoming me with open arms when I finish flying puts a smile on my face as I climb into the bomber and Ken Tasker slams the door. The engines start, and we taxi out to the runway to join the long line of B-17s taking off. My headache is agony, but I fix my mind on soon being a communications officer. Maybe the thought will make me feel better.

As we climb into the frigid air at high altitude and adjust our oxygen masks, it quickly becomes clear that the new pilot is having trouble, and it's bad. He can't seem to fly a B-17. While the bomber fleet wings southeast across France above scattered, fleecy clouds, we have his terrible flying to add to our worries about fighters and antiaircraft. He can't keep the big plane in formation, and it alternately strays far away from the squadron and then zooms in so close to another bomber that I hold my breath, waiting for us to collide. I remember the bombers from the 92nd Group that smashed into each other on the cold mission to Brunswick in late January. The intercom is strangely silent except for the copilot's exasperated shouts of, "Watch out for that plane!" At one point, the front half of our B-17 drifts about eight feet beneath the tail section of another bomber. I duck. The other plane looks gigantic just above my head. Flying this way is as scary as being attacked by fighters. Our B-17G jerks back and forth as the pilot tries to control it. I don't merely tremble, I shake.

By a miracle, we reach the target outside of Nancy. A barrage of antiaircraft fire awaits us with a hundred puffs of black smoke filled with flashes of shells exploding. Beneath the bursts is our target. We plunge into the antiaircraft fire. Blasts rock the B-17. Shrapnel snaps through its skin. Flashes of exploding shells surround us. They're bound to hit us! Down go the bombs to cover the airfield in flashes, fire, and smoke. I sigh as we turn from the target and leave a sky filled with black smoke rising from the burning airfield.

The ride back is no better. Repeatedly, our B-17 narrowly misses ramming into another plane. The squadron formation becomes loose, as other pilots pull away to give our bomber a wide berth. By the time we approach the coast, our plane has drifted far away from the main formation. The pilot seems to have solved the problem of almost crashing into nearby planes by remaining far from them. We're flying two hundred yards from the 92nd Group's formation.

It's fine unless German fighters appear. Without the covering fire of the formation's guns, fighters will pick us off quickly.

BANG! A bright flash startles me as a shower of splinters stings my face. I gape at a three-inch hole torn in the floor a foot from me. A big hole in the cabin's ceiling shows blue sky. An antiaircraft shell exploded under the plane and a large piece of shrapnel shot upward through the radio room and just missed me. Ken and Ed stare at me while I shake and gaze at the holes. Instead of following the formation along a safe route, our pilot blundered away from it and into range of an antiaircraft gun crew on the coast. They tracked us and fired a single shell. If it had been set to explode a little higher, it would have blown us from the sky. As it is, a piece of shrapnel nearly killed me, and other pieces ripped holes in the bomber. It's another close call, and I'm tired of close calls.

Somehow, we get back to the base, and the new pilot makes a bumpy landing. The B-17 hits the runway hard, bounces into the air and comes down even harder. At interrogation, the pilot insists on doing all the talking. He describes a mission with little resemblance to the one that we just flew. While Lloyd and Jerome stare skeptically at the new pilot, I drink my two ounces of Scotch and remember that I have now finished twenty-one missions. Only nine left. Somehow, counting down on the final ten makes me feel better.

That evening, I lie on my bed and listen to music on the Armed Forces Network. I have a letter from Pearleen and one from Jane. Pearleen's letter is as bright and cheerful as ever. She is a wonderful friend. Jane's letter is full of funny happenings in London and repeated encouragement for me. She says that she loves me and she "simply can't wait until we're together again." I lie quietly for a time and think of Pearleen and Jane. I talk with John Sloan for an hour and read a lesson from my latest university course. By then, it's time for two barbiturate capsules and blessed sleep.

April 27, 1944. Eyes tightly closed, I wait for the intelligence captain to uncover the map. Do I hear groans? No. Do I hear sighs of relief? Yes! I open my eyes and see that the red line stops at the French coast. This should be an easy mission. We're going to the Bois Coquerel area of France to bomb a secret V-1 site.

I don't have any trouble climbing into the bomber for a trip to the French coast, but once we are in the air, there is a lot of trouble. I forgot about our new pilot. Look out! We're going to hit that bomber! The pilot yanks our big plane away. A couple of feet more, and we would have collided. My heart takes time to stop racing while I close my eyes and try to stop trembling. I've been flying too long for this nonsense. I hope I haven't survived twenty-one missions, only to die in a midair collision. The copilot is yelling and swearing again. Finally, we move away from the other bombers and fly alone. We drop our bombs nowhere near the rest of the 92nd Bomb Group's bomb pattern and turn for home. I sigh and cross my fingers. All we have to do is make it home without a collision. Fortunately, the pilot continues to fly some distance from the formation. Doesn't the commander in the lead plane see this?

We land, and I smile. I survived my twenty-second mission. There are only eight left, but how long can my luck last with this pilot? I hope I transfer to the other group soon, before he kills all of us.

When we finish with interrogation and our two ounces of Scotch, I find Jerome Charbonneau spitting with anger. He is a top-notch guy, and a veteran of the 92nd Bomb Group.

"This guy can't fly, and we don't deserve to get killed by his screw ups," Charbonneau says, pacing back and forth.

He is really angry. He looks ready to punch someone. It's a good thing that the pilot isn't around, but he left after he described his perfect flight at interrogation, while we stood with open-mouthed amazement at his story. Maybe he was afraid that we would say something. No, he seems stuck on himself, unless that is a cover for being nervous about his inability to fly in formation. He must know how close he has come to killing everyone, including himself.

"What the hell can we do?" Lloyd asks.

"We can damn well complain," Jerome says. "We don't have to fly with a bad pilot."

We follow Charbonneau and troop into the office of the squadron operations officer, a major and a good man. Charbonneau states the complaint clearly. I wonder whether we'll all be arrested for insubordination, but the copilot and navigator enter

while Charbonneau is talking, and the two veteran flyers back everything he says. That does it. The operations officer promises action.

That night, my hand trembles while I read Jane's letter. I think
of the times that we have been together, how she smiles, how her
eyes light up when she sees me, and how wonderful she makes me
feel. I sigh and read her letter again. She will be disappointed if she
does not get a letter, so I shakily scribble a note, hoping that she
can read it. Once it is finished, I reach for the barbiturate capsules.

CHAPTER 27

I Don't Think They Like Us

April 29, 1944. I awaken to the sound of the 92nd Group's bombers roaring into the air. The rumble shakes the building and builds to a thunderous crescendo as more and more of the heavily loaded bombers struggle into the air and circle above our roofs. Then, the thunder slowly fades as the bomber formation climbs away from the airbase on its way to Europe.

At a breakfast of powdered eggs (I will never become accustomed to those things, but you have to eat something), Spam, waxy butter, excellent toast, and strong coffee, I hear that the group is on its way to Berlin. Whew! My luck has held again. The thought of flying all the way to Berlin with that administrator-pilot trying to stay in formation is too awful to imagine. I hope fervently that the operations officer somehow can find another pilot to join our crew, and our albatross of a pilot can go back to administering whatever he administers. In doing so, the operations officer would probably save the 92nd Group from losing two aircraft, when he finally collides with another bomber, and it would save the lives of twenty men.

As I cover my powdered eggs with ketchup to make them remotely edible, a corporal hurries into the combat mess. A bad feeling grips me. Sure enough, he sees me and rushes over.

"I'm supposed to get you to the flight line right away," he puffs. "There's a major flying in, and he wants you there quick."

"Wonderful," I say, as I grab a slice of toast to take with me. "On second thought, flying with the major saves me from eating these God-awful powdered eggs."

"I thought you guys got real eggs," he says as we hurry outside.

"We only get them before a mission, when we're too nervous to enjoy them."

He puts the jeep in gear and speeds off down the road, while I hang on. We must be doing seventy miles per hour on the narrow road. Where do they get these jeep drivers? Just as I'm convinced that he is going to kill both of us, we screech to a stop to get my flight gear, and then speed around the perimeter track to a silver B-17G that sits gleaming in the sunshine. The silver ones are a pretty sight. Grease-stained mechanics turn the propellers and check the plane. A staff car pulls up behind us. Out pops the major and his lieutenants.

"Well, sport," he says, "you've had time to think about it. How about transferring to our outfit as a communications officer?"

"I'd like to very much."

"Good man! OK, let's get going."

He hands me the secret codes, and we all climb into the bomber. I can't suppress a bout of tension as I face another mission. We've already had one mighty close call on these flights. How long can we do this before they shoot us down? On the other hand, we have made it safely through a number of them. Surprisingly, I feel that we will make it through today's flight over the Pas de Calais. In fact, I am getting an optimistic outlook, even without any urging from Jane. Of course, her letters never stop being upbeat about our future together. Maybe it is having an effect. Whatever it is, I feel better. After all, I am almost finished with flying missions, and I may become a ground-based communications officer before I have to fly all of the remaining missions.

The engines roar to life, and the big bomber vibrates from the four engine's power. We taxi out along an empty perimeter track, thunder down the runway, and climb into sunny, blue sky. The ride south is almost pleasant. Four aspirins have dulled my headache, although they make my stomach burn. My mind is full of excitement about becoming a communications officer. I keep thinking that I will be safely on the ground then. No more flights over Germany. Will this be the last combat mission that I have to fly? There's nothing like wishful thinking.

The countryside passing below is a lovely green of fields and forests. England is so beautiful. Off to the west are hills. Tiny villages are everywhere and cities dot the landscape, all connected by roads and railroad tracks. Trains speed along the tracks, leaving trails of coal smoke. Trucks are the principal vehicles on roads, and I see long convoys of military vehicles moving south. As we fly over southern England, I gaze at military camps that I have not seen previously. The south of England—that area south of London—is a vast collection of armies. There are long rows of tents and parks filled with tanks, trucks, jeeps, and artillery guns. An immense amount of military gear is moving to the south coast. It looks like the invasion is getting very close, probably just a few weeks away. From my seat above it, the operation looks like a motion picture from Hollywood. Will the armies cross the twenty miles between Dover and Calais to land on the Pas de Calais? I am certain that an invasion across the English Channel to the Pas de Calais is the reason why we keep flying over the Pas de Calais. I assume that the major and his boys are collecting intelligence.

After a steep climb to a chilly 15,000 feet while I put on my oxygen mask, we sweep over the coastal cliffs, and I gaze down at sunlight glinting on blue water. The Channel is pretty today. It is also surprisingly empty, so I turn my attention to the sky. The closer we get to the French coast, the more likely is the chance of meeting German fighter planes. We race along silently for a time. The pilot applies full power and points toward a spot on the approaching French coast. I remember that German radar has tracked us since we left England. I watch the sky and listen on the radio for an abort message. A quick glance shows the French coast racing toward us. We charge across it, but now I am too intent on the sky to spend much time admiring the beauty of France. I glance down to see an engine pulling a long train of flat cars carrying German tanks. The Pas de Calais is filling with tanks and guns. There must be a whole German army down there.

"Ready with the camera," the navigator calls.

I open the trap door, flop onto the floor, and put my hand on the camera controls. The camera seems to be in good working order, just as the photo technician told me.

"Camera's ready," I reply.

There is a pause. I hear antiaircraft fire bursting around us. That's a first. The Germans are getting touchy.

The radio emits our call letters and a burst of code. I jump up, write the message from memory, and decode it quickly.

"Major, we have an abort message!"

"OK, let's get the hell out of here!" he barks.

The bomber banks sharply to head north as he applies full power. The surge pushes me back in my seat. The coast is just ahead, and he puts us into a shallow dive to increase speed. The big plane begins to hum, and then sing, and then vibrate as he increases speed. We cross the French coast, and I gaze upward. Two German fighter planes are coming toward us from the east.

"Fighters are closing on us from three o'clock high!" I yell.

"I see them," the major says. "I don't think they like us."

While I watch the fighters approach, our plane roars out over the twenty miles of English Channel. The English coast is closer by the minute, as our shallow dive speeds us along. The fighters don't try to head us off. Instead, they continue to fly along the French coast.

"They seem to be ignoring us," I report.

"That's what I expected," the major says. "They just wanted to shoo us away, although they would have popped us if we'd given them the chance."

"Did you guys see what was ahead when we crossed the coast?" the navigator says. "It looked like they were bringing in big reinforcements."

"They didn't want us to take pictures of it," the major says.

Back on the ground at the base, I gather up my gear. The major saunters over and shakes hands.

"OK, sport," he says, "I figure this was the last mission that we fly from here. As soon as I get back to my office, I'll get the paperwork going on your transfer and direct commission. Just relax and try to avoid any more bomber missions. I'll see what I can do to help out on that."

"Thank you. I appreciate it."

He waves and gets into a waiting car with his lieutenants. They speed away around the perimeter track. I trudge to a waiting jeep for a ride back to get rid of my flying gear and return to my quarters.

"Where you been?" Ken Tasker says. "Were you flying again?"

I nod.

"I had to fly on another errand."

He grins, shakes his head, and walks off.

"Oh, somebody's sure got it in for you," he calls back. "You're an unlucky guy."

I lie back on my bunk and sigh. All of a sudden, I feel pretty lucky. That was my twenty-third mission. Even if I didn't transfer to a safe job, I have just seven missions left to fly, and only six of them have the potential to be tough. This is good because I have had enough scares and close calls. If I can avoid bomber missions until the transfer comes through, I will survive to go home after the war in Europe ends. I can also hold Jane in my arms all of the time, and I know where that will lead.

But nothing is certain in war.

CHAPTER 28

Ten Days with Jane

It's the first day of May. The sun shines and my world smiles. I live on aspirin, barbiturate, amphetamine, and paregoric, but they keep me flying, and I only have to survive seven missions. I've flown twenty-three times into that cold sky, where death is so quick and unexpected. There were too many close calls, but I'm still here. I never thought that I would live this long. Now, if a transfer to the major's group occurs before I fly any more missions, my days of combat are over. What could be a rosier outlook than that?

Squadron operations removed the administrator-pilot from our crew, which caused much joy and celebration among us. Unfortunately, there were no available pilots that were not members of crews, so the squadron operations officer disbanded our crew. Now, one or another of us will fly only if a crew needs a replacement. We are sort of like the steno pool in a big office, we wait around to fill in if a crew member is sick or injured. If I can avoid being a replacement for a few weeks, my promotion and transfer to the major's group will occur, and this new lieutenant (me, that is) will keep his feet planted on the ground as a communications officer.

The world brightens further when I get a call to squadron headquarters. The first sergeant stands in the office with a big grin.

"This is your lucky day," he says. "I don't know how you rate it, but group headquarters has given you a ten-day leave, beginning today."

I detect the hand of the major arranging the time off to keep me from combat until the transfer comes through. This will be ten days when no one can shoot at me.

"OK, get out of here as fast as you can," the first sergeant says. "You don't want someone to change his mind and cancel your leave, so move!"

I grab my ten-day leave order and run back to my quarters. I have not seen Lloyd or Greg since yesterday, and Ken and Ed are not around at the moment, so I pack my bag and leave without being able to say goodbye to those great guys.

Most flyers on a ten-day leave go north to Edinburgh, Scotland, but I head south to London and Jane. Spring is here, and the panorama passing outside the window of my compartment on the train is a delicate green. The ladies and gentlemen in my compartment probably think that I am an idiot because I smile at everything. But I can't stop smiling. I am on my way to see Jane, and it looks like we will have a life together.

Two hours later, I arrive at Jane's flat to awaken her and tell her, between kisses, that we can spend ten days together. She screams and kisses me more. I have never seen her so happy. This experience of a first romance is wonderful.

"We shall go away, love," she says. "I know a place that's lovely and peaceful. You can rest, and I shall have ten days to make you well. By the time I finish, you will be tip-top."

Chattering excitedly, she dresses quickly and rushes away to the theater to arrange time off. I stretch out on her bed and gaze at the familiar ceiling of her bedroom. I feel the best that I have felt in months. I have never known a girl like Jane. She actually loves me. *She loves me!* I shake my head in wonder. I never dreamed that I would fall in love with an English girl. I also never thought that I had a future, except to die on a bombing mission, but can we have a future together? Is it what she wants? I think that she does, but I wish I understood women.

By the time Jane returns, she has our destination set. I marvel at how quickly she arranges things and packs. She sings while she bustles around the flat. It's clear that she is happy.

"I've never seen anyone get ready so fast," I say.

"I'm so frightfully excited. I simply can't wait to get you alone, all to myself, for ten days."

"We're alone here."

"Oh, you silly boy, I mean truly alone—away from the bloody war. I want to be away from air raids and noisy streets and crowded

sidewalks and drunken soldiers and the whole lot of it. I want peace
and quiet so I can work my wiles on you."

"You've already worked your wiles on me."

"Just you wait, love. Just you wait."

We soon sit together in the comfort of a first-class compartment
on a train racing westward out of London. Again, Jane looks like
Hollywood's picture of a proper librarian—a pretty, blond librarian—as she gazes coolly through her glasses at the well-dressed passengers in our compartment. Her blond hair is pulled back into the
usual, neat bun on the back of her head, with not a hair out of
place. A pert little hat perches on her head, and she wears an attractive blue suit that we purchased somewhere. I notice a gold wed-
ding band on her finger.

"It belonged to my grandmother," she whispers in response to
my questioning look. "Mum gave it to me to wear when I marry, but
I'll wear it now so we look proper at the inn where we'll stay."

"Just like that, I acquired a wife," I whisper with a grin.

"You acquired her some time ago, darling," she says with a
bewitching look that turns me to jelly. "You simply didn't know it."

I gape, as usual, causing her to smile smugly.

The vista outside the window is bright green and sparkling in
sunshine. It matches my rising spirits as Jane and I watch the changing panorama of dark forests, open fields, far-off hills, and nearby
villages that go past while the train speeds along the track. I have
noticed that most English in first class do not speak, unlike Americans on a train. The well-dressed English read a newspaper, gaze
out the window, or stare at a point above my head. It's interesting,
but I would rather watch the scenery passing outside, while Jane sits
primly beside me.

After several hours of dashing through one town after another
on its way westward, the train slows while rows of small houses and
sheds appear outside. They are soon replaced by two-story, dark
gray or brown stone houses and commercial buildings. The train
slows more, and our car sways while it rumbles over switches and
crossovers, while grimy railroad workers watch us pass. The train
snakes into a city, and we pass buildings that appear to be very old.
Hissing and clanging, the engine pulls us into a large station and

squeals to a halt. Jane rises while the other passengers file out through the door to the platform beside us.

"We have arrived, love" she says with an excited grin. "This is Bath."

She pronounces it something like "Bahth" and chatters breathlessly while we hurry from the station and climb into a taxi. Her instructions to the driver are so rapid and British that they go right past me, but he nods with half-closed eyes and away we go. We drive past shops and stone buildings while Jane hugs my arm. Soon, we leave Bath, speed down a highway through rural countryside for a time, and then turn off onto a narrow road. From there, we turn onto one country lane after another until the taxi pulls up at a small inn located in a village. Jane says that the inn dates back to the 1700s. It is breathtaking. Downstairs, I see a restaurant and pub. Big, dark beams cross the ceilings.

Upstairs, our large, airy room is clean and bright. The trim is white, and the walls are white with pink flowers. The huge bed is amazingly soft. When I sink into it, I feel as if I am floating in water. Jane whips off her hat and glasses, wiggles out of her suit, loosens her hair, dons a robe, and cuddles beside me, far from bombing raids, London crowds, and war.

"Isn't this nice?" she says.

"It is heaven."

"You may lie here for ten days, if you like, while I pamper you with sweets and love and all manner of pleasures."

"Being here with you is all I want. This is the happiest that I've been in a long, long time." I turn to face her. "I owe you so much. You're the reason that I haven't gone crazy these past months."

"Darling, I will do anything in the world for you."

To have this pretty blonde say that to me overwhelms me. How can I be so lucky?

Outside, the sun shines, and I hear birds singing. When did I last have the chance to lie at ease and listen to birds sing? A dog barks in the distance. Otherwise, the village is so quiet that I can hear the breeze blowing in through the window to make the lacy, white curtains swing. I turn and gaze into lustrous, blue eyes.

"Jane, I've wanted to ask you a question for a long time. You say you love me, and I'm sure you do, but why me? You must have dozens of men after you. I'm not handsome, and I have health problems from flying. Why have you even looked twice at me? It may sound silly, but I would really like to know."

She smiles tenderly.

"When I first saw you at the theater, I thought you were just another sex-crazed Yank who thought that I would simply beg you to give me a quick one, and you could brag about it to your friends. A lot of Yanks think they are God's gift to us sex-starved British girls. But then I felt that something about you was different. That is why I agreed to have dinner with you. By the time we finished dinner, I was attracted to you, and after we talked more at my flat, I couldn't let you go. I felt that I had found the man that I always dreamed of finding. Everything that has happened since then tells me that I was correct."

She gazes at me with a calculating look.

"And what about you? Why haven't you loved me and left me as so many Yanks do to our British lasses?"

"The morning after we spent our first night together, I looked at you all dressed to go to the Park Lane, and something clicked. You were everything that I ever dreamed about in a girl. After that, I wanted to be with you all the time."

We lie silently for many minutes. Eventually, Jane stirs and gazes at me.

"What is your wish, sire?" she asks. "To lie here? To sleep? To dream? To eat? To have your way with me?"

"How would you like to take a long walk?"

"Oh, that is indeed romantic. It says that you are not merely interested in my nude body."

"I'm interested in every inch of you and everything about you."

"I'm happy to hear it. I shall find some walking clothes."

Outside, Jane and I explore the village. It is tiny, and I count about thirty homes. There may be more that I don't see, but the place is still very small. Many of the homes are cottages with thatched roofs, but there are some attractive, two-story homes. Most houses have flower boxes under the windows, and I smile to see flowers that look like pansies beginning to bloom in some boxes. Red and orange and yellow tulips grow in flower beds. The few villagers that we see go about their business without staring at us. When we finish walking around the village, Jane turns to me.

"We can go north, south, east, or west. What do you wish?"

"Let's begin by going north."

Hand in hand, we walk down country lanes, across open fields, over hills, and through stands of open woodland where I stop to gaze at, and listen to, an amazing populace of birds chirping and singing. The sky is clear. The sun shines, and except for birds, it is blissfully quiet. Toward day's end, we wander back to the inn, tired but relaxed. Before dinner, we meet the residents of the two other rooms at the inn. Both couples are elderly and English, and they seem to be fascinated by the American flyer and his English wife.

Everyone dresses for dinner, and the inn rewards us with what Jane says is excellent sherry and a delicious meal that finishes with cheese and a fruit tart. I gaze across the table at Jane.

"I've been saving some good news to tell you."

Her blue eyes widen and stare at me.

"I do welcome good news. What is it, love?"

"Sometime soon, I will transfer to another group as a communications officer. I'll be a lieutenant, but the most important thing is that I won't fly any more. There'll be no more danger and no chance of being killed, unless I get hit by a truck or something."

Her eyes open wide. Her mouth opens, and her face seems to radiate.

"Darling, that's smashing!" she gasps. "This is the best news that I have heard in ages. You will be safe!"

I see tears filling her eyes. This girl is really emotional. Pearleen never cried, so I never before had to cope with a girl's tears. Jane turns me to jelly each time the tears come.

"Jane, please don't cry. This is really happy news."

"Oh, love, I know I'm a silly cow, but I'm so happy. I worry about you every day. I sometimes hear the bombers go out. I simply know that you are on one of them, and I pray that you will return safely. When another of your letters comes, I hold it against my heart and feel so relieved that you are safe. Now, I will be able to stop worrying."

"The doctor says I should feel much better after I start my new job. In fact, I should soon be almost normal. It's good news all around."

"You were to return to the United States when you complete your thirty missions. I hate the thought of you leaving. What will happen in your new assignment? Will you still return to America?"

"No, I'll be in England until the war ends. We can be together all that time. Think of the happy times that we can have together."

"Oh, darling, I would like that very much," she says with a big smile.

The next day brings a long walk to the west. When we return, a tail-wagging dog meets us. Jane picks up a stick and throws it, sending the dog in a happy chase for the stick. When the dog prances back with the stick in its mouth, we begin a session of throw the stick and bring it back. Each day after that, the dog waits outside the inn for us to play throw-the-stick with it.

When we return from another walk the following day, we find a gray-striped cat at the inn. While we sit in the quiet pub with a pint of Guinness, the cat pussyfoots around to carefully sniff us and check us out. We quickly make friends with it. Cats seem to like me. I tell Jane how my father felt that "a boy should have a dog." But when he brought a dog home for me, I had little interest in it, so he gave it away. Again and still again, he brought home a different breed of dog, and each time had the same result. Years later, my mother found a tiny, gray and white, abandoned kitten crying by our back door. Within minutes, the kitten and I fell in love with each other. Since mothers know everything, I asked her whether it was a boy cat or girl cat. She took a quick look and pronounced it a girl, so I named it Ginny, the name of a singer with one of the big bands. But it soon became clear that Ginny was a vigorous male.

I tended Ginny, played with him, and treasured him. He grew into a big, tough tomcat, universally feared by the neighborhood dogs. After their first experience with a painful swipe from his claws, accompanied by a growl that would do justice to a wildcat, they ran when he strutted through the neighborhood with his tail straight up. But with me, he purred, rubbed against me, and slept in my lap. Before I left for combat in England, he rubbed his cheek against my face repeatedly. My mother felt that he sensed that I was leaving, and he was telling me goodbye. Now, my mother tells me in letters that Ginny sits patiently and stares at the front door, waiting for me to return. Hearing this brings tears to Jane's eyes. She loves animals, and the local dogs and cats seem to sense this.

During the next day's walk, things take a turn. We sit on a big rock beside a path leading through open woodland. It is a bright afternoon, and I admire tiny, white flowers that grow in an open space across the path from us. The peaceful setting is a striking contrast to the horror of war. In fact, our entire stay in the village brings peace that I have not felt since I left the university.

"Are you happy, love?" Jane says.

"I couldn't be happier." I smile at her. "Being with you makes everything right."

She cocks her head and stares at me.

"I wonder what the future holds for us."

I can tell that she is trying to be light, but I sense that this is a serious question to her. I realize that it also is a serious question for me. I'm an idiot concerning romance, but I have never been as happy in my young life as I have been with Jane. I see that it's time for a decision, but I must be careful. We're suddenly talking about serious stuff that affects two people's lives. I take a deep breath and look at her pretty face.

"You know that I haven't felt that I have a future," I say, "but once I stop flying, we could have a future. Would you   ?"

My throat suddenly closes, and I can hardly get out those last words, but she gazes at me with a little smile that women have probably worn for hundreds of years at times like this.

"Yes, darling, go on," she says.

She's way ahead of me.

"Jane, I—I—" I begin to say, but my mouth seems to be filled with talcum powder, and my throat has closed.

I gaze helplessly at her. I am afraid that she will either laugh or become angry with me, but she does neither. She cups my face in her hands and smiles. Her eyes glisten, and her face seems to glow.

"I love you," she says. "You have told me in your letters that you love me. Is that what you are trying to tell me now?"

I nod helplessly.

"I thought as much," she says. "Try again and remember that you are not speaking to Parliament. It is the woman who loves you that is listening."

I nod my head and try again.

"I love you," I gasp.

For a moment, a chill grips me as I wonder if I have just jinxed us by letting things get too serious too soon, but I dismiss the thought when I see the happiness on Jane's face and feel the same happiness inside me.

"And our future will be together?" she says. "Do you want that?"

I nod.

"You have made me very happy, and I shall not try at the moment to get you to pop the question, as you Yanks put it." She giggles. "We might sit here all night."

We spend a long time holding each other, while birds sing and insects chirp around us.

That evening, as we enjoy another delicious dinner, we see the gray cat stepping carefully past the restaurant entrance.

"I would dearly love to have a cat," Jane says. "I would very much like to make friends with Ginny and pamper him the way I want to pamper you."

"Ginny will love you. He'll sleep on your lap."

Later, we settle into the huge bed. There is a new bond between us. We love each other, and we look forward to being together forever.

"How are you feeling, darling?" Jane says softly.

"I feel better than I ever have in my life. How about you? Are you happy?"

"Darling, I'm ecstatic. I see happiness ahead for us."

The next morning, I wake up to an amazing realization. Jane had been so passionate the previous evening that I forgot to take my sleeping capsules, but I slept through the night without a nightmare. I turn to see if Jane is awake, and face her blue eyes gazing intently at me. When I tell her, she smiles triumphantly.

"I knew that something good had happened. You were sleeping so peacefully."

At breakfast, I look up from my eggs, bacon, and toast to the kipper that Jane is preparing to devour. It sits there, a medium-size, brown fish with big eyes.

"I suppose at breakfast ten years from now, I will still have one of your smoked fish staring at me from your plate."

She giggles.

"Ten years from now, I will have taught you to simply adore kippers."

"Ugh."

"Well, perhaps not, and I will instead eat your beloved eggs and other bewildering, American things, such as hamburgers, which do not contain a bit of ham."

"Or hot dogs, which do not—"

"Please do not pursue that thought while I am eating."

"OK, but how about eating doughnuts?"

"That is going too far. I shall be quite firm about it."

At that, we burst into laughter. It feels good to laugh.

"Love, you seem almost a different person. You are so relaxed and happy."

"I feel like the person I was before I began flying bombing missions, except I feel even better." I reach across the table and take her hand. I believe I can say it now. "I love you, and I'm looking forward to a wonderful future—with you."

Somehow, I get the words out. She smiles.

"Would you like to have a change from long walks?" Jane asks. "Today, would you like to go into Bath to see the Roman baths?"

"So that's why they call the place Bath. I am certainly bright not to have thought of it."

"I think you are quite brilliant—a bit innocent—but brilliant."

"If I'm so brilliant, how did I let myself get into the military?"

We get a ride into Bath with the innkeeper. We cross the River Avon on the Pultaney Bridge, a stone, covered bridge that has shops lining both sides of the bridge itself. Amazing! With a cheery wave, the innkeeper drops us off on the west side of the bridge. I gape at the buildings and shops of a spectacular, ancient city. Jane has obviously been here before. After a moment to get her bearings, she takes my arm, heads south for two or three blocks, and stops. I stare upward at the Abbey, a breathtaking cathedral that soars into the blue. We enter and gaze at handsome, stone archways, vaulted ceilings, and immense, stained glass windows.

After we leisurely inspect the Abbey, Jane steers me down the street a short distance to face an imposing building with Roman figures carved into the stonework.

"This is the Roman bath, love," Jane says.

We enter, and I gaze down at a vast, rectangular pool of green water. It resembles a huge swimming pool. I wonder if the green comes from minerals in the water, thermal bacteria, or from the pool's finish. The pool has no roof over it, but a stone deck runs around it on the lower level, and a covered balcony runs around it where we stand. At intervals along our balcony are stone statues of Roman soldiers and statesmen.

"The Roman bath is 2,000 years old," Jane says. "As I understand it, water from mountains to the north goes deep within the earth and emerges at a spring under this building. The water is very hot. If I recall correctly, it comes from the earth at something like 120 degrees, and it comes out in amazing quantity. I heard that the spring puts out something like 240,000 gallons per day."

The Roman bath is amazingly intricate, with two levels, many rooms, and several smaller baths. Jane and I wander through its passageways. In a deep chamber, we gaze at the water intake for the baths via a huge conduit.

"The Romans built the water system," Jane says. "I was told that they fashioned lead pipes to conduct the water."

In a section of the bath called The Pump Room, we sample the water, said to have medicinal powers. Jane says that the taste is unusual. I say that the taste is terrible.

After lunch, we explore Bath. It has a medieval look that I find fascinating, but Jane is interested in shopping. Some people are drug addicts. Jane is a shopping addict. Bath has numerous alleys, called passages, lined with shops. Jane attacks these until I believe that she has visited every shop in central Bath. Only then do we take a taxi back to the inn.

We discuss a trip to Stonehenge, but the next morning brings a gray dawn, with rain pelting the window, so we sleep late and spend the day talking happily about our future. Jane has a million more questions about life in the United States. I tell her that the American military has made marriage between American military personnel and English citizens a complicated procedure. I suspect that it is to discourage brief romances that will end quickly in divorce. I heard that the military will send shiploads of British brides to the United States after the war ends, and I promise to get the needed information.

The days in the country pass in idyllic togetherness. Again and again, I think of how I have never felt so relaxed and happy since I put on a uniform a million, miserable years ago.

Toward the end of our stay, we sit on a log beside a country lane outside the village. Jane's doe-like eyes gaze at me through her glasses.

"Darling, I believe it would be fitting now for you to meet my parents. Are you willing?"

"Yes, I would like that."

She gives me an adoring smile.

"We will have a wonderful future, darling," she says.

A cold fist grips my heart. I should not have let this get so serious. I'm afraid it will jinx us. Wait! I'm a scientist. There is no such thing as jinxing, and Jane looks so happy. We hold each other while we sit joyfully in a peaceful oasis in the midst of war.

As with anything wonderful, the ten days eventually end. Rested and happy, we return to London for a hopeful goodbye at St. Pancras Station.

"Next time that I see you, we should have something to celebrate," she says through tears. "I simply can't wait."

"My transfer will probably be waiting when I get to the base, and I'll write immediately to tell you. When we see each other again, we'll celebrate and make plans. Now, please make that pretty face smile for me. I want to keep your face in my memory until I see you again."

With that adoring puppy dog look in her blue eyes behind glasses, she smiles.

"I'll be waiting," she says. "I am so happy."

"I'll see you soon."

"I love you."

"And I love you."

After many kisses, I run to board the London, Midland, and Scotland Railroad for the familiar trip to Wellingboro. As I enter the station, I turn and look back. She waves and smiles while tears run down her cheeks.

CHAPTER 29

Trouble Ahead

By mid-May, the nature of air operations has changed noticeably. Our fighters have destroyed huge numbers of German planes, and our destruction of aircraft factories and supporting industries has limited the Germans' ability to replace them. In fact, allied bombing has destroyed much of German industry. The result has been fewer attacks on our missions to France and western Germany. In eastern Germany, you can still expect vicious attacks, but the overall result has been good. I heard that our goal is to have the air free of German planes when our troops invade France.

Missions have become a bit less wearing. The new B-17G is much more comfortable than the B-17F, and our fighters sweep the sky ahead of the bomber formation and provide close cover. Still, missions are always dangerous.

As for me, I feel like a million dollars. I want to jump over the moon. A new job is ahead, and a pretty blonde who loves me is waiting in London. At 92nd Group headquarters, I search out the personnel clerk that handled my transfer to the new group and ask him where my transfer stands.

"No news," he says. "All the papers have been approved here and at your new group. The transfer would normally go through fast, but your direct commission to lieutenant is tied to it, so it has to go through Bomber Command for approval, and that's likely to take a month. One of the guys there told me that they are awfully busy right now, but I figure that it should be here soon."

I'm sure that I look disappointed.

"Hey, don't sweat it," he says. "You had a ten-day leave, and it got you off operations. I heard that you're supposed to stay off missions unless there's an emergency. Sit back and wait for the colonel to pin those gold bars on you. Then, you can give me five bucks for being the first guy to salute you, and you can pack up and go to your new home."

During the following days, I loaf at the base while it runs its usual operations. I write to Jane and work on my university lesson. Lloyd is away somewhere, but I sometimes see Ken, Ed, and Greg. They are available to fill in if a crew needs a gunner. I don't dare tell them about the transfer, because the major drilled into me the need for secrecy about our flights. I don't know whether it applies to my transfer, but I can't take any chances. I hate it that I can't tell them. I don't like secrets.

While Jane and I were at the village, I heard no news from the outside world. It was wonderful, but now I must join the world again. The BBC reports that the invasion of Europe is expected to come any day. British and American light and medium bombers are hitting targets all over France, especially air bases, railroad yards, and bridges. The Soviet Army is attacking on a broad front in the East. Allied forces in Italy are poised to capture Rome, and our Pacific forces are pushing the Japanese off one island after another. One of the clerks in my building said that he saw convoys of troops, tanks, and guns filling the nearby roads heading south, so the invasion must be very close. I don't tell anyone, but I bet that they will invade the Pas de Calais. That would explain our hush-hush flights.

While I was gone, the 92nd Group flew three missions to Berlin, one to Merseburg, one to Stettin, and several to France. Despite these tough targets, the group lost only two bombers. Two months ago, we would have lost more than a dozen on those missions. It shows how opposition by German fighters is weakening.

I walk in the country for relaxation. One day, I saunter for about ten miles and enter the ancient village of Bozeat, to the southwest of Podington. I thought that the buildings in Podington looked old, but this place appears to date back even further. Once I begin acting like a tourist, several villagers are happy to tell me about its history. It dates all the way back to the Iron Age. There are Roman earthworks and evidence of a Saxon village here. The place certainly looks ancient, with weathered cottages and worn bricks in walls and shops that appear to have been there for hundreds of years. I visit St. Mary's Church (another St. Mary's), a handsome church of ancient, tan stone. They tell me that it was built in about 1130, a fact that blows my mind, but they say that its beginnings are even earlier. It was built on the site of a church dating back to the sixth century. I think that Bozeat is an unusual name, but the villagers can't tell me the name's origin. One says that he believes that Bosa was an ancient Saxon name, and zeat, or something similar, meant gate, but I gather that they really don't know. It is a fascinating village, and it gives me the eerie feeling of connecting with an England of so long ago that Roman soldiers tramped across the countryside.

The next day, I am off to Wollaston, a town to the west of Podington and about four miles south of Wellingboro. The day is bright, the birds sing, and the walk makes me feel even better than yesterday. I find Wollaston to be much larger than Podington village. It looks to have around 3,000 people living there. Naturally, it has a High Street that is narrow and lined on both sides by old, brick buildings containing shops and homes. I wander along High Street and London Road, and Queen's Road, and Rotten Row. The people are busy—too busy to stop and talk with an American tourist—but in the shops, I learn a bit about Wollaston. The town is industrial and, like so many of the villages and towns in the area, manufactures shoes and boots. As I expected, the town dates back for centuries. St. Mary's Church (still another St. Mary's) is a handsome edifice of light brown stone that dates from the 1300s. One shopkeeper tells me that the town originally had a Saxon name. It was something like Wulflaf's Town, which converted over the centuries to Wollaston. Another told me that the oldest part of Wollaston is Beacon Hill, which is actually the earthwork of an ancient castle that dates back to the 1100s. Thus, I spend a pleasant day in Wollaston and even get a ride back to Podington for a short walk back to the airbase.

My tour of nearby towns and villages continues when I get a ride to Olney, a small town south of Bozeat and about twenty miles south-southwest of Podington. Like Bozeat, Olney is ancient and exudes character. You can feel the connection all the way back to the Middle Ages in its homes and shops and churches. I meet people that are eager to tell me about the town, and one promptly stuns me by saying that the first recorded mention of Olney was in 878 in the Treaty of Wedmore. I don't know the Treaty of Wedmore, but I learn from my new acquaintances that it was a treaty between the Saxons and the English that divided England into a northern part ruled by the Saxons from Denmark, and a southern part ruled by the English. As I stand in the town market, I am overwhelmed by the thought of standing in a place that dates back that far. I rest on the bank of the tree-lined River Ouse until it is time to return to the airbase.

Visiting nearby villages and towns is fun, but I have a chance to go back to Cambridge again, and I jump at it. This time, the pleasure of being at a great university is heightened when I encounter the Cavendish Laboratory. Every scientist worth the name knows that the Cavendish has some of the world's greatest physicists. It is a thrill just to see it. The visit gives me one pang of unhappiness when I think how much I miss university life. Maybe all of our bombing can help beat the Nazis and end this miserable war. Then, I can take Jane to America and get back to the university.

I'm asleep early in the morning of Saturday, May 20. A terrific explosion slams the building and nearly knocks me out of bed. I stagger to a window. A huge pall of black smoke rises from the airfield and towers above us. As I watch, another blast, and still another, shake the ground and rock our building. They are followed by two more detonations. Smoke billows high into the air and covers the field.

"What happened?" Ken says as we all gather at the windows.

"Are the Germans bombing us?" someone asks.

"There's a mission today," Ed says. "I bet a plane's bombs went off accidentally."

That makes sense. We dress and hurry to the airfield while more smoke boils upward and towers ever-higher in the sky. The mass of smoke is awesome. As we near the field, the source of smoke and explosions becomes clear in an inferno that we face. Halfway down the runway, two bombers burn fiercely. From the position of their rudders, it looks like they ran head-on into each other. Past the end of the runway, another column of smoke rises, and someone says that it's from another burning bomber.

It takes time before we piece together the story of the accident. The airbase was thick with fog when the 92nd Group's bombers prepared to take off. A B-17 flown by Lieutenant Jack Pearl, one of our new pilots, couldn't make it off the ground and crashed into the woods beyond the end of the runway. Hearing this, the control tower ordered takeoffs to stop. The next B-17 in line was already rolling down the runway. Hearing the order, it skidded to a stop and turned around to return to its take off position. But the next bomber in line failed to hear the call from the control tower and continued to speed down the foggy runway. Suddenly, there was the first plane. The B-17s crashed head-on and exploded in flames. Several crewmembers jumped from the burning planes before the bombs aboard the B-17s detonated. The final blast came from the bombs on the B-17 that crashed beyond the end of the runway. Eventually, we hear that crashes and explosions killed eighteen crewmembers of the three bombers. What a tragedy!

The 92nd Bomb Group will be out of action while workers clean up the wreckage and repair the runway. Repair crews work day and night. By Tuesday, May 23, the group can take off to bomb Saarbrucken, followed by a mission to Berlin on May 24. As had happened all month, I do not fly on these missions. I relax and wait for my transfer from the group. The word I get is that the transfer and promotion will come any day now.

I want to go back to London to see Jane, but I must fly on errands with Colonel Brousseau on Tuesday, Wednesday, Thursday, and Friday. I admire the countryside while I ride along on these low-altitude flights. On Saturday, I don't get a call to fly, so I check again on my transfer. Any day now, the clerk says.

That night, I get a shock. My name is on the bulletin board for a mission the next day with a crew that I don't know.

"This is a surprise," I say to the first sergeant.

"It's a fairly new crew," he says. "Their radio operator left a fork, tines up, in a cup on the floor by his double deck bunk. He wasn't watching when he jumped off the top bunk. His foot landed on the fork and ran the tines into it. What a dumb-ass trick. The upshot is that he's crippled and can't fly. The orders are that you don't fly unless there's an emergency, but we don't have another radio operator available, so it's an emergency, and you'll have to go." He smiles. "Maybe your transfer will be waiting when you get back."

I nod unhappily and leave. I have a bad feeling about this. A headache begins on my way back to my barracks. When I get ready for bed, I notice that I'm trembling. There's only one thing to do. Out come the barbiturate capsules and I swallow two.

May 28, 1944. My bad feeling about the mission is there as soon as a voice from the darkness calls and someone shakes me awake from a drugged sleep. Lloyd, Ed, Ken, and Greg are sleeping peacefully, and I envy them. Unhappy at facing a mission, I wait for two amphetamines to take effect during my usual breakfast of fried eggs, fried Spam, toast, and coffee. I secretly hoped that I was finished with bombing missions, but there is always someone who messes up, so I must fly one more time. I hope that guy's foot is OK by the time we return.

The bad feeling gets worse while I sit nervously on a bench in the briefing room, waiting for the curtain covering the map to draw back. The buzz of conversation halts when the briefing officers, captains and lieutenants, stride to the front of the room. I cross my fingers and shut my eyes. I hear muttering among the seated flyers. Is it good or bad? I open my eyes and peer at the long, red line on the map. A cold fist grips me. The line extends all the way across Germany. We are flying a tremendous distance to bomb a synthetic oil factory at Ruhland, in southeastern Germany. It is not too far from Sorau, our target on that disastrous mission on April 11, when the group lost eight planes, and we carried poor, dead John Kindred to the target and back. German fighters will have hours to attack us. I wonder if it will be a repeat of the April 11 killing.

By the time a truck drops me at my assigned B-17G, my head is splitting, despite four aspirins. I shouldn't take that many. The doctor said that I could bleed to death on a mission if I take that much aspirin, but I can't fly with a headache this bad. The pain is pure agony. I shake like a person with palsy. There is nothing like a nasty mission to wipe out all the good from ten days with Jane in a peaceful village. I try to hide my shaking when I meet the new crew, but they must notice that I'm pretty weird.

The pilot is Victor Trost, a first lieutenant with an easy smile and an air of competence. The copilot, Richard Funk, is small, wiry, and friendly. The navigator is Franklin Burks from Arkansas, an affable, literate fellow. The sergeant bombardier is Joseph Topolosky, quiet but smiling as we shake hands. The flight engineer is Bill Honaker, young, handsome, and definitely a ladies' man. The ball-turret gunner is Samuel Johnson, a freckled redhead from Steubenville, Ohio, and a thoroughly nice guy. The waist gunner is Milt Powell from Texas, tall, rugged, and courteous. The tail gunner is George Keith, another handsome one and as friendly as they come. They look good to me. As long as I have to fly, I'm happy it's with them. I only hope that they don't think I'm too strange, but they seem to understand my weirdness when I say that this is my twenty-fourth mission. Everyone knows that some of the veterans have "combat fatigue" and act weird.

This time, I have to force myself to climb into the bomber. Every cell in my body yells to me, "Leave! Run! You made it twenty-three times. Don't take any more chances!" All of my confidence is gone. Still, I smile at George Keith and Milt Powell while I clomp through the waist compartment to enter the radio room. Today, there is no camera and no chaff. The compartment is neat and clean, and the radio mechanic says that everything is in top shape. I'm not surprised. The bomber looks new. He gives me a pat on the shoulder for luck and leaves.

Doors slam shut, and the engines start. A cold fist grabs me. I don't want to go. I want to jump out and run, because something tells me that this is the mission that kills me. It's an awful feeling, but I close my eyes, grit my teeth, and sit quietly at my desk. If I don't go, the bomber doesn't go, because there is no one else. I look outside. How I feel doesn't matter now. The B-17 is rolling along the perimeter track, and I can't get out.

We roar into clear, blue sky and climb while circling to assemble the 327th Bomb Squadron, the 92nd Bomb Group, and the 40th Combat Wing formations. The sixty-three B-17s of our bomber fleet join the armada of other combat wings of the 1st Air Division and turn eastward toward the rising sun. Still climbing and getting colder, we reach 10,000 feet above the earth and don oxygen masks as we cross the English coast. After twenty-three missions, I'm still not accustomed to frigid oxygen in my lungs. The North Sea sparkles in sunlight while we cross it. Holland is its usual, pretty landscape of lakes, rivers, and canals surrounded by bright, green fields. Germany is a patchwork of green and brown squares surrounding cities that are centers of networks of roads and railroad tracks radiating from them. I note in my log a record of trains, barges, and everything else that I think may be interesting to group intelligence.

Europe is pretty at the end of May. The intercom is quiet for a long time while we fly over Germany. I gaze down at familiar rivers— the Rhine first, then the Leine, the Weser, and finally the Elbe. We now are deep inside Germany. My trembling has become outright shaking, and my heart beats fast. When will German fighters hit us? My headache is so bad that I'm becoming nauseated. Don't let it happen, I tell myself. If you clog your oxygen mask, you will die.

To take my mind off my throbbing head and heaving stomach, I look back along the top of the bomber. Far behind us, it looks like a big formation of B-24 bombers is over Merseburg, probably bombing the synthetic oil plants. The sky back there is black from the anti-aircraft barrage, and bursts surround the bombers. I see stuttering flashes of the blasts, and black puffs of smoke surround the huge, central cloud of blackness. A shell hits a B-24. The big plane explodes in the familiar ball of boiling, orange fire. Pieces of the B-24 trail black smoke as they drop toward the ground below. The guys in the plane didn't have a chance. Another B-24 is going down in flames, leaving a long trail of black smoke. Still, I envy the planes in the B-24 formation. They are turning away from the target and heading home. We still have a long way to go to reach Ruhland.

"Fighters!" someone yells.

I see ten silver FW-190s. They turn in our direction and dive. A cold fist grabs my insides, and I'm paralyzed as I watch them. They bank and slash through another group in our combat wing. Fire gushes from a B-17, like water from broken pipe. The plane turns over on its back and spirals down while it blazes from nose to tail. No one gets out. I brace for another attack, but none comes. From beneath the plane in the ball turret, Sam reports that the German fighters have moved below and behind us, and are attacking another Group.

We fly on in sunshine, but broken clouds increasingly hide the land below. Where's Ruhland? I don't like being this far into eastern Germany. It brings back too many memories of the terrible April 11 raid aimed at Sorau, where thick cloud sent us to Stettin.

The 1st Air Division's combat wings separate. Some head for Ruhland, and others go toward Dessau. Now we have fewer bombers to fight off German attacks. It is a lonely feeling to be this deep in Germany.

"Fighters!" someone yells on the intercom.

Here they come! Fighters glint in the sunshine as they slam through B-17 formations that seem to be scattered all over the sky. It's a bad arrangement to fight off German attacks. A B-17 explodes in that familiar ball of boiling fire. Other bombers catch fire, while streams of tracer bullets crisscross in the sky. Parachutes appear beneath some burning B-17s, but the rest dive toward the ground, trailing long tails of flames, while they carry their doomed crews down with them.

The 92nd Group has been fortunate thus far. If we have had any attacks, I have not seen them. But the strikes on other Groups have scattered bombers all over the sky. They are everywhere. Still, we press on. My mouth is dry, and the headache is so bad that it makes me even more nauseated. "Don't vomit into your oxygen mask!" I beg myself.

At last, we reach the initial point and turn toward the target. Up comes the antiaircraft fire in a ragged, black box of smoke and flashes of explosions erupting ahead of us. We plunge into the barrage and fly through a cloud of black puffs of smoke from bursting antiaircraft shells. The bomber jumps and rocks from the blasts. The bomb bay doors open, and I look down at clouds with a few breaks that show a city beneath us. We must fly as straight and level as possible to get the bombs placed correctly on the target. This is dangerous because the antiaircraft gunners have their best shot at us. I grit my teeth, waiting for the bombs to drop. Nothing. They don't drop. The group bombardier can't see the target.

We turn away from the target. I sigh. At least we're away from the antiaircraft. Now, if the German fighters that I can see in the distance don't get us, I may survive this unexpected mission.

Wait! We're not leaving the target! The bomber formation turns in a wide circle. No! Let's get away while we can! But I remember that Colonel Brousseau is leading the formation, and come hell or high water, he is determined to hit the target. He's right, of course. We have come all this way to bomb the synthetic oil plant at Ruhland. If we don't destroy it today, we will have to make the long trip across Germany again, maybe tomorrow, and opposition on the way in could be much worse. He continues to lead the fleet of bombers in a wide turn. I bet the German fighters off there in the distance think we're crazy, but we head right back toward Ruhland. Up comes the antiaircraft fire again. The cloud of smoke over the city from exploded shells is pure blackness, and the bursts are closer. I wince as the B-17 rocks and bounces from the force of the blasts. I shake so badly that I can hardly move, but I gaze down through open bomb bay doors. Through a break in the clouds, I see buildings far below us. The bombs drop. I can't see what happens because clouds already cover the target. We turn away. The bomb bay doors close and we head for home.

England is a long way from a spot in Germany southeast of Berlin. I spend the return flight trembling while I expect an attack by German fighters at any minute. To my surprise, we make it unscathed to the coast and let down over the North Sea until we reach the beautiful green of England. I never thought that I would survive this one.

At interrogation, I gulp down my two ounces of Scotch. It burns going down, but I wish that I had more—lots more. I'd like anything that would blot out the terror in my mind that has returned after this mission over Germany. Sitting mute while the crew answers questions about the flight, I realize that my combat fatigue has returned, and it's worse. I should tell the flight surgeon, but he might put me in a mental hospital, and my transfer could fall through.

The only good thing about today is that this mission was my twenty-fourth. Only six left if my transfer doesn't come through first, and the final one of those is supposed to be an easy one, so there are only five stinkers to face.

The Eighth Air Force lost thirty bombers today, while our fighters shot down sixty Germans. Our guys keep shooting them down, but the Germans keep having fighters to hit us. Will it stop before one of those fighters gets the plane I'm in?

I skip dinner and return to my quarters with the hope that my transfer is waiting, but it is not. It should be any day now. A letter from Jane is waiting. I will read it several times and then take two sleeping capsules and crawl into bed. If the capsules do their usual job, they will keep the nightmares away.

"Hey, there's a mission on for tomorrow," someone says.

I don't think that I can face another mission. Maybe the guy I replaced is OK again, or maybe this crew will get a rest, but I had better check. I force myself to get out of bed and stagger to squadron headquarters. I peer dizzily at the bulletin board as the barbiturates begin to overcome me. My heart sinks. There is the same crew, and my name is on the list to fly with it in the morning. A feeling of doom grips me stronger than ever.

"Holy smoke, I'm on to fly again tomorrow," I say to the first sergeant as he walks into the squadron office.

"That guy with the hurt foot still can't fly, so you'll have to replace him, but your transfer is probably on its way here. I bet this will be your last mission."

"I hope so," I say as I leave. "I really hope that this is the last one."

It's only later that the double meaning of my wish hits me. "Last mission" could mean that I'll return to find my transfer and commission waiting. It could also mean that I won't return.

I force that thought from my mind. Despite drowsiness, I scribble a letter to Jane that is full of how much I love her, and how I look forward to our future. When I finish, I smile. Maybe it's the effect of the barbiturate, but things strike me as looking better. After tomorrow's mission, there will be only five left to fly. But before I fly on those, my commission and transfer will arrive. All decked out in my new, officer's uniform, I can go to London and look ahead to the future with Jane. Everything is coming up good. What can possibly go wrong?

CHAPTER 30

Disaster

*M*ay *29, 1944.* A bright light sears my eyes, and something shakes me. I fight to wake up but feel like I'm drowning. Something grips my shoulder. I cry out and open my eyes. A flashlight beam is in my face.

"Take it easy," a voice says from the darkness behind the flashlight. "You awake now? Breakfast in thirty minutes."

I nod and try to stand, but I'm so dizzy from two sleeping capsules that I fall back on the bed. Whoa! The room is whirling!

"Hey, are you OK?" the voice says. "You want me to call the medics? You sure as hell don't look to be in no shape to fly."

I shake my head.

"I'll be OK. I just have to get my pills."

My trembling hands fumble until I dig out my package of amphetamine tablets. After several shaky tries, I fish two out and swallow them.

I sit quietly for five minutes. Then, with quivering hands, I dress in flying coveralls. Wow, I'm shaking all over. Even my head won't hold still. Poor old head. The pain throbs with every beat of my heart. I consider taking aspirin, but I don't want to double over with stomach pain again, and I can't take a chance on my stomach bleeding during a mission. I wipe away tears that the headache pain brings to my eyes and stumble to the latrine before I climb aboard the waiting truck. The rest of the crew is silent when I enter, slump over, and close my eyes. The ride is a blur. By the time I get hot coffee at breakfast (after the usual dose of paregoric), the amphetamine is working, and I feel better. I see the crew that I'll fly with (the same as yesterday) sitting several tables away, but I don't join them. I silently eat my breakfast and think about Jane. The more I think of her, the better I feel. I'm glad that I wrote to her last night

220

to tell her how much I love her. We plan to visit her parents. You know what that means.

The invasion of France will be any day now, and we will bomb the French coast daily to help our ground troops. Those will be easy missions. After today, I will have only five missions left, and five days of bombing the French coast will finish my thirty missions fairly safely, even if my transfer has not come. Maybe today will be the first of the missions to the French coast.

But at briefing, my heart sinks when the captain pulls back the curtain. I stare at a red line stretching far across Germany, while the captain tells us that we are going to bomb an aircraft factory outside of Cottbus, a city in eastern Germany. It is southeast of Berlin again, almost to the Polish border. German fighters will have plenty of time to get at us. We made it across Germany yesterday. Can our luck hold today? General Doolittle must feel confident, because the Eighth Air Force will break up into small units to bomb many targets in eastern Germany. Will our group be alone when we reach Cottbus? Our fighters will have a difficult time helping everyone. Still, I bet my transfer will be waiting when we get back.

After briefing, I decide that I won't need to wear my electrically-heated suit. On the new B-17G, the cabin is cold at the end of May, but not frigid. Flying coveralls and leather jacket should be enough, so I grab my yellow life jacket and parachute harness. While I do this, I mutter things about the guy who ran the fork into his foot. Then, with a sigh, I grab helmet, throat microphone, oxygen mask, and parachute and stumble toward the truck. On the trip along the perimeter track, I listen to the crew's banter and dream of a bright future with Jane stretching before me.

Silver B-17G No. 42-97314 glistens in morning sunlight. The new silver ones are striking. The sky is blue, and the weather looks good. After a long, dark winter, it's nice to see sunshine and feel mild temperatures. I follow the crew toward the bomber's open door but stop to gaze at the green fields next to the airbase that has been my home. I feel the breeze and listen to birds singing in trees beyond the fence.

"Hey, are you coming?" George Keith calls from the bomber's open door.

Everyone else is on board. The airfield is quiet. Richard Funk looks at me from the copilot's window. He waves to me to get aboard.

"I'm coming," I call to Keith. "I was just enjoying the morning."

I take a last look at the English country beyond the fence and walk over to climb into the B-17. The radio mechanic there reports that everything is in tip-top shape.

"Good luck, old buddy," he says. "How many times have I told you that?" he says with a grin. "I heard a rumor that you're going to be a communications officer. That's really good."

He shakes hands and hurries away. The bomber's door slams shut.

Now it's all business. I check the armored vest in my compartment, check the medical kit, and switch on the radio receiver. I plug earphones, microphone, and oxygen mask into receptacles in the wall. Everything works. Finally, I sit down at my desk and study the secret codes and call letters for today's mission. I begin to write in my log. Outside my window, a tan bird with brown wings sits on the fence. If that nice, elderly birdwatcher lady was here, she could tell me what it is. I stop and admire it until it flies off when the first engine coughs and roars into action.

With much squealing of brakes, the 92nd Bomb Group's four-engine B-17G bombers taxi along the perimeter track and line up to take off. I've watched it twenty-five times now. There goes the first one down the runway, followed by the second and third. It's always a struggle to get into the air with a load of bombs and a full load of gas, but when our turn to take off comes, Victor Trost handles it well. He's a good pilot.

I watch us climb and join the squadron formation. Is it six planes or seven? I can't be certain, but I hope that it's seven. The more guns we have, the safer I feel. While we continue to climb above England, the squadron slides into the group formation and the group joins the combat wing. Our silver fleet of some sixty planes heads east, climbing steadily above 10,000 feet while I try to make my oxygen mask fit comfortably on my face—an impossible task. The sunshine is bright, but it's chilly in the radio room. Outside, I see armadas of bombers all over the sky. The Eighth Air Force is sending out more than 800 bombers today.

We cross the North Sea, and it sparkles in sunshine. I hear the chatter of gunfire as gunners test-fire their machine guns. When the bomber fleet crosses the Dutch coast, everyone is alert, and the gunners scan the sky. I gaze down at Holland. I'm always fascinated by how much of it is water. Rivers, lakes, and canals are everywhere. I think of the Dutch people down there and the stinking Nazis that have enslaved them.

Moving steadily eastward, we cross into Germany and drone high above familiar rivers. One by one, as time passes, we cross the Rhine, Weser, Leine, and Elbe. They are beautiful rivers as they sparkle in the sunshine. Barges seem to be a big thing in Germany. The radio has nothing interesting, so I glance around the azure sky for German fighters and then return to gazing at the landscape far below. We pass south of Berlin as it sits in haze, or maybe it is smoke. I wonder if the RAF bombed it last night.

The bomber armada breaks up as combat wings and individual groups turn away to head for their targets. Soon, the 40th Combat Wing is alone, heading southeast. There is no sign of fighter escort. I don't like being in a small formation deep inside eastern Germany. I hope German fighters don't see us. If they do, we are in trouble. Everyone is silent as we fly above green countryside.

"We're at the IP," Franklin Burks calls.

Thank goodness, we're almost halfway through the mission. Can we get in and out of Germany for a second day without being attacked?

"Bomb bay doors coming open," Joe Topolosky calls.

I watch the doors open to reveal green fields below us. This part of Germany doesn't seem to be as intensely farmed as western Germany.

"Bomb bay doors are open," I reply.

As I peer down through the open doors, a cold fist grabs me. German FW-190 fighters are directly below us! Where did they come from? How did they sneak up on us? They are at about 12,000 feet, but their red noses are pointed upward while they climb toward us, and sunlight glints off their silver bodies.

"Bandits directly below us!" I call. "They're about 6,000 feet below, but they're climbing."

As I watch the fighters climb, an airfield bordered by several, large buildings comes into view on the ground below. Those are certainly the buildings of the aircraft factory. Did the intelligence officer say that this factory assembles FW-190 fighters? I hope that these aren't test pilots climbing toward us, because those guys are likely to be very good.

Our bombs drop. I wonder if they will hit the German fighters that have pulled slightly ahead of us while they continue to climb from several thousand feet below. Bright, orange flashes march across the airfield and the factory buildings. Debris flies in all directions before a boiling curtain of smoke and flames covers the wrecked buildings.

"All bombs away. Bomb bay doors closing," I call as I watch the doors shut.

Our little formation turns away from the target and heads northwest toward home, but I know we're not going to get there without attacks by those FW-190 fighters. As we drone along, the intercom is silent. I tremble. I know what is coming at our bombers soon. I only hope that we can survive it. Thirty minutes pass.

"Here they come!" someone calls.

Guns on the 92nd Group's bombers stutter. Our B-17 bobs and weaves as Victor Trost takes evasive action. Our forward guns begin firing. Gunfire becomes continuous, then frenzied. Here come the Germans! The B-17 beside us bursts into a flaming torch. An FW-190 races past so close that I see the pilot looking down at me through the Plexiglas roof of the radio room. For a frozen second, we stare at each other. Another FW-190 flashes past even closer. Our bomber bounces from its passage. On our right, the blazing B-17 is engulfed in fire as it falls away toward the ground. I don't see anyone get out.

"They're turning around and coming back right at us!" the tail gunner yells.

I can't see the fighters. They must be about level or a little below us. Our guns open up, firing to the rear. The pilot bobs and weaves the B-17 in a desperate attempt to evade the fighters' attack. Our guns reach a crescendo of frantic firing, but over their racket, I hear a sound like a string of firecrackers banging. The noise races toward me as the bangs become louder. I turn to look out the window, and sharp blasts erupt beside me. *BANG! BANG! BANG!* Pieces of hot metal drive into my upper leg, like a gang of swordsmen ramming red-hot blades into me. The force knocks my legs out from under me, and I crash to the deck. Everything turns black, and then light. I find myself lying on the deck while I stare upward at blue sky beyond the Plexiglas roof. What am I doing down here? I grab the edge of my desk and pull myself up so that I can stagger to my feet. As I do, I'm dizzy, and I feel a torrent of warm liquid flowing down my leg, like lava from a volcano. I touch my hand to the shredded coveralls on my leg, and it comes back covered with blood. My leg is numb from hip to knee. Blood flows over my boot and pools on the deck.

"I'm hit," I call, but the intercom is dead.

The next thing that I see shakes me like nothing ever has. Through the window, I gape at our bomber's right wing blazing. A long trail of orange fire flares out behind it. Within a minute, the plane will explode or be engulfed in flames that will burn me to death. I must get out! Dizzy and panic stricken, I grab my parachute and yank open the door to the bomb bay. I'll jump, the doors won't hold me, and I'll fall free of the fire. I glance outside and stop. The fire is out! I stare, dumbfounded. I can't believe what I see. It's a miracle! It's a downright miracle, but will the fire stay out?

We have to get out of here! The German fighters will turn around and blast us again, and we won't survive it. I stare at the plane's wing, where gasoline pours from the shredded metal. It could ignite again in an instant.

The world is getting dark. I'm cold and feel like I'm going to pass out. Milt, the waist gunner, staggers into the radio room. His ashen face is bloody, and blood comes from wounds on his arm and leg. His face shows pain.

"I'm hurt," he says.

I nod, but suddenly dizzy, I slump into the chair at my desk and grasp the desk to keep from falling. Blood still flows down my leg and spreads across the deck. I have to stop the blood flow before I bleed to death, and I have to help Milt. He slides down to the deck and rests weakly against the side of the compartment. I wonder if he's about to pass out too. I hear a noise and peer up through the

Plexiglas roof to see a green flare rise into the sky. The guys in front must have fired it to ask for help from any friendly fighters that might see it. I press my hand hard against my leg to try to stop the flow of blood. At first, the leg was numb, but now it begins to throb with increasing pain. The pain is getting worse! As I grab the medical kit, I glance outside and see with relief that the fire is still out.

A few minutes later, the greatest sight in the world appears, as a pair of American P-51 fighters circle above our B-17. The sky is clear of German fighters. I'm doubly glad the P-51s are above us because I see that the 92nd Group's formation of bombers is far above and ahead of us. Why have we fallen so far behind? I'm puzzled until I notice our engines. Two of the four engines are smashed, their propellers stationary. A third engine shows damage and runs badly. It stutters and sounds like a washing machine that is about to quit. We're staying in the air due to one good engine and one damaged one. The plane is shredded with holes. Pieces of it are gone. It looks like a flying junkyard. I don't see how Trost and Funk are keeping it in the air. Thank God for good pilots, and thank God that Boeing made such a tough airplane. I had heard of how much punishment a B-17 can take and still fly. I believe it.

The door from the bomb bay opens and Joe Topolosky, the bombardier, enters. He is white and trembling, and he has no oxygen mask.

"Help Milt," I say while I press gauze pads against my leg and tape them tightly. That seems to slow the loss of blood. I have certainly lost enough, but my concern is about the fire starting again from the gasoline pouring from the wing.

"OK," he says, grabbing the medical kit. "The plane's wrecked. They're doing everything they can to keep it flying, but we're losing altitude fast. We're already down to 10,000 feet, so you can get rid of your oxygen mask."

I pull my mask off. It feels better to be no longer hampered by it.

"We must be dropping awful fast," I say.

Joe nods.

"We can't stay up on two engines, especially when one is not working well at all. The pilot wants us to throw out everything possible to lighten the ship. At the rate we're going down, we'll never make it out of Germany. Also, even if we can maintain our altitude, we're losing so much gas that there is no way we can get back to England. We're going to try to reach Sweden."

To get there, we'll have to fly from southeast Germany to northeast Germany across the whole of eastern Germany. But what's the alternative? The distance to Sweden is not as great as the distance to England, but it is a mighty long way through air where we may meet German fighters at any time. If we throw out our guns, we'll be sitting ducks, but it occurs to me that we're sitting ducks anyway for German fighters that happen by. A single B-17 can't defend itself against an FW-190. It will destroy us on its first attack. Trying to reach Sweden is a desperate move, but Trost is right. It's our only choice. Somehow, he and Funk are keeping us in the air, although I can't see how.

Joe gives me a morphine syringe, and I jab the needle into my leg. I bind the wounds tightly with more tape, and it seems to stop the bleeding. I should sprinkle sulfa on the wounds, but I don't want to let up on the pressure that has stopped me from losing any more blood. I'm woozy enough as it is. My blood is all over the deck below my desk.

George Keith, Sam Johnson, and Joe Topolosky drag heavy ammunition boxes and guns to the rear door and throw them out. Despite his wounds, Milt Powell staggers to his feet to help them. While they work, I check my bandage to be certain that it has stopped the bleeding. It is wrapped tightly around my leg, and it looks like the pressure from the bandage has done the trick. At least I don't feel blood pouring down my leg or see it oozing through the bandage. I'm dizzy, but I detach cables and fasteners from the big, radio transmitter. The gunners pull it from the bulkhead, manhandle it to the rear door of the plane, and throw it out. I do the same for the radio receiver and the navigation receiver and out they go. I look at the transmitter and receiver that the pilot uses and shake my head. They are small. I don't know whether the cable from the pilot to these radios was cut when the fighters hit us. The intercom was cut, but if the cable to the radio was not, the pilot might need to use them if we are lucky enough to reach Sweden.

I gaze stupefied at the armored vest that I must have shed when I was preparing to snap on my parachute, although I don't remember doing it. The fabric on the vest is slashed, and the armor has deep dents. If I had not worn it, I would be dead. As if I'm not shaking enough, a big shudder wracks me. One of the gunners throws out my armored vest. It saved my life. Now, the final thing that it can do to help me is to remove its weight from the descending plane. As the gunners continue to throw out everything that they can pry loose from the plane, I think of the trail of aircraft parts that we are leaving across eastern Germany. I hope that we have not hit any civilians with something falling from the sky, although it would be nice if a big piece hit a Nazi.

Fire and sparks burst from the wing. A cold fist grabs me. Flame flickers along the edge of the wing. I stare frozen as it creeps toward the hole where gasoline streams from the wing. Pointing to the fire, I start to call to the gunners, but the flame sputters like a Fourth of July sparkler and goes out. Whew!

I gaze unhappily at the secret IFF transmitter. It is heavy, and we must throw it out, but it contains an explosive charge, and it is my responsibility to set off the charge to destroy it to keep it out of enemy hands. The problem is that gasoline leaking from the plane's tanks has filled the radio room with fumes. Will the explosion of the charge inside the IFF ignite the gasoline-air mixture and blow up the plane?

"If we toss it out, it should wreck when it hits the ground," Sam Johnson says hopefully.

"Yeah," Keith says. "Dropping from this altitude, it's going to smash to bits when it hits."

Reluctantly, I shake my head. I don't want to be the person who gives German bombers a way to get into England, like foxes in a hen house. I gaze at two, red buttons on the IFF transmitter. You have to push them simultaneously to set off the dynamite charge inside the black box. I put two fingers on them, close my eyes, and push. There's a sharp report, like a shotgun firing, and the sides of the IFF transmitter bulge outward. I breathe again. We didn't blow up. I disconnect the IFF from the front bulkhead, and the gunners grab the bulged box and toss it out.

The gunners even throw out sheepskin clothing, oxygen masks, and other little things, in a desperate attempt to lighten the ship. I chew up the rice paper containing my secret codes and contribute the few ounces of the codes' plastic cover and my clipboard to the mass thrown out.

I look outside, and my heart leaps. The north coast of Germany is in sight. Beyond it stretches the Baltic Sea. I never dreamed that we could get this far before a German fighter shot us down. The German fighter controller certainly sees us and has tracked us northward across Germany. I wonder if he figures that we are heading for Sweden. Why waste gas on us? If we make it, plane and crew will be out of the war permanently.

Even though we are approaching the German coast, we are much lower than the last time that I looked. The ground gets closer by the minute. Do Germans down there want to lynch us? We have to lighten the bomber more. If not, we'll never make it to Sweden, but as I peer around, it looks like the crew has thrown out everything that it can. Sam Johnson, the ball turret gunner, points to the big, heavy ball turret in the floor of the B-17.

"Let's get that out," he says.

I stare at him. How can we do it? The turret is bolted into the floor. But Sam is the ball turret expert and produces a set of tools for taking out the ball turret. I then remember that each B-17 is equipped with a set because you can't make a belly landing with the ball turret hanging under the plane, so you unfasten it and drop it. In this case, we need to get rid of its tremendous weight. Sam and the gunners go to work on the bolts. I'm dizzy again. Everything is getting dark. They threw out my desk chair, so I sink to the floor and watch them work on the ball turret.

After a time, the dizziness passes, so I stand and look outside. The coast is closer, but so is the ground. I get a bad thought. Coasts have antiaircraft batteries. As low and slow as we are, one shot can blow us out of the sky. While the gunners work on the bolts holding the turret in place, I watch the coast move toward us at a snail's pace. Nearer and nearer it comes. It's coming faster. Now, it seems to speed toward us. Here it is! It is directly beneath us. I wince and wait for an antiaircraft shell to hit us, but nothing occurs. We pass over white surf, and I look down on water not far below. We are out of Germany and over the Baltic Sea, but we are terribly low. Still, if we can keep going, we can get away from German territorial water and into the part of the Baltic controlled by Sweden.

A noise turns my head toward the gunners. They have removed the bolts of the ball turret, but it is stuck. They push and pound on it.

A flash catches my eye. Flame licks out from the right wing again. Hypnotized, I watch it flutter along the wing. If we have a fire now, I doubt that we can make it down to a water landing before the bomber explodes. The flame spits out a shower of sparks like another Fourth of July sparkler and goes out. My heart slows to a gallop. How many more close calls can we survive?

When I look back at the gunners, Sam hangs like an orangutan from a strut on the roof of the plane. He stomps as hard as he can on the ball turret while the others pry on it. I hold my breath. Watch out, Sam! The heavy turret comes loose and drops from the plane. I peer down through a big hole in the floor. The turret and the mast that attaches it to the plane's roof girder turn over and over like a giant lollipop as they fall toward the water. Sam hangs precariously above the hole, but the gunners grab him and pull him to safety. We all stare at the big hole that we now have in the bomber's floor. You slip through that, and you are finished. I wonder if I should put on my parachute.

Joe Topolosky reappears to say that dropping the heavy turret has slowed our descent, but we should prepare for a crash landing, whether it's in the water or in Sweden. I gaze down at the gray water of the Baltic Sea. At least we're not over Germany. That's hopeful. We won't be beaten to death by a bunch of German civilians.

If we can get far enough away from Germany, even a landing in the water might get us picked up by a Swedish boat. I wonder if our life rafts are intact. I still don't know how to launch them. I look back at the German coast. I'll be happy when it's out of sight.

We sit in the radio room and look at each other. Everyone is white and obviously shaken. I check my leg. The wounds aren't bleeding, and the leg is numb with morphine. I imagine that I can feel the metal in there. Milt got it worse than I did, and he looks to be in a lot of pain. The flight is out of our hands now. It's up to the pilot, copilot, and navigator. We sit inert and drained as minute after minute creeps by. I peer back. The German coast is out of sight. I sigh with relief. We are somewhere over the Baltic.

I have a few minutes to think. If we reach Sweden, I know that the Swedish government will intern us. As I learned back at Podington, it is not like being a prisoner of war. An internee is treated much better—something like a guest who can't leave. I remember hearing that internees in Sweden live in hotels, apartment buildings, or houses. The food is said to be very good. You wear civilian clothing and cast aside all semblance of being a member of the military. It sounds a million times better than being taken prisoner in Germany. But there is a down side. By international convention, we will be required to stay in Sweden until the end of the war in Europe. If the war winds down, there is an outside chance that the Swedish government will release us earlier, but we will be required to go directly to the United States. We can no longer be in the European Theater of Operations.

A thought hits me: Jane! She will not hear from me and won't know what happened. She may think that I was killed. I heard that internees can't communicate with England for security reasons, and communication with the United States is limited. I will not be able to get in touch with Jane until the war ends and the Swedish government releases me. This is the thing that I didn't want to occur. She won't know what happened to me. It will break her heart.

George Keith yells and points outside. Two fighter planes have pulled alongside. For a moment, fear seizes me at the thought of German fighters toying with us while they prepare to destroy us. Then, I see that the insignia on the nearest fighter is not the hated swastika. It's a circle containing three crowns. These are Swedish fighters! They are escorting us. I gaze ahead and see the coastline. We seem to creep toward it for many minutes, but then it comes at us rapidly. We have lost so much altitude that we sweep very low over the coast. I gaze with relief at green fields and roads and neat villages beneath us. We are so low that I feel as if I can almost reach down and touch a church steeple. I feel us descending rapidly. An airfield must be close. The pilot sends Joe Topolosky back again.

"Prepare for a hard landing," he shouts.

I gaze out and see flame flicker along the edge of the wing. No! Not when we're so close. It disappears, flickers again, and goes out.

We are very low. Trees and houses are just beneath our wings. The gunners and I sit down lined up with our backs to the front bulkhead of the radio room. The engine noise dies, and we brace for whatever is coming. The engines stop. There is silence as we seem to float above the ground. I feel a heavy jar, followed by a heavier jolt, and I realize that we are skidding across the ground on the plane's belly. Dirt pours into the plane through the hole in the floor where the ball turret rested. The force of our skid presses us against the bulkhead. The hole in the plane's underside digs a mountain of dirt that piles up in the waist compartment and acts as a brake. The odor of freshly plowed soil fills the air.

The bomber stops. Fearing fire, we struggle to our feet. My leg is now stiff and numb, but I hobble behind the others to climb on hands and knees over the mass of dirt in the waist compartment. The gunners kick open the door at the rear of the plane and tumble out. I stagger along behind them until I stumble through the door and fall down. Slowly, I get to my feet and gaze around. The B-17 lies on its belly, its propellers bent around the engines. Trucks and an ambulance pull up. Rifle-carrying soldiers in gray uniforms pour from the trucks and surround us, but many smile.

"Welcome to Sweden," an officer shouts. "Do you have any wounded persons aboard your aircraft?"

Now, there is no more doubt. We are in Sweden, a neutral country, and our fate is set by international agreement. Sweden will intern us for the rest of the war, however long it may last. With luck, it may send us back to the United States when the war in Europe finally ends. Until then, our fate is in their hands. In any event, we will live comfortably and safely until it is time to go home.

I take a deep breath and gaze around at the green field and trees surrounding it. My leg is beginning to hurt again, and my neck is sore, but wonder of wonders, my headache is gone. I have an empty ache in my heart for Jane, but one thing is certain on this sunny afternoon of May 29, 1944. There will be no more combat missions and no more facing death in the savage sky over Germany.

Epilogue

The Government of Sweden interned me. Doctors at a hospital in Malmö tended my wounds, and a Swedish officer in gray-uniform and shiny, black boots lectured me on Sweden's strict rules governing my behavior. He warned of prison if I tried to escape from Sweden. Try to escape? I was in a beautiful country with no one shooting at me. Only an idiot would want to escape. Sweden also required me to discard my uniform for civilian clothing. It felt wonderfully comfortable after wearing a uniform for so long.

A train ride through a breathtaking landscape of forests, hills, lakes, and villages took me to Loka Brun, a small cluster of resort hotels and houses on a placid lake in a valley surrounded by wooded hills in central Sweden. In this peaceful setting, I settled into an attractive room in Villa von Essen, a two-story, four-bedroom house on a hillside. Two maids, Karen and Ruth, made beds and kept the house spotless. Neither spoke English, but one morning, Ruth, a shy, young blonde, smiled at me and said sweetly, "Shut the goddamn door." I could see that American culture had reached Loka Brun. Karen helped me learn Swedish, while I helped her with English.

Internees dined on very good food in a hotel that housed many of the Americans. The hotel's public rooms were elegant, and it was difficult to comprehend the transition from fire and death to this quiet life. At the time, there were about 500 American internees in Sweden, housed in several communities.

When we bathed, we encountered the Swedish custom of a community bath. I also noted that the Swedes had no hesitation about bathing nude in nearby lakes. It took time to become comfortable with these customs.

A squad of Swedish soldiers was at Loka Brun, but their function seemed more to keep curious Swedes away than to keep us
there. We could take a charcoal-burning taxi (Sweden was short on
gasoline) to the nearby town of Filipstad to shop. I continued to
receive my regular pay, 50 percent additional flight pay, 20 percent
additional overseas pay, and a daily allowance of even more money.
Thus, in Filipstad, I bought a handsome radio, a record player, a big
collection of records of American music, clothing of all sorts, and
anything that caught my eye.

I fretted constantly about Jane. I could not get a letter to her.
No contact was permitted between Sweden and England. I only had
heavily restricted communication with the United States. My letters
went to the American Legation in Stockholm. There, the thor-
oughly-censored letters went by diplomatic pouch to the Pentagon
in Washington. They were censored more, placed in new envelopes,
and forwarded to the addressee, a process that took weeks and was
intended to conceal where I was. When my mother wrote, she sent
the letter to the Pentagon, and many weeks later, it arrived in Loka
Brun. Since Sweden was almost surrounded by German-occupied
territory, it is surprising that we could communicate at all.

I also could visit Stockholm. After the blackout in England,
Stockholm's lights and activity were a wonderland. I stayed at the
Hotel Continental and enjoyed great restaurants, theaters, and
stores. I especially liked NK, a large, department store on Hamn-
gatan. It had handsome merchandise and an attractive, American
woman to help me shop. A perpetual tourist, I had all the time in
the world to go sightseeing in this old, yet very modern, city built on
a cluster of islands.

But we had to be careful. German and Allied agents, all pretending that they were something else, filled Stockholm. On our
first trip to Stockholm, Richard Funk, Franklin Burks, Sam Johnson,
and I were dining in Blanch's restaurant. As we discussed how we
survived our last mission, the waiter brought us a note. It said that
the man sitting at the next table was a German agent. When we
began talking, he had the headwaiter move him to that table. We
stopped discussing the mission and spoke of how the Nazis were
slime. Later, the man who sent the note stopped by our table. He

was from the American Legation and told us never to discuss anything military in Stockholm. It was a hotbed of spies. After that I peered curiously at people in Stockholm, wondering which ones were spies.

Thus, I spent the summer lazing at Loka Brun. I read books, listened to music, took long walks along the lake, and felt my headaches disappear and nightmares subside. On the radio, the BBC reported the Allied invasion of Normandy in June, the breakout from the beachhead in July, the defeat of German armies in France and liberation of Paris in August, the occupation of most of Belgium in September, and invasion of the German Rhineland in October. The BBC said that, once the Allied armies crossed the Rhine, they would defeat Germany quickly.

At the end of October, the American Military Attaché ordered me to move to Stockholm. I got the stunning news that the Government of Sweden had released me from internment. I packed clothing, Rolleiflex camera, and the many presents purchased at NK into suitcases. I gave a tearful Karen my radio, record player, and records. After a wistful last look at Loka Brun, I left for Stockholm.

The American Legation put me in a nice room in the attractive State Hotel in Sodertalje, a Stockholm suburb. A Legation officer told me to be ready to leave at a moment's notice. I waited and waited and waited. Then, without warning, a car came and whisked me to the Grand Hotel Saltsjobaden, an old-fashioned waterfront hotel on the other side of Stockholm from Sodertalje. I settled down for another, long wait, but the next night, a car sped me to Bromma Airfield, Stockholm's airport. Planes of many nations, including swastika-bearing German planes, were there, but the car whisked me to an unmarked, black transport plane on the far side of the field. After I boarded, I learned that Berndt Balchen, the famous, Arctic explorer, was now a colonel in the U.S. Air Force and commanded several transport planes that flew at night over German-occupied Norway between Stockholm and Leuchars, Scotland. They carried secret agents and all manner of unknown characters. Whispers around the cabin were that a member of the Swedish Royal Family was on board. It was a dangerous flight. German night fighters tried to shoot down these planes, so we flew in darkness in a black plane. During a tense time, we crossed over German-occupied Norway and finally landed safely in Scotland.

A stipulation of my release was that I must leave Europe immediately and not fight against Germany again. Eighth Air Force officers and a hard-faced American civilian swore me to secrecy about everything relating to Sweden and Colonel Balchen's planes. They sent me to the 92nd Group to pick up uniforms and records. When I changed trains, some American soldiers overheard me getting information about train times. Noting my European-style clothing, they asked if I was an American spy. I told them that I was not, so they gathered around and wanted to know what I was doing in England. When I said that I was not permitted to tell them, they decided that I was a spy.

At the 92nd group, Ken Tasker, Lloyd Lyons, Greg Araujo, Ed Norton, and all the flyers that I knew were gone, replaced by fresh-faced kids, but John Sloan and Dick Shaw were there, and we had a great reunion.

I had a few hours free, so I jumped aboard a train for London. With growing excitement, I hurried to the theater. Jane was not there. She had left in late June, but no one knew where she went. Frantic, I rushed to her flat. A married couple now lived there. No one in the building knew where she had gone, and she had left no forwarding address. I had never thought to get her parent's address in Herefordshire, or to give her my address in the United States. Despite searching for many months, I never saw Jane again.

An overnight train carried me to Prestwick, Scotland, to board a gleaming DC-4 passenger plane. It was Thanksgiving Day, 1944. The plane stopped at Reykjavik, Iceland, to refuel and feed the passengers Thanksgiving dinner. Stuffed, we flew on, with a distant view of icy Greenland, and landed at Stephenville, Newfoundland, for another Thanksgiving dinner. Thoroughly stuffed, we flew down the east coast to land at New York's LaGuardia Airport. The breathtaking New York skyline made me realize that, unlike so many of my friends, I had somehow survived. But the air force had pleasant surprises. To make up for my months of internment, it was giving me thirty days leave at home, followed by several weeks of relaxation at a Miami Beach hotel. I also finally got that elusive commission as a second lieutenant, and before I left the Air Force, I was promoted to first lieutenant. I would have traded it all for a chance to return instantly to the university, but good things (such as university study) often come to those who wait just a little longer.

Stackpole Military History Series

Real battles. Real soldiers. Real stories.

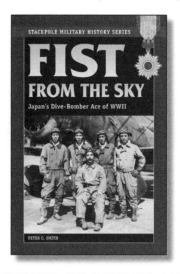

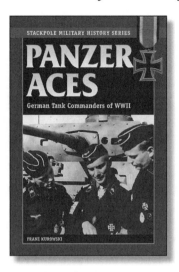

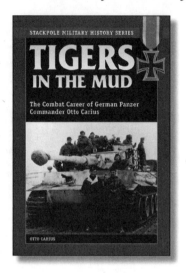